ON PRAYER

ON PRAYER

by

Karl Rahner, S.J.

PAULIST PRESS DEUS BOOKS

NEW YORK   PARAMUS   TORONTO

A Deus Book Edition of Paulist Press, 1968, by special arrangement with Clonmore & Reynolds, Ltd.

NIHIL OBSTAT:
Joannes O'Donoghue
Censor Theol. Dep.

IMPRIMATUR:
✠ Joannes Carolus
Archiep. Dublinen. Hiberniae Primas

July MCMLXVII

The Nihil Obstat and Imprimatur are official declarations that a book or pamphlet is free of doctrinal or moral error. No implication is contained therein that those who have granted the Nihil Obstat and Imprimatur agree with the contents, opinions or statements expressed.

Cover Design: Morris Berman

Published by Paulist Press
Editorial Office: 1865 Broadway, N.Y., N.Y. 10023
Business Office: 400 Sette Drive, Paramus, N.J. 07652

Manufactured in the
United States of America
by Our Sunday Visitor Press

CONTENTS

THOU WILT OPEN MY HEART.

THE life of men is made up of many and varied activities. Deep in the heart of men is the longing, fitfully glimpsed and but half realised, to gather up all these strivings into an intense pursuit of one all-embracing objective worthy of the toil and tears and devotion of the human heart. Such is the half-shaped dream; but the reality is a picture of heaped-up activities, where the trivial jostles the less trivial, and the less trivial elbows the important things, and there is no unity of design, nor any intensity of single, concentrated purpose. There is no real perspective of values: what is essentially trivial but immediately urgent, looms large and commands attention; while what is essentially important, but not immediately urgent or insistent, is relegated to the hazy recesses of the background. But the thing of greatest importance is not always what is demanded by the needs of the moment.

A man may turn from it all; and immediately the noise of his activities sinks to silence as, in a spirit of reverence and love, he speaks to God in prayer. With one swift upward glance of his soul, he has got as near as his finite nature will allow him, to that sublime fusion of all his activities into one glowing point of heat and of light. Only in Heaven can he fully achieve this synthesis of all his faculties, of all the energies of his being, in the contemplation of the Beatific Vision. Here on earth, hedged in by the things of the senses, such synthesis is impossible to men; and yet, in prayer, though " through a glass in a dark manner ", a man looks upon God and comes as near as he can to that unity of action and purpose for which his heart has a deep and secret longing. Prayer is, therefore, one of the essentials of our life—the food we feed to our souls in order that this deep and secret longing may live into eternal life.

But there is no compulsion to pray: we can freely decide to pray or to neglect prayer. When we say that prayer is necessary, we mean necessary for the highest part of man's nature; and just as the highest part of man—his soul—is often ignored, so too is prayer. For prayer is not easy. It is not the speaking of many words, or the hypnotic spell of the recited formula; it is the raising of the heart and mind to God in constantly renewed acts of love. We must go forward to grapple with prayer, as Jacob wrestled with the angel. We must lift high our lamp of Faith that it may show us what prayer is, and what are its power and dignity. Into the darkness we must whisper our prayer: *Lord, teach us how to pray.*

The idea is sometimes entertained that we know what prayer is, that we know how to pray, and that therefore we have simply to put our knowledge into practice. However, like so many other ideas which we regard as ordinary currency of knowledge—ideas about the nature of kindness, generosity, charity, silence, understanding, and so forth—our ideas of what prayer is and how we should pray are far from clear. We must question those ideas and thereby come to realize that, so far from the idea of prayer being something which leaps to us spontaneously from the front line of obvious ideas, it is a concept which it will take us our whole life to fathom, and a practice which our whole life will be too short to perfect.

We speak for our times: there probably was an era when the knowledge and practice of prayer were more familiar to men. There was almost certainly a time when men's spiritual arteries were less hardened; for instance, the very trowels and hods of the builders of Chartres Cathedral must have prayed, for the hands holding them were speaking a prayer in stone. But our spiritual climate has changed, and we have become spiritually hardened. The process has been a slow one, each generation inheriting the hardness and spiritual insensitivity of its predecessor, to hand it on to its successor as a legacy of yet greater hardness and spiritual insensitivity But the tradition of prayer has come down to us, and we give it some frigid respect. Prayer lives among us as the wraith of what it was. It lives on bored and casual lips that know nothing of prayer as earth's hymn of praise. Dry hearts offer their dry homage; eyes flit constantly to a watch which ticks its way towards the time of that really important appointment. God will understand and excuse this somewhat prefunctory discharge of one's spiritual duties; there are so many important things to be done. So God receives a crust of worship served distractedly on an ill-washed plate. But He has His honourable place in our scheme of things. We call on Him as we would to our insurance office; we pay grudgingly and we seek eagerly for our bonus. Our hands outstretched in prayer are mercenary hands; they show a certain near-parody of spiritual eagerness only when we are asking for something. This, of course, though witnessing to that hardening of the spiritual arteries we spoke of, is better than complete spiritual sclerosis. But what a travesty of prayer it really is! It is surely but the odour of an empty vase.

What, then, is prayer? We shall see that it is by no means easy to answer this question. When we have said all that is in our minds about prayer, it is inevitably found that we have said a lot *about* prayer and yet very little about what prayer *is*. Let us begin with one simple fact, so often regarded as a spiritual cliché that we tend to pass too lightly over it. Prayer is the opening of the heart to God. To understand this primary condition of prayer, both as a fact and as a reality to be lived, it is necessary to consider what precisely is meant by " the opening of the heart ", and what are the obstacles to this opening.

It is a well established psychological fact that actions deliberately and consciously performed are motivated by unconscious urges, are controlled by emotions long buried in the recesses of our being; so that, what appear to be actions done in the full light of consciousness, are but the shadows and symbols of buried urges which now suddenly become active beyond the reach of our conscious will. What appeared, therefore, as straightforward acts consciously controlled, are shown to be, as it were, a mirror held up to the true inner reality of ourselves. Thus we come to realise, with a rush of panic, that what we regard as actions posited by us are in reality but aspects of our real selves: they are *us*.

Let us try to further this idea by means of an analogy. Many of us remember those long nights in an air-raid shelter during the war, when we stood in abysmal loneliness among a crowd of terror-stricken people, waiting for death. In the darkness, we felt the coldness of fear chilling our hearts, and it was in vain that we put up a show of courage and stiff upper lip: our brave words were hollow, and fell as husks about our feet, leaving only silence and the vigil that might be the vigil of death. Then suddenly the explosion came, and the shower of débris to bury us. Let this be taken as the symbol of modern life. We have indeed crawled out from the powdered shelters; we have resumed our daily lives with a great show of bravery and pretence of enjoyment; but the truth is that many of us are as though we had remained buried in the débris, because we have suffered no change of heart through having been brushed by the wing of death. However far fetched it may sound, it remains true that externals are but the shadow of what has taken place in the depths of our hearts. Our hearts are obstructed, buried under débris.

Let us be quite clear about one fundamental fact of human existence. Unless it is set free by God into that infinite freedom wherein alone it can realise itself, our heart becomes hedged in by mean limitations, by suffering, by hopelessness, by the daily commonplaces that chain us down. Like the insatiable cormorant, the human heart then begins to feed upon itself. It becomes a welter of vanities, a sour well of bitterness and despair, a prison from which there is no escape. We may seek to escape by travel—forgetting the warning that " one may change the sky overhead, but not the mind within"; we may seek oblivious immersion in work or in that sick unrest that is miscalled pleasure; we may seek to stifle our loneliness amid the laughter of men. But there is no escape from that ceaselessly nagging sense of utter loneliness and of helpless conviction that the world is futile. We know that we are in hectic flight from ourselves; that we cannot stand still for a moment because the voices within us will say we have not moved at all—that we are still in the puddle of futility. We are like a person who appears to be in good health, but is really being gnawed by an incurable disease. A little stab of pain suddenly coming in the midst of enjoyment, reminds such a person that all this is mere pretence and that he is shadowed by death.

We may choose any form of escapism dictated by our

taste for pleasure and by the limits of our resources; we may build our house of happiness with what bricks we choose, or wander at large to gather the roses of pleasure. Yet, at a thought, the shades of our prison house are again stiflingly about us: we realise that we have but crawled from the misery of one cell to that of another— or, to revert to our metaphor, we have simply hollowed out another place in the same débris. Filling our lives is the same futility, frustration, monotony, chatter and all that weary swirl of pointless strivings we call human life. There are many, of course, who sit contentedly in the dust, feasting on the store they have, conversing brilliantly with their neighbours, still rooting for the truffles of pleasure, still dreaming and planning, apparently oblivious of the fact that the shelter has collapsed and that there are tons of débris between them and the light. Yet, even such hide-bound optimists, with their blinkered minds, will suddenly be jolted into the realisation that they are breathing the dust, that there is death in the air, and bitterness in the dregs of life's pleasures.

But in the dust of the powdered shelter, there are also the stoics who claim to know that the position is hopeless, and who stand up to proclaim this barren truth; who lift up the lamp only to show that there is really nothing but dryness and despair. They speak sternly to the poor wretch who shudders from them, in the icy grip of his sudden realisation that he is utterly alone, that his diet must be dust, that there is nothing beyond the inevitable blow of death. They tell him he must learn self-control by facing calmly up to the fact that there is no escape, and the poor wretch accepts this state of stultifying despair so that he comes to accept it as the ordained order of things. He is convinced that there can be no other state, that he has awakened from the illusions of life, that he has put aside like the toys of his childhood those dreams and ideals with which he used to feed his soul. He has experienced his bitter epiphany of despair.

Those who have settled down to this chronic despair preserve their self-control, appear to be leading—and regard themselves as leading—a perfectly natural life. They behave reasonably, work conscientiously, observe standards of decency, marry, found a settled home, discuss

11

the arts and sciences. Occasionally they like to indulge in a little speculation about the meaning and value of human life, or to listen to such speculation. But all this is a mere façade to conceal the real man—to hide that wound from which the heart is bleeding to spiritual death, but about which one may not speak because it is "bad form" to indulge in what one of their number has once called "spiritual nudism". All this is a mere pretence at ignoring the prison whose exit is blocked by the débris of their own hearts. Within that prison, their real self is hopelessly trapped—that self which does not wear the spectacles of humanist sophistication, that raw self which sees unerringly into the hollow heart of earthly life, and judges it to be empty, futile and subject to death.

Modern philosophy has invented a new and flattering mask for the countenance of despair. Man's true dignity, it says, is to realise that there is nothing beyond the material things around him, that he himself is no more intrinsically permanent than the trees and the grass "that today is and tomorrow is cast into the oven", that human life has no more meaning than is summed up in the terrible words: "from day to day we ripe and ripe, and from day to day we rot and rot". There is no true human dignity except that of facing up calmly and bravely to the absolute worthlessness of human existence. A man's wisdom is to be measured by his realisation of his own utter lack of any significance. This so-called philosophy of despair has been formulated by one such philosopher as "an icy silence in face of the eternal silence of the alleged Divine"; and the same author (Camus) claims for this philosophy that it establishes "a meaningless and godless world which thinks clearly and which no longer hopes".

There is, of course, a certain *positive* realisation of one's fundamental nothingness which may be the beginning of salvation: "of myself, I can do nothing" said Saint Paul: and those who have come to such a realization may be already close to establishing the kingdom of God in their hearts. The philosophical despair of which we have spoken above, is simply perverted pride: it is as though a man should say—"I shall calmly despise my whole existence because it does not make me a god ". Such a man comes to take pride in his realisation of his very worthlessness, as though it were a positive achievement which gave him dignity. " Greatness has changed its field: it is now to be looked for in resoluteness and sacrifice without hope ", writes Camus. What a parody of human life we have here, in this picture of man's finest qualities being exercised in an affirmation of worthlessness and sheer negation! The head remains " bloody but unbowed ", and the eyes look forward unflinchingly to where there is no hope, no destiny, no line of light rimming the eternal hills. How different is the positive sense of its own nothingness characteristic of the truly Christian soul! For this realization is simply a measuring of ourselves against the greatness of our Creator, and a casting out of all that is petty and earthly in us so that we may remove all obstacles to the indwelling of the strength of God in our bodies chosen by Him to be His " temples ". It was from a realisation—a positive, fruitful realisation—of his own nothingness and worthlessness, that Saint Paul made his magnificent boast: " I can do all things in him that strengtheneth me." It is a great paradox to those who have not the eyes of faith, that such abasement and such audacity can exist together, almost as cause and effect, in the Christian soul.

Stripped of its mask of sophism, this philosophical despair is revealed as mere negativity—as ordinary, barren despair dressed in fine feathers. Behind the words and the lofty protestations of the modern philosophers, there is simply emptiness and frantic self-deception. They are like those deceptive ruins one sometimes sees, where a sound façade, viewed from a distance, gives the illusion of a house standing four-square and solid; but, viewed at nearer range, is revealed as an empty shell housing only heaps of the débris that once were roof and walls and windows open to the light. But such philosophers claim to stand upright in the heart of this shell, boldly denying the existence of those heaps of débris because they assert that the roof and the walls were mere illusions; and yet, under that débris, are buried their true freedom, their faith, their hope of an eternal destiny, for they have never learned the secret of the freedom of the adopted sons of God.

Even the Christian must be on his guard lest his own house has crumbled to some extent, and some of his true greatness been buried under its débris. The façade here will take the form of a dry discharging of prescribed duties wherein the heart has long ceased to play a living role. The danger of such crumbling is that it happens with great silence: it is rather a process of noiseless dry rot than such a fall of masonry as would jolt the attention. Thus the débris will silently gather; and mere observance of the externals of religious practices will not save the living reality of religion from becoming choked and buried beneath it.

A true realisation of one's worthlessness is fruitful and positive, because it is a realisation that what is subject to death in us is unworthy of claiming the allegiance of our hearts. It is the realisation that the most carefully planned projects, the most lofty ideals, the most impassioned strivings, are meaningless except as inspired by, and directed towards, the Eternal Power in Whom alone we "live and move and have our being". This is the conviction which enables a Christian to delve deeper and deeper into the realisation of his own nothingness and helplessness, because only thus can the power of God live in him. It was this truth that Christ put so vividly when He said: "Unless the seed falling into the ground die, itself remaineth alone; but if it die, it bringeth forth fruit". It is in the darkness of one's knowledge of complete personal worthlessness that the light of the presence of God begins to dawn: it is in the realisation of one's own utter powerlessness that the power of God becomes active, springing up into Life Everlasting.

Thoughts such as these should inspire the Christian who has allowed his soul to become filled with noise and bustle, to realise that God is awaiting the silence of his heart so that He may speak His word of power. He is awaiting that moment when the Christian ceases to spin fine words as a cloak for inner emptiness, to heap up dry prayer and arid observance of externals, to listen to the heart's moan of despair at the burden of life; for in that moment, He knows that the Christian will turn and say: "My existence has no meaning except as the manifestation of Thy Power and Glory through my weakness

14

and nothingness." The soul then realises the truth of the words that " he who will save his life must lose it "— that obsessive anxiety for happiness in this world leads only to the hovel of despair, not to the palace of wisdom. Every day becomes a renewed miracle, wherein the soul grows in deeper knowledge of its own powerlessness, and knows the growing power of God within the depths of its being. What once seemed a sterile sense of utter emptiness, proves to be but the greyness before the dawn of Grace in the soul. The heart is buried in the sense of its own futility, but there is no need to seek an exit of escape, because God is present. It would be fatal to turn from this blessed realisation of one's loneliness and futility, to seek comfort from things that have no power to comfort us, because they are but shards that can hold no water. In a fresh affirmation of faith and love, the soul must descend deeply into the knowledge of its own worthlessness, for only by doing so can it find God. It is not *despite* the fact of our nothingness that we find God, but *because* of our realisation that we are as nothing in His sight and that the world is dust and ashes except as the means of loving and serving Him. Deep cries unto deep: the depth of our nothingness unto the depth of the power and majesty and wisdom of God.

With this new awareness of God, comes deep and lasting peace—a calm which is not deceptive, a confidence without fear, a security that needs no reassurance, a power that lives in powerlessness, a life that springs up in the shadow of death. Nothing is left in us but God and our faith in God. We find our happiness, our strength, our power to face all sorrow, in the thought that God is with us and that we are His. In this peace, our heart learns to commune silently with God in a living union with Him. The dry formulas of prayer on dry lips, are replaced by that silent communion of heart with heart which comes with the sense of God's nearness to us and our utter, loving dependence on Him. This colloquy of the heart with God cannot be expressed in words, because it is a silent reaching out towards God with reverential fear and sublime trust. It is a complete silent oblation of self, and an entire surrender to God.

And here again we come upon one of the exalted

mysteries of the spiritual life. In thus abandoning himself to God, the Chrisitan can cry out with Saint Paul: " I live, now not I, but Christ liveth in me "—because the pulsating centre of his life has ceased to be other than the Life and Power of God dwelling within him. Yet, by a splendid paradox, it can be said that in ceasing to be himself the centre of his life, he becomes more entirely at one with himself; because God is more the true centre of our being that we are ourselves. The sheer Immensity of God urges us to realise our being to its fullest through transcending the limitations imposed by choosing to remain our own centre. For we now know that within those limitations there is no salvation, but only emptiness and frustration. The darker and more difficult the ways leading to this peace, the more intense is the love in hearts that have sought refuge from the threat of God's judgments by sweet submission to God Himself. Peace has come because the heart has opened to admit the presence of God, saying: " O God of my heart, and the God that is my portion forever. Abba, father. Have mercy on us." The Christian surrenders unconditionally, listens to the inspirations of God now breathing their power within him, filling him with a reverence and awe wherein is the healing power of eternal love. In this new freedom from thraldom to self, every word and act becomes a lived prayer, because the presence of God suffuses the whole pattern of living. Here is real prayer: here is the Power of God set free at last to spring up in the acknowledged barrenness of the human heart.

To reach this blessed state of peace of soul demands an initial step into the unknown, and therefore a decision which must be freely taken and which cannot be imposed. A man may cling to his philosophy of despair, his creed of life's utter meaninglessness, as a drowning man clings to a plank; and it is as little use to tell him that he can relinquish this philosophy and yet find happiness, as it is to impress on the drowning man that he should release his hold, that he really can swim, when he is convinced that he cannot and that he will undoubtedly drown. As long as he clings to the plank, he cannot put this assurance to the test, and must float aimlessly; for he wants, not an assurance that he can swim, but almost an advance guarantee that the water itself will bear him up. But no such guarantee can be given. So, too, a man may look for such an impossible guarantee before he relinquishes his philosophy of despair by praying; and yet, he must take the initial step of laying aside this paralysing anxiety. If he feels himself incapable of praying, he must nevertheless kneel, join his hands, speak words of prayer even if he feels that these words come only from his lips and that his heart remains unmoved. For such a conviction as to the insincerity of his prayer may be the last defence offered by his philosophy of despair against inevitable defeat. "I believe, Lord: help Thou my unbelief", must be his prayer; and there is nothing insincere in such a humble admission of one's weakness of faith and one's difficulty in believing.

It is vain to plead inability, for in this matter, 'inability' is simply an excuse for making no effort. There is no inability preventing this decision, and one's greatest guilt may be to acquiesce in the idea that one cannot decide. But the ways of God are inscrutable; for if a man really longs for the strength to decide, and realises but is not obsessed by his own weakness, it is through that very weakness that God will work his salvation. Why should you not kneel, join your hands, speak the words of prayer, even when you feel that your heart is not in what you are doing? Is it the fear of insincerity? Is it insincerity to do what you feel you can do—force the body at least to do what you feel the heart cannot achieve but yet desires? You have got no right to stifle those longings deep within you for the possession of a key to the true meaning, the happiness, the exhilarating truth of life in God. The very fact that you repeat with such anguish: "I cannot do it," is already an admission that this is something longed for as good, and indeed an acknowledgement of a duty to seek this good. Your own free decision and your acting upon it will open the way to grace, but you cannot expect grace to come unsought. You cannot command the feelings of your heart. True; but there is one thing you can do. You can kneel down and tell God that your heart is dry and hard, but yet longs for Him. You can force yourself to pray.

In His Passion and Death, Christ has shown us how

the sense of being abandoned by God can be the dawn of God's presence in our dried and wearied hearts. For in this, as in every other aspect of our life, Christ has shown us how we must act by Himself undergoing the same desolation in His Heart for us and for our guidance. The Garden of Olives was the desolation of Christ in order that it might become the consolation of all human desolation, for Christ is the living heart of the world. Christ crushed to the earth, His sweat becoming as drops of blood trickling down unto the ground, His whole human nature shrinking from the agony upon which He had entered, is the God-Man forcing Himself to make a human prayer. In the silence of the Garden, Christ knelt alone, His whole being filled with the darkness of a seeming abandonment by the Father. Yet, overcoming the shrinking fear of His human nature, and with immense courage, He prayed: " Not my will but thine be done."

In that moment, all the desolation of the world, all the emptiness of human hearts, was lifted up and sanctified through Christ. We attain to profound union with God by uniting ourselves in our desolation with the Agony of Christ. He is the Way. " Thou wast walking in thy ways, a vagabond," writes Saint Augustine; " straying through wooded places, through rough places, torn in all thy limbs. Thou wast seeking a home, that is, a sort of settlement of thy spirit, where thou mightest say, it is well; and might say this in security, at rest from all un-easiness, from every trial, in a word from every captivity; and thou didst not find it. What shall I say? Did one come to show thee the way? There came to thee *the Way itself* . . ." (In Ps. LXX, Serm. ii, 3—Przywara p. 199). Our prayer in union with the agonizing Christ is a prayer of pure faith, and in the words which we struggle to say, we shall find His strength beginning to live in us. We shall receive grace to grow in holiness of heart unto ripeness for Heaven, because we have learned to unite our darkness with the desolation of Christ. " My pain cometh," writes Saint Augustine, " there will come my rest also; my trouble cometh, there will come my purgation also." (In Ps. LXI, 11—Przywara p. 469).

We have said very little in this chapter about prayer itself, but we have made an approach to the subject and, we hope, given an impulse also. We must try to develop a facility in opening our hearts to God, so that it may become a living reality in our prayer, and we may descend fruitfully into the depths of our heart, rather than deceive ourselves with a spurious philosophy of stiff-lipped despair. We must find courage by facing squarely up to the fact that there can be no complete rest for the soul, but rather disillusionment and bitterness, in the things whose end is the abyss of death. For deep in our hearts there is a profound restlessness, because God has given us a thirst for the Infinite, for the Incomprehensible, for Himself: " Thou hast made us for Thyself, O Lord," cried out Saint Augustine, " and our heart is restless until it rests in Thee." Deep in our buried heart, we find this seed of the Divine, this restless reaching out towards something infinitely beyond the things of this world; and we find strength to pray:

Our Father Who art in the depths of my heart, transforming its hollow emptiness into a heaven on earth; *Hallowed be Thy Name,* even in the death-like silence of my ignorance and my lack of faith; *Thy Kingdom come* in the very midst of my desolation; *Thy will be done* in me, even if it means pain and death; *Thy will be done* in me, for Thy will is my true life; *Give us this day our daily bread,* for I am utterly dependent upon Thy Divine Providence; *Forgive us our trespasses*—those sins which are ultimately but treason against Thy love for us, and therefore treason against myself; *Deliver us from evil*—from the evil of centering our lives upon ourselves, in order that we may learn that Thou art the centre of all, and that only in Thee can we find freedom worthy of the sons of God.

Perhaps, indeed, we may not really use so many words; but as we repeat the words of the Lord's Prayer, God will open our hearts that the warmth of these feelings may steal into the hard and stony places made arid by the bitterness of life.

II.

THE HOLY GHOST IN OUR PRAYER.

ONCE we have opened our hearts, we no longer seek to escape from ourselves; and where we formerly experienced an aridity empty of God, we now feel the joy of His Presence. In the depths of our heart we find the courage to say: " Our Father." We would never have the audacity, of our own accord, to address our Creator with such familiarity. Whence, therefore, do we derive the courage and the right to approach our Creator and speak to Him as His sons?

One thing in particular fills us with confidence: we speak these words in union with the Divine Son, Our Lord Jesus Christ. Christ adores the Father 'in spirit and in truth,' being born of the Father from all eternity. As God made man, Christ has adopted us as His brothers and co-heirs to His glory in the bosom of the Father; and that we may realise the full significance of that adoption, He teaches us to join with Him in saying: " Our Father." This prayer is the spirit of the New Law of Love proclaimed by Christ. No longer are we to look on God as the Almighty Judge and know nothing of His love for men. In Christ we have seen that love incarnate, and in the strength of that love we dare to say—*audemus dicere*—" Our Father". There is God and there are ourselves; and between us and God there is the stretch of infinity which our minds can never grasp. God, the all-Perfect, the all-Sufficient, the all-Holy; we, hanging by a thread of the mercy of God, utterly dependent on Him, dust in His sight. Only through Christ and at the bidding of Christ could men find the audacity to speak thus to God from the abyss of their own nothingness.

The Incarnation is our great source of inspiration in prayer. " In stooping without defiling Himself," wrote the famous seventeenth century mystic, Cardinal Berulle, " God the Son raises us; in His union with the Father, He purifies us; in Incarnating Himself, He deifies us . . ."

By assuming our nature, Christ became one of us in all things, sin alone excepted. In the bosom of His Father, He worshipped God from all eternity; and when He was made man, He worshipped with human lips and human thoughts. He invites us to join with Him in that worship, and by that invitation, by the sublime words in which He adopted us as His brothers, He swept away the cold fear which makes the creature crouch low in its own dust silent before the majesty of God or speaking only some trembling words of fear. Through Christ, men found a new dignity—that dignity which St. Paul flung as a magnificent challenge to the early Christians : " For know ye not that ye are the sons of God, and if sons, heirs also; heirs indeed of God and joint-heirs with Christ." We are no longer afraid—no longer dumb with the sense of our nothingness. We accept it, and the more intense our knowledge of the unapproachable majesty of God the greater our exaltation in accepting Christ's invitation to join our prayer with His and to say " Our Father ". We find the strength to pray through the realization that we do not pray alone, but " through Jesus Christ Our Lord " in union with the Church, His Mystical Body.

But our prayer must also be inspired by the Holy Spirit, the Third Person of the Blessed Trinity. Let us consider this more closely. We must find a place in our lives for the Holy Spirit, that this Spirit may pray in us and with us. There is a craving for the divine deeply stamped in our nature, whether we acknowledge it, or choke it with sin and worldliness; there is a divine discontent in us which made St. Augustine cry out: " Thou hast made us for Thyself, O Lord, and our hearts are restless until they rest in Thee." Only when the gates of our life are flung wide to the Spirit of God can this discontent be allayed; only when our souls become living temples of the Holy Spirit can that rest be ours.

We are the heirs to the ages, and we have inherited a strange confusion. Within the past few decades, there has been a craving for untrammelled freedom, because men will tolerate only such restraints as they choose to impose on themselves. This is the result of several centuries of spiritual lawlessness, in which men have ' progressively ' flung from them the authority of the Church, state, custom, tradition, in the name of what they called the "chainless spirit" of Man. Men claimed to be masters of their fate and captains of their soul. 'Freedom' became synonymous with true manhood; and so we invented free science, free love, *laissez faire* economy, free thought, free press, free expression, and a thousand other freedoms which we fondly imagined were adding cubit upon cubit to our human stature. There were moments of sublime, even if myopic, greatness in that struggle for freedom; there were far more frequent moments in which it was merely stupid rebellion against all restraint, an unworthy thirst for license and lawlessness. But men were so busy crying Freedom up and down the highways of life, that they had not perception to see that they were forging for themselves a new slavery. This was not an external slavery, as symbolised in the figure of the Dictator with his iron heel on the necks of a whole nation, and the smoking crematoria of his concentration camps as the sign of his power; nor was it even the slavery of poverty and hunger in the aftermath of war. It was an internal slavery, a chaining of the minds of men with fetters forged by themselves. Lust, ambition, greed and covetousness took command within the souls of men, in the places that had been swept clear of all hoary authority in the name of Freedom.

" See how kindred murder kin:
'Tis the vintage-time for death and sin:
Blood, like new wine, bubbles within:
Till Despair smothers
The struggling world, which slaves and tyrants win."

Men became slaves to the tyranny of their own passions, and began to reap the dry and withered harvest of their own despair. Life became meaningless, and the hearts of men were weary and dry of hope. Every man was free to be his own slave, and to live a life that was a miserable parody of the sublime freedom of a child of God for which he had been destined from eternity.

In the Middle Ages—the ages of Faith—men lived with their knowledge that God and eternity were waiting beyond the rim of human life; and that the greatness of man should be measured in the light of that fact. With the Renaissance and the Reformation, however, men lowered their eyes from the rim of life edged with eternity, and thought they could find a new freedom by making man the measure of man. The word 'man' itself was promoted to the dignity of a capital letter: the proper study of mankind was to be Man in all his dignity and freedom, sufficient unto himself, seeing only with his own eyes, believing only what was approved as 'rational' by his own mind. He began to take himself very seriously: he was 'rational' and he must fling wide human horizons before him, he must live fully, he must love passionately, he must follow knowledge like a sinking star, he must pass on the burning torch of human freedom undimmed. Science, art and poetry sought to fathom the secrets of life, "brooding over the dark abyss intent to hear its voices," as one poet said. The French Revolution enthroned beautiful women as Goddesses of Reason on the very altars of Catholic churches, heaped flowers in their honour, burned incense in their homage. In its very excess, this was a true picture of how men were turning in on themselves in a kind of worship of their own natures. And yet, the final result of all this was that the idea of Man became debased. No longer was he a being of great personal dignity, but simply a collection of atoms flung together fortuitously, a mere conduit by which the 'Life Force' passed from one generation to the next. He became the plaything of blind and ruthless forces; he saw himself as a cork tossed aimlessly on a dark ocean he could not fathom. He himself had little real and vital personality, because he had lost the answer to "the heavy and the weary weight of all this unintelligible world."

But the grip of materialism on the thoughts of men was loosened, in our century, by the developments in Psychoanalysis and Depth Psychology. Nineteenth century materialism had swept into oblivion all mysticism and all metaphysics, as outmoded ideas from a pre-scientific age. The province of the human mind was to be all knowledge, and mysteries had no place in it because mysteries could not be expressed in those clear scientific concepts which had become the new intellectual gods of men. There were, of course, strange irrational stirrings and cravings in men's souls, but these would be met by the new panacea—enlightenment. Morality was to be a matter of what was cricket and was was not cricket, assisted by a traditional behaviour; and, of course, an excellent police system was to be the guardian of good order. With the coming of Freud, however, men suddenly realized that they were living complacently in a half-world; that within themselves was another strange world full of blind forces and imperious instincts—the world of the unconscious, of whose very existence men had been unaware, and which they now found to fit very uneasily into the categories of materialism. The era of psychoanalysis had come, and the non-material element in man could no longer be ignored. Men became more and more aware that the springs of motivation and activity, which they had claimed to explain rationally, were in reality the expression of strange laws in an irrational and disturbing part of themselves. They groped into the newly discovered country of the unconscious, questioning its mysteries, gathering some vague answers; they became aware of it as a region where neat and satisfying 'clear scientific concepts' had no place, but where realities were but the prelude to greater realities, horizons suddenly swallowed up in greater horizons. It had been claimed that man was the measure of all things; and now men experienced a bitter awakening to the fact that they could not measure themselves nor fathom their own being.

The result of all this was that men lost any clear conception of what is their own nature, and what the aim and purpose of that nature. Now a complete mystery to themselves, men saw their neat and trimmed ideas degenerating into a writhing coil of cravings and blind possibilities. Which of these cravings expressed the real essence of Man? To which of the forces in their nature were men to abandon themselves? Were they to abandon themselves, in a spirit of Nietzschean *amor fati*, to lust or greed, to humanism or selfishness, to omniscient but barren intelligence, to intense living in the conviction that the grave takes all? Should men take up an attitude towards their own lives, or just drift with the current of experience and of pleasure? But by drifting, do not men miss the whole meaning of their existence, by shirking a decision? In the face of the new chaos suddenly revealed within their own nature, men could take the way of determination and decisive action. These glimpses of strange infinities within us are pointers to a thirst for Infinity, for God, which has been placed by our Creator in the very depths of our nature. We must not seize on these infinities—these "magic casements opening" into the recesses of our being—as idols to be enthroned in our lives. Their very multiplicity would only increase that modern disease we have called *Angst* and which is a vague dread accompanying the apprehension of freedom and limitless possibilities, but without a definite object. The far flung horizons within us must lead us to the Infinity of God, if we are to find peace and rest.

Where does God enter into all this? The first question that suggests itself is whether experience can reveal everything in the limitlessness of the soul. Has God been discovered among the infinities of the soul? Or has all this groping into the depths of the soul been a mere unearthing of rubble, of cheap and valueless knowledge, while the image of God revealed in these infinities has remained undiscovered? To answer these questions, we must turn to the Word of God. There is indeed something more in our souls than can be revealed by daily experience, by modern psychiatry or psychology, by mystical communion with nature, by the exaltation of art or of love—in short, by any attempts of the human mind to grasp infinity. All such fail to reach the ultimate meaning of man's nature, the image of the Divine stamped on mankind. No matter what riches are revealed in human nature, Man can never prove worthy of the adoration of men, and the questing mind must ultimately turn from it all in bewilderment to seek enlightenment from the Word of God. Through the Word of God, we learn that deep in our own nature God dwells, and that this is no mere metaphor for the reflection of the infinite things within us, but the expression of a literal truth. God, the Infinite, the Incomprehensible, has been pleased to create man in the image of His own infinity, and to take up His abode in the souls of men. By realizing this truth, we escape being enslaved by the finite things in our nature which would delude us with the pretence of our own Godless infinity, and we are lifted far above that only infinity which we can indeed claim—the infinity of our own weakness and limitations.

God is within us, not merely in the sense that by adopting us He sets us free from our own terrifying loneliness, though this in itself is a greater happiness than the world can give us. Knowing that we are dust in His sight, and humbly accepting the measureless distance between Him and us, we adore Him as more than just the Cause of our liberation. Without Him, we could not know ourselves as we really are. We raise our eyes to God and cry to Him, nothingness speaking to Eternal Being; and yet, we know with a rush of joy that He is the very source of our being, the meaning of our existence, and that, through grace, we are partakers in His Divine Life.

God is within us, as He has himself testified. We are "the temples of the Holy Ghost" and "the spirit of God" dwells within us as our true infinity. This spirit broods over us, filling us with the abundance of the plenitude of life, anointing us and sealing our hearts with a celestial seal. The earnest and first taste of life everlasting, He satisfies our insatiable craving for knowledge of what we are and what we mean. He is the Life in which our death is swallowed up. He is our unbounded happiness, through Whom we know a tearless joy even in the valley of tears. When we are weary and heavy in mind and heart, He is our secret source of consolation. We know that we often grope in the half-light of our own folly; and we find courage in the realisation that He is within us and that we can call on Him for guidance. We find the eternal love of God dwelling within us, even though our hearts are selfish and narrow; behind the dryness of our years we know there lives His eternal freshness; He is the sky of serene joy behind our heavy clouds of sorrow; in Him we find confidence to face the tasks from which we shudder; He is true liberty, through Whom our souls take wing towards eternal bliss.

To many, all this may seem the poetic weavings of mere wishful thinking, since we are not really aware that we have such treasure within us. This objection, however, is based on an outmoded idea; for the surface mind, thinking only in terms of materialistic being—that is to say, admitting the existence of consciousness alone—is an anachronism surviving from the " enlightenment " of the eighteenth and nineteenth centuries. Today, we know that the mind of man is not consciousness alone, and that below the level of consciousness are infinite possibilities, unfathomed depths, unmeasured horizons. We are far from having surveyed the range of our own nature. To use a homely comparison, we have as yet lived in a paltry gate-lodge, while in reality our heart is a stately mansion where dwell the hopes of all our happiness and where a glorious personal destiny awaits our shaping. It is a well-known fact, of course, that psychiatry has reached down into the depths of our nature and has stirred up much that may seem indeed slimy and repulsive, so that our soul might seem rather an abode of hate and lust and greed fit for a devil's habitation rather than for the temple of God. And yet, we must nourish our faith, in order that we may know the splendid message of joy in all this. The depths in us are not pools of stagnant bitterness, but the waters of infinity springing up into eternal life. It is easy to stir up the slime; but it needs faith to see, behind and through all these dark forces, a much more powerful force—the power of the presence of the Holy Ghost. We can conquer the depths of our own nature and thereby realize ourselves to the fullest, only by an adoring belief and acceptance of this Divine Presence. Thus we make ourselves *living* temples, through conscious acceptance of the Divine in the depths of our being. Only through such acceptance do we open our hearts and our lives to the full power of the Holy Ghost.

All this does not occur if we ourselves do not invite the Holy Ghost to speak live-giving words in our souls. He speaks within us in answer to the words He hears from us; and when once we have heard His voice, the depths of our being are no longer a tangle of conflicting urges and shoreless immensities, but a window opening on real Infinity and a place alight with the fructifying presence of God. The bewildering infinities of human longings become swallowed up in His true and incomprehensible Infinity: in the mysterious designs of God, we become partakers, in our own finite way, of God's infinity. We cannot truly know ourselves except through this realization that our whole nature is in the image of God's immensity.

This brings us back to the subject of prayer. The Spirit of God dwelling within us as a great light in all our darkness, is the source of our prayer. He is not only God before Whom we kneel in supplication; He is working in us and for us, by His inspirations, especially when we are engaged in that most important of all our activities— prayer. In itself, our prayer consists of but dry words in arid minds; our pious feelings are in themselves but sickly plants languishing in the poor soil of our souls. But, through the power of the Holy Ghost within us, the words of our prayers become winged words, light-filled words, words that rise to the throne of God; and our pious feelings take deeper root, and blossom into spiritual strength and beauty. Thus, through our prayer, the Holy Spirit within us worships the Father and pleads for us " with unspeakable groanings "; and sometimes in our prayer we shall experience something of God's eternal joy in His own infinity and splendour. Herein is the secret of the great dignity of human prayer.

Since we are partakers in the Divine Nature, our prayer has a greater power than lies in mere human words. We pray, not only with what is human in us, but with what is divine. Mighty things, far beyond our understanding, occur within us when we say: " Our Father ". They may seem to us to be drily spoken and to savour of presumption; but when sincerely spoken, the inner reality to which they correspond is something glorious. We are baptized children of God, professing our belief in Him and our love for Him; therefore the Spirit of God truly lives within us and speaks in us. Through the Holy Ghost dwelling within us, the words: " Our Father " are filled with a power of worship which links them with the praise of God by the Angelic choirs in Heaven.

We may not know for what we should ask when we pray; but it suffices that God knows. Our pleadings may seem to lose themselves unheard somewhere in the cold silent expanses that separate us from God; and yet, God not only hears us, but calls to us from His Immensity. In this faith, we cast out fear. Only God knows the depths of the human soul, and there is nothing hidden from Him. When He searches the depths in us, He does not find mere emptiness, aimlessness, the coiling and un-coiling of urges and passions, twisted and thwarted being; He sees His own Divine Spirit, and listens to the " unspeakable groanings " of that Spirit pleading in the prayer of the human soul. He hears those pleadings as His own pleadings in which the chaos of our hearts and of our lives is touched with Divine order and transformed into praise worthy of God.

The Holy Ghost is our help in prayer. When we are overcome with fatigue and spiritual dryness, so that the words we speak seem to fall heavy and lifeless about our feet, He prays within us with that freshness of praise we cannot command. When our lack of faith seems to wither the prayer on our very lips, He speaks words within us and for us which are not the image but the very substance of Divine Worship worshipping the Divine. Sometimes what we really think and feel seems to lag far behind the fervent words we speak in our prayer: we say—"My God, I love Thee"—and feel that the words are echoing only in our own hollowness. We then find courage and strength in the realization that the Holy Ghost dwelling within us is giving the true meaning to the words, speaking them with us in an adoring rapture of love. Always when we pray sincerely, from however dry a heart, the Spirit of God prays within us.

The Holy Ghost helps us, not only in our interior experience of prayer, but also by giving to our prayer a new and more exalted significance. Through Him, our prayer becomes one with the pure harmony of angelic prayer eternally rising like incense to the Blessed Trinity. The Spirit of God prays in us. This is the source of the confidence which enables us to pray. The Spirit of God prays in us. Herein is the sublime dignity of our prayer, and the inspiration urging us " always to pray and not to faint ". The unfailing power of our prayer is the Spirit of God praying within us. Because of this, our prayers are real, however arid the words on our lips and however dry our hearts. Because the Spirit of God prays within us, our prayer will become as a fountain springing up unto life everlasting.

Our prayer is made worthy of God through the Spirit of God. Before we begin to pray, let us silence the echoes from the commonplaces of life, that a deep interior silence may take possession of our souls. Only in that silence can the finer things within us be heard, and only when there is silence of the heart can grace work in us to inspire our prayer. Into that silence, the Spirit of the Father and of the Son will speak. Sometimes, through the actual grace of sensible devotion, we may be keenly aware of that voice in a rapture of joy; more often, we must believe in faith that He is speaking in us, with us and for us, that His words are being silently spoken in the depths of our being and in the Being of the Eternal Father. We must not do anything to hinder this speaking of the Holy Ghost through our prayer. We must speak His word: *Our Father,* with reverence and love. For this is true prayer.

THE PRAYER OF LOVE.

OUR love of God and our prayer have one difficulty in common. They will succeed only if we lose the very thought of what we are doing in the thought of Him for Whom we are doing it. To be concerned mainly with the correct way to love or the correct way to pray, entails almost inevitable failure in the realization of either activity. It is useful to consider these matters in retrospect by meditating on the nature of the love of God and on the nature of prayer; it is useful to attempt to describe what the act of love or the activity of prayer really entails. Yet, to some extent, such meditation destroys the very act itself, for we cannot really perform an act and at the same time be preoccupied with the mechanics of our doing it. We succeed in prayer and in love only when we lose ourselves in both, and are no longer aware of *how* we are praying or in *what manner* we are loving. Our age is particularly given to introspection and the analysis of motive and action, with the result that we are often deprived of the power to act through sheer preoccupation with how the act is to be done. In the spiritual sphere, we become entangled in our own speculative thoughts about God and about the modes of our prayer, instead of entering into union with God through meditation and love. We lose our zest for the object of the activity in our zeal for the activity itself. Thus we become tangled with the very means to activity, and we cannot act. Our age is imprisoned in its own subjectivity. The modern tendency is to call on even the most exalted moments of the human mind to stand and unfold themselves, declare their identity, state what they are and how they ' work '; for the modern mind is fearful of mistaking the image and the symbol for the reality, of mistaking for pure spiritual currency what is in reality the cleverly deceptive coinage of baser cravings. All this creates a closed circle of sterile questioning in which men imprison themselves. Instead of leading men to reach out for the desired object, this kind of self-questioning leads only to further self-questioning and to a sterility in which there is no answer and no activity.

Today, we tend to judge our thoughts and feelings in themselves, and not by reference to the exalted nature of the object towards which they tend. This is a wrong attitude, because it leads to feelings of disillusionment in which our activities cease to have any real significance for us. Thus disillusioned, we are inclined to avoid altogether such acts as deliberate raising of mind and heart to God in prayer and love. God becomes for us the Ineffable, the Incomprehensible; and we live out our years in His sight dumb in mind and heart. He sees our good works on earth, our " little nameless unremembered acts of kindness " towards our neighbour, our fundamental decency, and the patience with which we bear the weight of " all this unintelligible world ". We live, as it were, with our backs to God, knowing indeed that He is watching us, but never turning to speak to Him because we fear the very act of prayer. Hence the cult of a religion so prevalent today, which could be described as anonymous morality: *I don't pray and that sort of thing, but I am as decent a man as the next,* is the way this cult is usually worded. Those who still " pray and that sort of thing " are regarded as naïve, unanalytical, incapable of realizing that they are confusing God with their own thoughts and feelings *about* God. The proper attitude is, of course, to live decently and avoid the dangers of self-deception in all this praying and church-going. The Modern Mind has come to regard prayer and expression of one's love of God as at best redundant, and at worst mawkish and effeminate.

Let us examine more closely this fear of " direct " religion. On analysis, it is found to be an aspect of the modern fear of introspection: the fear of being caught up in a circle of subjectivity which sets off from the self and returns to the self, its only fruits being inner loneliness and a sense of futility. This fear freezes the springs of prayer, because prayer is regarded as something which inevitably leads *inwards* to the self, whereas the tendency is rather to reach *outwards* away from the self. Prayer is indeed such a " reaching out " to the Infinity of God, and has a significance far beyond the limitations of this earthly life. It is because modern man tends to suspect everything reaching beyond the narrow sweep of the five senses and of human reason, that he shrinks from the supernatural, except perhaps to the extent of passive belief. The great masters of the spiritual life have emphasised that the objective relationship existing between God and men demands a positive attitude in which men look up to God in faith, worship, hope and love, rather than adopt a remote, negative attitude in which they worship God indirectly through something other than God. All things lead to the direct worship of God Himself. Though Incomprehensible and above all His works, God can be known through His works. He has spoken to us in the Person of His Son, and it was in human words that the Son spoke to us of the Father. God has poured forth His Spirit into our hearts, but we know this only through the words of the Son. Therefore we may, and indeed we must, lift up our minds to God Himself, praise Him in our hearts, worship Him explicitly and publicly, honour Him, take courage to speak to Him and to call Him ' Father '.

All our activities take their meaning from Him. What our minds can know of Him, we love in Him, but mind and heart reach out to seize on the Unknown, the Incomprehensible, the Infinite. A thirst for the Infinite has been made part of the very essence of the human soul; and hence Saint Augustine's famous words: "Thou hast made us for Thyself, O Lord, and our heart is restless until it rests in Thee." While we remain on earth, we see things " through a glass, in a dark manner," as Saint Paul puts it, and the Spirit of God given to us remains a hidden God. That this is so, however, does not dispense us from the duty of Faith, for it is through Faith that our thirst for the Eternal finds its expression. Through Faith, man dares to reach away from himself towards a glory which as yet he can but glimpse, until that Faith is swallowed up in the Eternal Light wherein he meets his God face to face.

If God is regarded as the unknown factor which, being beyond the range of our practical life, can be ignored or at most accepted passively as one might accept the presence of an onlooker, then we can never experience a nearness to God, and our vague religion will pale, to all intents and purposes, into atheism. We must invoke the Mystery of God, ponder it, live with it, learn to love it; so that, even though it remains a mystery, it becomes a reality in our life.

Prayer is a lifting up of the heart, a directing of the mind, to God. In the language of Christian thought, love is that pure fulness of prayer in which man gathers up all his activities into a direct communication with God. The Commandment of Love is more than the fulfilment of the Law: it is also the essence of all true prayer. There is no need for specific formulae and set words in prayer, because in prayer we speak freely with God, offering our petitions, confessing our guilt, worshipping the infinite attributes of God. Men find themselves by yielding themselves entirely to God, and above all by giving to Him a love of which He alone is worthy—unconditionally, boundlessly, eternally worthy. Since the fulness of prayer is the love of God, it is through that love that we must learn what prayer really is.

What is the love of God, and how can we attain it so as to learn how to pray? We are told that this love shows itself in particular through the observance of the Commandments. This is indeed true; but it is not the whole truth. The love of God must precede and be the motive of such observance. Many efforts have been made to describe the love of God in the human soul. It is true, of course, that those who know how to talk about the love of God do not necessarily possess a greater measure of it. It remains nonetheless true, however, that when we hear others speak of the love of God, we come to realise how lacking we are in this love.

In speaking about the Divine Mysteries, even Holy Scripture had to fall back on thoughts and images drawn from human life. We may begin, therefore, from our human experience of human love. When one person loves another with a pure and unselfish love, that love gives some idea of the love we must bear to God, except that our love of God must be deeper, more unselfish, more unconditional, because it is directed towards God Himself.

The word *love* covers a variety of human relationships so that it is necessary to determine what one means by the term. The love we speak of here is certainly not the narrow and selfish idea of sexual lust. Even in cases where it does not degrade itself to promiscuity or excessive indulgence, sexuality falls short of the perfection of the ideal *love* in the context: *love of God*. On the other hand, the love of which we speak must not be confused with a feeling of benevolence which, even though it may prehaps be unselfish, is fundamentally supine. For this love is something essentially positive, passionate, arising from the very recesses of a man's soul, shattering his egotism, surging upward from the dust of its nothingness to its glory in the worshipping of the Infinite. Through such love, we lose ourselves in our union with One immeasurably greater than ourselves, Who has become the sole meaning of life for us.

Unselfishness is the essential quality of love, wherein the soul rejoices at the very existence of the beloved. It is a radiant release from the self, experienced when a man learns to break through the imprisoning walls of his own egotism and give himself to another. Beforehand, his life was a miserable one, cribbed and cabined: now it has taken on " an ampler ether, a diviner air " by escaping from its own self-shackles through giving itself to another. In complete forgetfulness of self, this love clings to the beloved. The happiness of the beloved is the happiness of him who loves. To love in this manner, is to have escaped from the prison of selfishness without being trapped into another prison. For this love of one person for another not only reveals the value of the beloved person, but opens up vistas of the mysterious and radiant wonders of the whole creation. In fact, this exchange of pure and unselfish love between two persons becomes the reflection and symbol of that Love which embraces all things—the Love of God.

But this love between two persons can lead to happiness or to misery. The secret of its happiness lies in the recognition by both parties, that through this love a greater love must be born. Their love for one another must meet in and be exalted by the greater Love. Again, the essence of human love is the realization that in giving

35

oneself, one has received in return the gift of another. This gives a greater sense of security than when lived within oneself; for it is not good for a man to be alone. From the union of two loving hearts arise that thoughtful serving of one another and that unselfishness and fidelity which are at once the safeguards and the hallmarks of love.

Let us endeavour to love God in this fundamental way. Let us seek Him, the Almighty and Holy One, before Whom we are as dust. Forgetting ourselves, surrendering to Him our whole being, uniting ourselves to Him with every fibre of our souls, let us fling ourselves wide to God; and we shall know that bliss, at once yearning and sweet, which pervades us when we give to Him our whole being and our whole world. My Lord and my God! To Thee we may surrender ourselves entirely. Through Thee, what is hard in us becomes tender; and in our pure worship of Thee, we may reveal what we keep hidden from all. We can open our hearts freely to Thee, whispering to Thee what we are and what we do, our successes and our failures, our sorrows and our joys. In yielding ourselves entirely to Thee, we have no fear of being deceived. We lay our most precious treasures at Thy feet, and we know that our loving enthusiasm in doing so will not turn to the disillusion and bitterness of a betrayed love.

This love cries out to God in the depths of our hearts. All the powers of the soul well up to meet Him, and there is no ebb. God becomes the centre of our life, nearer to us than we are to ourselves, loved with a greater love than we bear to ourselves, loved unselfishly for His own sake. It is stained through with the inspired knowledge that it is He Who has first loved us. God never fails to answer the call of love rising to Him from the shadows of this valley of tears, because this love is utterly unselfish, faithful and gentle, seeking nothing but a return of love. It loves God rather than merely loving the reward which is promised to that love; for in the love itself, it is rewarded. Trials do not daunt it, nor is it quenched by the waters of sorrow. It is something quiet and hidden; at once bold and timorous; always marked with reverence for the Divine Mysteries, familiarity never breeding an absence of awe and wonder. It is not the love of a human person, but the love of God; and therefore the Infinite Greatness of the Object of love will be reflected in the reverence, humility and burning ardour of the lover. For the love of God is holy and sublime—and eternal.

This love is the true love of God, the Infinite One, Who dwells in our hearts in a mysterious manner that we cannot understand. It is the love of the Holy One, Who alone is worthy of adoration. We love Him with Whom we are to come face to face in life everlasting; Him Who is our Creator and our Lord; the Eternal Father, Son and Holy Ghost—three Divine Persons in one God. We love Him Who first loved us, Who gave us existence and life, in Whom we live and move and have our being, Who loves us even when we have turned our backs on Him. He is patient, faithful and wise; He is the God of our hearts and the God Who is our portion forever. Infinity lies between His Immensity and our nothingness, but this very Infinity is a challenge to our love inasmuch as it emphasises how much our whole life is dependent upon His adorable Providence. In awe and worship, we entrust our life into the hands of this beloved God. The more radiant His divine beauty and love, the more that love exceeds any conception we can have of love. By grace, the Divine becomes more living and real in us, so that thereby God becomes to us father and mother, brother and sister, our hearts growing more intimately united with His Divine Heart. Love is the soul's answer to the inscrutability of God's judgments and ways: the less able the soul finds itself to understand God, the more urgently its love reaches out towards Him. Overwhelmed by our utter nothingness in the face of God, we pray the more fervently: "My God, I love Thee "—words which are the highest expression of love that any man can offer. In the mystery of the love he bears towards an Infinite God, man realises what is most exalted in his nature.

But we must not misunderstand the nature of this love. True, it burns with the sacred fire of selflessness and self-oblation which is characteristic of all human love—be it only the fire where love turns to pain through its own yearning. While this is so, however, the fire of the love of God has a higher nature, because its power is not *in itself* but derives from the fact that it is a flame of love rising to *God*. Hence it is that this love becomes true Christian love only when sanctified by Grace.

Several considerations flow from this. The love of God is indeed the highest exaltation of human nature; but it must be constantly preserved, through being continually sanctified, from degenerating into a mere expression of one's own presumptuous ability to become like unto God through one's own paltry resources. Nor should it become an expression of burning impatience to win God by our own efforts—to seize Him, as it were, by sheer power of will. The true love of God can exist only in a heart which is humbled by the unattainable majesty and unapproachable holiness of the Everlasting God. To be redeemed from ourselves, we must humble ourselves in adoration of the Almighty. We must control our thirst for that grace of sensible devotion which makes us experience the *nearness* of God: this must be left entirely in His hands, since what matters to us is only the doing of His holy will. The fire of our longing for God is pure only when it is kindled in us by the will of God. The love of God demands perseverence and self-restraint; and this is possible only by the grace of Him Who, dwelling eternally in the bosom of His Father, yet "emptied himself" to serve that Father in silent obedience in a sinful world.

The greatest and purest upsurge of human love falls short of that love which God wishes to receive from us. The divine paradox here is that we must love God with a love implanted in us by God; for this love, like everything we have received, and even like that Beatific Vision which we hope for in Everlasting Life, is a free gift of God, beyond our power to achieve or to merit by our own unaided efforts. Between us and God is the gulf between nothingness and Infinity. If our love reaches God across that abyss, it is solely because, through His Holy Spirit, God has cast into our hearts His own supreme Love, in which our sinfulness and our nothingness has been swallowed up. "God has first loved us": Love has stooped to our nothingness and kindled itself in us. We were unworthy of this Love, and it is only through this Love that we can offer our love to God. For what is our love, but, as it were, a frightened surrender to that Divine Love that has been cast into our hearts as the fire which Christ said He had come "to cast upon the earth" with the desire that it "should be enkindled"? All our efforts to love would fail hopelessly, were they not mysteriously transformed, freely lifted to a higher plane above the reach of human effort, by Divine Love, through which we attain to that true love worthy of God and of redeemed creatures destined to enjoy the Beatific Vision. This true love of God becomes a living reality in us when we bear in mind that it is rooted in, and is the free gift of, God's love for us. Therefore our prayer of love must be: "Thou, O Lord, lovest me. Grant me the grace to open my heart to that love, that I may love Thee."

How are we to know that this love lives in us? The deepest things in a man are not those which abide his question most readily, nor about which he is most ready to speak. A love stronger than death can live unsuspected within a man. But our own honest opinion of ourselves is that we love God only in a half-hearted way —that, indeed, our love is often no more than a resolution and intention to love Him, far from that "with thy whole heart and with thy whole soul, with all thy mind and with all thy strength" which He Himself demands of us. Yet, we must love God more and more: otherwise, we shall have in the end to face the bitter realisation that our life has been useless because devoid of real love. We shall stand at the outer rim of our years like an errant child at the grave of a mother whose love for him he realizes too late to make a return of love.

It is said that we cannot command love—that we cannot *resolve* and *intend* to love—because the waters of love rise in obedience to their own mysterious laws. This is indeed true of merely human love. Yet, of one thing we can be certain. He who has honestly resolved to seek the love of God, may be said to possess that love already in his heart. For that very resolution is a proof that the grace of God has descended into the depths of his heart to kindle there a longing for God's love. What we must do is to set no obstacle to the growth of this love within us, so that it may pervade our whole being more and more. We must ask Him Who is the object of our love to give us the sweetly compelling power of His Grace; to reach into the depths of our soul, and set a spring of love there so that its waters may make fertile the dry and barren places of our lovelessness.

We often feel that our heart is stony, and that we have no power to warm it with love. There is, however, one thing we can all do: we can heed the first feeble stirrings of a love for God, the first timid longing of our restless hearts for God. The busy cares of life make us dusty and tired, so that even life's joys may become insipid. There are times when we feel cold and alone, our friends become as strangers to us, and even the love of our dearest fails to satisfy a deep longing in our innermost soul. Our world seems a meaningless tangle of empty hurryings to and fro, where the new turns out to be but the old wearing another face, where day follows pointless day, where knowledge arduously gathered lies cold and inert in the soul. Life ebbs, wealth becomes as sand running through one's fingers, friendship grows cold, the senses become blunted and without response. Such is every man's lot, but we do not regard such things as our real sufferings. For, in addition, there is all the bitterness that can fill the heart of a man—desolation, grief, distress and suffering both of body and of soul.

Grace comes when we are made to realise the futility and ephemeral nature of all things under the sun, and it is typical of human nature to resist this realisation. When one thing turns to dust and ashes for us, we turn from it hopefully to something else, and so the restless search goes on. This seed of restlessness placed in the human heart, though at first sight it may appear an unwholesome thing, is in reality a great blessing. For when a man has discovered that all his fevered searching leads only to blank walls of disillusion, he begins to experience a new realisation which makes a way for the love of God in his heart. There is only one object of love—God—that can fill the soul of man to its immortal girth—that can quench that thirst which drives a man restlessly on and on. God alone can possess us fully and satisfy us entirely. Hence, that disillusionment which makes the heart cry out its "vanity of vanities" over all earthly things, is essential to all Christians. It reveals to us that only One is capable of seizing upon our entire being, and that we must surrender to Him in unbounded love. Reeling under the impact of this disillusion, yet neither despairing nor blinding ourselves with any deception, we begin to grope towards the love of God which comes to us as "something else" about which we are as yet vague and uncertain, but which we know this world cannot give us. When, under the guidance of Grace, we recognize this vague yearning as a thirst for Infinity, for God, the love of God comes alive in our souls. Deeply implanted in human nature is a man's longing for the God of his heart and the God Who is his portion forever. All earthly things wither to disillusion, and of himself a man begins to seek God Who alone is Love. In Him alone does the heart find rest.

The way of quiet and grateful joy may also lead to our discovery of the love of God dwelling within us. Someone does us a great kindness, we are freed from a crippling fear or a heavy sorrow, and we feel a surge of deep joy and calm. Behind that change from sorrow to joy, from oppression of heart to freedom, we sense something greater. We read into this joy a reflection of eternal light, and in our gratitude, we know that we have met God and that He has blessed us. We are filled with a sense of His goodness, His greatness, His sublime mercy. We feel His nearness to us, and the luminous shadow of His blessing, awakening our love.

When we are thus visited by God through sorrow or through joy we must nourish the inward urge to love awakened in our souls. We must not turn from that timid longing for God that raises its small voice to speak to us of His love. It is a whispering voice which is quickly drowned if we do not shut out the clamouring noises of this world, the eager elbowing voices of business and pleasure. We must create in ourselves that interior silence in which we can subdue the restlessness of our heart, and breathe our silent prayer: "O God, near unto me, great and above all things, Thou alone art good. I love Thee."

In thus awakening the love of God within us, we have but begun. This first small stirring of love within us must survive in our day-to-day life. It must prove itself in faithful obedience and in love of our neighbour. It does not develop into firm and authentic love of God unless God transforms it, through the power of His Holy Spirit, into that love which alone can unite a man with God. Nevertheless, we must not underestimate the importance of these first feelings of sensible tenderness towards God, those first feeble steps of our own, wherein Grace comes to us amid the work of our own hands. For it is in this way that the true love of God is born within our heart.

This mysterious rising of the waters of love within the hidden depths of our soul, this longing for God which requires only our willing consent, could well up with greater power if we had not choked its source with the dust of our sins. We experience in practice the truth of Christ's words: " Blessed are the clean of heart, for they shall see God." Only a person whose heart is pure, or who has at least a sincere and active desire for this purity of heart, can truly love God, the Source of all goodness and all purity. Repeated grievous sins extinguish the love of God in the soul; and venial sin and bad habits impede its growth. We observe the strict duties of the Christian life, perhaps, but we regard as unnecessary and supererogatory anything beyond what is strictly prescribed. Our conscience is easily satisfied, and we have no real anxiety about our salvation. We show a reluctance to prayer and the reception of the Sacraments, and our spiritual obligations are things to be got through as expediently as possible so as to get back to what we regard as the more pleasant things in life. Now, all this prevents us from loving God with our whole heart. We stand before God as persons who are spiritually blind and dumb.

The soul that loves God welcomes the sense of God's love in the performance of every duty, thereby transforming each duty into an act of love. The sin-ridden self-centred soul, however, fears that God may demand that which it is unwilling to give, and is therefore reluctant to meet God. We must obey the promptings of our conscience, by earnestly and perseveringly doing our duty in every moment of our life. By doing so, we bring God into our daily life, and we draw nearer to Him. We grow in the knowledge of His holiness and His goodness, and thus cultivate that purity of heart through which the soul becomes united with God. In this way, we begin to love God with our whole heart and our whole soul, with our whole mind and our whole strength.

We must foster the first stirring of our heart, and we must keep our heart pure in readiness for the love of God. Above all, however, we must pray for the gift of divine love and for that purity which is essential to its presence. It is in the hands of God to control the beginning, the growth and the perfection of sacred love in us, according to His own Divine Will; for He has first loved us. The first stirring of sacred love within us was the effect of His grace. He, and He alone, can purify our hearts. We must pray for this grace, and for an increase of His love. We may well fear that our hearts will become cold to God's love, and may wonder whether indeed we do not love darkness more than we love light. All the more reason, therefore, to implore His compassionate mercy to give us ever increasing spiritual strength, so that His love may grow in our hearts.

O Jesus, give us a fear and love of Thy Holy Name, for Thou art ever present to guide and preserve those whom Thou hast established firmly in Thy love.

The love of God is the greatest grace which can be given to mankind. In it, human life achieves its true fulness, for in it we find happiness, an end to the restless searchings of our heart, and the very essence of Everlasting Life. No prayer is more certain to be heard than the petition that God may take us to His Heart, and that we may desire only the riches of His love.

Let us therefore pray: "Make me love Thee, my God; Neither in Heaven nor on earth have I anything but Thee, O God of my heart and my Portion forever. Make me cling to Thee. O beloved Lord, be Thou the centre of my heart: purify it that it may truly love Thee. Thy holiness, Thy beauty, Thy goodness are my happiness. Stay with me when I am tempted to leave Thee. Do not forsake me: make Thy love grow in me, for that love is eternal, and without Thee I am nothing. Through this love, I fervently hope to be united with Thee in Life Everlasting."

PRAYER IN EVERYDAY LIFE.

PRAYER is a voice from the depths of the heart, and there is nothing more sublime on earth than a pure heart filled with faith and charity. Prayer is the language in which the heart asks God to hear it, and to take it lovingly to His own heart. There is nothing more moving or more sublime that this loving attention on the part of the Eternal Father to the feeble stammering of His child. True prayer is prayer in the Holy Spirit. There is nothing more awe-inspiring or more sublime that this voice of the Spirit, at which all eternity trembles. The abyss between man and God is bridged when, on the wings of prayer, the feeble words of the creature are carried to the throne of the Creator. The voice of human supplication reaches to the heights wherein dwells the Majesty of God in eternal bliss. He who has truly understood what a sublime thing prayer is, must be stricken with awe indeed when he is about to pray.

How then can prayer be an everyday business, compatible with the monotony, uniformity, depression and dullness of our hearts, so tired and desiccated? Yet there must be something like prayer in everyday life, for the Scripture says that we ought " always to pray and not to faint." (Luke 18:1). St. Paul admonishes us to " pray at all times in the spirit " (Eph. 6:18), to " pray without ceasing " (I. Thess. 5:18) and to be " instant in prayer " (Rom. 12:12).

Let us consider two aspects of everyday prayer. We are to pray in everyday life, and we are to make everyday life our prayer.

We are to pray in everyday life. This should be regular prayer, practised without regard to our humours or likings. We mean here that prayer which, without being specifically enjoined, is practised from an innate sense of duty or as a cherished tradition—prayer at certain times, such as when retiring and before meals. Prayer in everyday life includes the Angelus, the Rosary said by the individual or by the family, and visits to the Blessed Sacrament outside the times of public service. Prayer in everyday life includes many pious customs we have inherited from our forefathers, such as our salutation when we pass a church or a Crucifix, the sign of the cross when we cut a new loaf of bread, the blessing received at night by children from their parents. All these things are essentially prayer in everyday life.

Such prayers have their own difficulties. Many of us find it hard even to remember them. In many Catholic countries they have fallen into disuse or oblivion. Those of us who still are Christians know that we are bound to such prayer at least by custom: yet in many places these customs have a precarious existence, since minds and hearts are filled with other things. We are told that modern man has no time for such prayers. They appear old-fashioned. They have become mere memories of childhood days. Never officially abolished, they drag on a miserable life without exercising any formative influence. We are inclined to think that, by dropping these relics of childhood, nothing would really be changed, for better or worse.

Prayer in everyday life is difficult. It is easily forgotten, since our rushed and fevered age does not foster and promote it. It thrives only in individual hearts, which, unconcerned with the disbelief of others, can instil their own vigour into everyday prayer from their own lively and personal faith.

It is difficult to prevent everyday prayer from disappearing imperceptibly and withering away. It is even more difficult to make everyday prayer *real* prayer and to prevent its degenerating into mere routine. We must ask ourselves how far our everyday prayer is more than mere words. Heart and mind are often far away from what we are saying. Instead of speaking heart to heart to God, we recite set formulas. Our main concern is to get through the formulas, and there is no attempt to establish vital contact with God. Thus everyday prayer becomes an everyday matter in the worst sense of the word. It becomes a superficial, mechanical, slipshod lip-service, the performance of an external task to be got through as quickly as possible in order to get back to more pleasant things.

Such prayer is, as it were, time grudgingly conceded to God, because this concession is better not omitted, lest we should get into His bad books. Thus we slip into that terrifying state of everyday Christian life, where in praying, our hearts remain far from God. Our lips honour God, but our heart does not join with them; and yet we imagine that we thus fulfil our duty towards God. Towards Him Who alone knows our heart, however, there is no fulfilment of duty unless our life and words are filled with the pure spiritual intention of the heart.

In many cases, a man suffers because of the difference between what his prayer is and what he knows it should be. He suffers from his heart's refusing to enter into the lofty words of adoration, praise, thanks, petition, awe or contrition, which are the subject and expression of prayer. He suffers from the contrast between his willingness to pray, often and every day, and his apparent incapability. His heart seems to be paralysed, and he fears he may be labelled a hypocrite through pretending to do something which in reality is beyond his power. He thinks that in sincerity towards himself and towards God, he must wait until the fountains in the depths of his heart spring up again, to provide the healing waters of grace, of spontaneous emotion and of vital spiritual experience, thus making true prayer possible in a sincere outpouring of the heart. This difficulty tempts many a responsible and good person to pray infrequently. These are persons whose everyday life becomes void of prayer, not because they have succumbed to the superficiality of mundane routine, but because they are conscientious and honest. They refuse to pray unless their prayer comes from the heart. They do not believe that it needs only the will of man to make his prayer the voice of the heart.

Nevertheless, in spite of all these difficulties, it remains true, as the wisdom of our forefathers and our own precious inheritance teach us, that we must make prayer part of our daily life. We must not restrict prayer to the rare moments of sensible devotion when prayer wells up spontaneously within us. Such moments do indeed occur as long as faith in God lives in the soul. We must realise the necessity of everyday prayer, which is both the prerequisite and the result of those great moments of spiritual exaltation.

There are, of course, considerable differences in the quality of various moments of prayer. There are certainly prayers, perhaps in but fleeting and rare moments, when an Angel of God touches our heart, and when our heart is filled with awe at the majesty of the real presence of God. In those moments we experience a veritable nostalgia for our eternal home. In those moments we are inspired by the hope of the peace of God, in contrition transforming our life, in love of the eternal Love. These moments must certainly be treasured more highly than the prayer of everyday life. We may indeed be inclined to confine the name of prayer to those rare moments.

Yet those moments of grace are indeed rare. What would they profit us if they did not really capture our whole life and lift it on their wings. How spiritually impoverished we would become if in the course of our life they became imperceptibly more rare and less urgent, like inspiration in the brain of a dilatory artist? Such danger of spiritual desiccation cannot be overcome except through daily prayer. Only by our daily prayer can we create the prerequisite for the great moments of real prayer. Only when we make the effort, however hard it may be, to keep our heart open, our mind awake, and our attention alert, can we be in readiness to avail of these great and rare moments of grace. In those moments, God will suddenly meet us anew, and we shall receive an impetus which will inspire us for some time to come. We must not miss that impetus. We must always be prepared for it. In an hour of trial, of temptation, of ecstatic joy or crushing sorrow, in an hour of unspeakable loneliness or abysmal suffering, we may be called upon to give an answer which can be rendered only in prayer, an answer decisive for time and eternity.

This openness of the heart, this alertness of the mind, this constant preparedness for the great hour, will not be ours unless we have followed the command of the Lord: "Watch and pray." We must then draw on the resources we have accumulated through everyday prayer. Not to pray daily means that we are ignoring God, not listening for His word, and not preparing every day for our decisive trials. Thus we are in danger of becoming gradually blind and deaf, indifferent and lazy. In fact, we will even become unable to notice the decisive moments when we are at the cross-roads of life. A sudden storm will find us without foundation. We will lose our bearings in any new or unexpected situation, unless we have accustomed ourselves to watching in prayer day by day. We will not stand our ground in that decisive hour when life and death are in the balance, because it will arrive imperceptibly without warning, and we will not be able to plead that we have been taken by surprise. We will not be permitted to say we did not foresee the consequences, when we have refused to keep alert, active and watchful through daily prayer. Important matters, both intellectual and spiritual, are decided by the degree of practice we have acquired at the moment of discharging them.

When the hour of God, of sensible devotion in prayer has passed, we must prevent it from becoming a mere fruitless memory. It must be continued, by patient cultivation, into our ordinary daily life. The routine of everyday life must be enlivened and transformed by that vision granted to us for a brief moment in charismatic prayer. This decisive transformation cannot take place except through everyday prayer. Under the burden and amid the toil of everyday life, we must wrestle with God's angel of grace. That grey Monday morning and that weary Saturday night must yet be transfigured to some extent by a reflection of eternal light. The fire of the spirit that descended upon us in an hour of fervour, must cast its transforming reflection over the hours of daily life. We must pray for the descent of this fire upon us, as earnestly as we can. Only in virtue of such prayer will the spirit of that fire really permeate our life, which after all is mostly woven of small grey moments. Everyday prayer is both the prerequisite and the fruitful expansion of the great hours of grace in the Christian life. For that reason alone, it is important and essential.

A further, even more important, reason for prayer in everyday life is the honour of God. God is the Lord not only of the holydays of life. He has created not only sublime things: it is His holy will that the little things also should live and that He should be glorified in what appear to us the insignificant monotonies of our life. We

49

are His servants not only in lofty cathedrals where His mysteries appear to us in overawing splendour and enrapturing beauty. We are His servants also in the field or the workshop, at the desk or at the washtub. All this is for the honour and glory of His Name. Therefore in this everyday life we must bear in mind that we belong to Him in every department of our lives. Through our whole life, His praise must rise up to heaven, and everything must be done in His Name. Again and again, we must utter the words that invoke His blessing upon our daily life. Hence we must be careful to pray daily.

Prayer in daily life may appear to us to be something as dreary as our daily life itself. It may have little room for lofty thoughts and sublime feelings. It is not a grand oratorio in a cathedral, but just a pious folksong, full of good intentions and straight from the heart, even if somewhat monotonous and simple. Prayer in everyday life is a prayer of fidelity and reliability. It is a prayer of unselfish, even apparently unrewarded service of God. It is the consecration by which the grey hours become bright and the little moments great. Such prayer does not seek a vital human experience, but only the glory of God. It is not a quest for experience, but for an increase of faith. It may sometimes seem very pedestrian: yet it carries us spiritually forward. Sometimes it seems to come merely from the lips, but it is better that at least the lips should continue to give praise to God rather than that a man should become silent altogether. When the lips speak, though the heart is silent, there is still hope that one day the heart will speak also. What in periods of spiritual aridity is described as mere lip-service in prayer, is in reality the prayer of a poor, yet faithful heart. Despite weakness, depression and weariness, a small shaft is again and again dug by honest labour, and through that shaft a ray of eternal light falls upon a heart buried by the débris of daily life.

We must pray in everyday life. Again and again, weariness and indifference must be overcome. We must endeavour to make our prayer a matter of our heart. We must make our daily prayer a deliberate attempt to turn our minds from busy concern with our mundane affairs, that we may be able to commune in a vital manner with God in the silence of our hearts. This cannot be done as long as we simply cling to a few set formulas which we have probably learnt as children.

We must pray regularly. We must strive to discharge in a *living* way and in *living* words, what we regard as our duty to pray. We must master our moods and feelings; and we can do so only by praying regularly.

It is only by grace that we can learn how to pray, but our willingness to pray and our perseverance in praying play an important part. We must learn to concentrate, in interior silence, on what we are about to do, namely to lift up our hearts. We must learn to speak to God without using set words; we must speak to Him of our necessities, of our daily life, in particular of that secret resistance against speaking to Him about our duties. We must speak to Him of our loved ones, of our moods, of the world and its needs, of the dead who have gone before us, and of Himself. Our words must tell of His greatness and distance, incomprehensible and yet wonderful, of His truth in contrast to our untruth, of His love and our selfishness. He is Life, while we are death; He is fulfilment while we are but longing. We must also learn to mute those things which keep us anxious and tensed, if we wish to attain to real interior quietude. The voice of our soul must become audible to us, that soul which is shy and uses so few, though such essential, words. Prayer is a song that can be sung only to God in the stillness of our hearts.

We must learn to make the reading of Holy Scripture really prayerful. Our evening prayer should give the scattered experiences of the day a unified meaning by directing them towards God. Rounded off with prayer, the day will enter into those deep recesses of the soul where the past is preserved without hatred or bitterness, in kindness and calm, in contrition without fear, in earnest dedication to God. We must learn to sanctify by prayer the dead moments in our daily life when we seem to have nothing to do, when we must wait or queue. The small annoyances and joys of the day can become reminders to us of God and of prayer. All these things can be learnt and practised. Make it your business to learn these things. Make it your habit to pray in everyday life.

51

Make everyday life your prayer. Happy is he who in his daily life returns again and again to prayer. Moreover, there is a higher aim to be achieved in the consecration of everyday life by prayer. Those who return again and again to prayer will never be completely overcome by everyday life; but the suffering of one's spiritual life from the cares of the world is not yet quite conquered. Even though we frequently pray in our daily life, this life itself seems to remain what it always was—a consistent, grey monotony. Our soul seems to continue its weary way on the road followed endlessly by the multitude with its innumerable trifles, its gossip and pretence, its curiosity and vanity. Our soul seems to remain in the marketplace where, from all quarters, the hawkers congregate to sell the petty goods of the world, and where in stultifying restlessness men, including ourselves, wander about offering their trifles. Our soul in daily life seems to be in a gigantic barn into which cartload after cart-load is brought, day by day, until it is filled to overflowing with mundane things. There is no end in sight. One day after the other, we go on in this way to the hour of our death, when all the goods and chattels which we called our life, will be swept away.

What will we be then and what will remain of us, whose life was nothing but the business of the day, idle talk and vain pretence? What will be the outcome of our life when at the last judgment the true essence of our hollow life and of the many days and long years that have remained empty, will be relentlessly revealed? Will anything remain beyond those few moments in which the grace of love or of an honest prayer to God shyly found a corner of our life otherwise filled with ephemeral rubbish?

It is of supreme importance to escape from this empty routine. Through the humdrum of our daily life we must find our way to Him Who alone is necessary, to Him Who alone is the Lord. Our everyday life must become a hymn of praise, indeed it must become in itself prayer. It is obvious that we cannot pray directly all the time. We cannot escape from daily routine, because it will go with us wherever we go. Everyday life is our life, and our everyday heart, our weary mind and our meagre love which abases all that is great, will ever remain with us. Thus we have to keep to the highway of our everyday life, its cares and duties. Nor must this routine be purely of intention. God must be sought and found in the things of our world. By regarding our daily duties as something performed for the honour and glory of God, we can convert what was hitherto soul-killing monotony, to a living worship of God in all our actions. Everyday life must become itself our prayer.

But it can become prayer only through unselfishness and love. If we are willing and understanding disciples, we cannot find a better means of growing in spirituality than through our everyday life. There are the long monotonous hours of work, for which often no recognition is given, the continuous and painful struggle which receives little reward, the weariness and the sacrifices of old age, disappointment and failure, adversity and misunderstanding. There are the many wishes denied to us, the many small humiliations, the almost inevitable opinionatedness of old age and the equally frequent inconsiderateness of youth. There are such things as physical discomfort, the inclemency of the elements, the friction of human contacts. Through these and a thousand other trials in which everyday life abounds, a man can learn to become calm and unselfish, if he only understands these task-masters, mundane and yet providential. He must willingly accept them, rather than try to ward them off. Such vicissitudes must be borne without complaint, as a matter of course. They must be accepted as incidental to the normal course of life.

In this way, we can use everyday life to fight our selfishness, slowly but certainly, since the guidance showered upon us by God in daily life is always certain and sure. In this way, the love of God will grow of itself in our hearts, a love both calm and chaste. It is men themselves who prevent the growth of this love. In everyday life we can mortify ourselves without vanity and without ostentation. Nobody will notice our efforts, and we ourselves will be scarcely aware of our mortification; yet, through the myriad occupations of our daily life, one defence after another will be thrown down, behind each of which our selfishness had entrenched itself. At last, when we have ceased to put up new defences, when we have learnt to accept our precarious human situation and rely on the grace of God, we will notice suddenly and almost cheerfully, that those defences were quite unnecessary. We will realise that it need not mean misfortune, if life deprives us of this or that joy hitherto regarded as indispensible. We need not despair when we fail or when our plans do not work out. Through everyday life, we are taught that we become rich in giving, that we advance spiritually through holy resignation, that we are blessed in sacrifice and that we find love when we give love to others. Thus a man becomes unselfish and free. This freedom makes us worthy of the supreme love of the ever free and infinite God, Who first loved us.

It is of supreme importance that we should achieve this conquest of our everyday life, because otherwise we allow ourselves to be dragged down to its level. Nothing can free us so much as this conquest. If we succeed, the love thus engendered will suffuse all the things of this world with the infinity of God, through a holy desire to exalt all the humdrum activities of daily life unto a hymn of praise to the glory of God. The cross of everyday life is the only means by which our selfishness can die, because in order to be utterly destroyed our selfishness must be ceaselessly crucified. This fruit of that cross will be a love born from the death of our selfishness. Thus, through love, fidelity, faith, preparedness and surrender to God, our everyday actions are tranformed into lived prayer.

Our life remains what it was, difficult, monotonous and unspectacular. It must remain what it is, for only in this way can it serve the love of God. Only in this way will it redeem us from ourselves. Through the sanctification of our everyday life, our desires, our reluctances, our stubbornness and our assertiveness, must be purified. Bitterness must cease to taste bitter. Routine must lose it monotony. Disappointment must cease to be sterile. Everyday life must train us to kindness, patience, peacefulness and understanding; to meekness and gentleness; to forbearance and endurance. In this way, everyday life becomes in itself *prayer*. All our interests are unified and exalted by the love of God; our scattered aims are given a specific direction towards God; our external life becomes the expression of our love of God. Thus, our life takes on a new meaning in the light of our Eternal Destiny.

Make everyday life your prayer. Pray for this great art of Christian living, as difficult to master as it is essentially simple in itself. Pray in everyday life, and so make everyday life your prayer. The sorrowful and fleeting days of our life, passed in monotony and banality, in commonplace pursuits and in toil, will merge with the Day of God, the great Day that has no evening. Let us pray daily for the coming of that Day, so that in us the words of St. Paul may be fulfilled: " I am confident of this very thing, that He Who hast begun the good work in you, will perfect it unto the day of Christ Jesus " (Phil. 1 : 6).

PRAYER IN OUR NEEDS.

OF all types of prayer, the one which is most often arraigned before the bar of human judgment is the prayer of petition. " I have prayed," cries the anguished, embittered human voice from the wilderness of its pain, " and God has been deaf to my pleadings." In human affairs, accusations and denunciations may be justified in certain cases; and we must remember that however clearly the innocence of the accused may be established, the very necessity for such defence is regarded as in some sense a tacit admission of guilt. From this point of view, it becomes immediately evident how difficult it is to defend the worth of the prayer of petition against those who denounce it as vain and useless. We must listen seriously and with great human sympathy to such denunciations, for they came from those on whom the burden of life has pressed most heavily and who think that God has failed them. Despite all this, however, we must renew our faith in such prayer, and uphold its vital necessity.

Life itself is the accused, and embittered hearts are the self-appointed judges. The witnesses for the prosecution are the great weary mass of those whose lives are shadowed with unhappiness, misery and pain. Their name is legion; for a vivid sense of one's own unhappiness is fostered in nearly all of us by brooding and self-pity. We may sift the evidence for the prosecution, and dismiss from the case those witnesses who are motivated by sheer insolence and petty grumbling, as well as those whose grounds for complaint are frivolous and unworthy of notice. Yet, when all this has been done, the poverty and misfortune of the vast majority of mankind qualify them to enter the witness stand in the case against the worth of prayers of petition. These witnesses come from everywhere, from all nations, age-groups and social classes; and they all voice the same denunciation, born of despair or disappointment, of incensed or weary scepticism about the prayer of petition. It is a monotonous cry that goes on and on.

"We have prayed," sobs the weary chorus, "but God has not answered. We have cried, but there has been no response. Our cheeks have been wet with burning tears, but in vain. Too well indeed could we have proved to Him that our little requests demanded no great concessions from Him Who is Almighty. Nay more, we could have shown how the granting of our requests would have been but the manifestation of His glory on earth, the furthering of His Kingdom among men. We could even have held out the cold threat that His lack of response was the annihilation of our belief in Him as a Father of mercy and compassion—or indeed our belief in His very existence. And we are justified in being embittered by His silence. File after file we lay before Him: the unheard prayers of children dying from starvation and of infants frozen by paralysis; the cries of children beaten to death, of exploited slaves and betrayed women, of those crushed by injustice, liquidated in concentration camps, mutilated and dishonoured. Only the silence of God meets those bewildered questions raised to heaven by perplexed minds in every age: Why do the wicked prosper, and the good fail? Why does the lightning strike both the good and the wicked? Why must children suffer for the sins of their parents? Why can truth be abused in such a brazen fashion? Why is world history a swirl of stupidity, meanness and brutality?

"We could continue by appealing to His honour and His glory, and above all to His Name Which He wills should be honoured among men. He must take care that his guiding Hand can be clearly seen in the world of men; otherwise, this world becomes a meaningless chaos wherein there is no evidence of His wisdom, His justice and his goodness. Surely this demands that His help should come to us so clearly marked as Divine that our enemies cannot dismiss it as due to natural causes and therefore proving nothing. May we not demand a greater warrant of success from God than that given us by the laws of chance? Otherwise, life becomes a mere lottery, and it makes no difference whether we pray before or after a purely accidental stroke of luck. It would be quite unscientific to ascribe to God what is simply the outcome of mere chance.

"We could have spoken to God of His Son, Who knows how we think and feel, since He has shared our human life. All this we could have done—and, indeed, all this we have done. Did we pray? Of course we did. Did we follow His own counsel, by subjecting the Kingdom of Heaven to the "violence" of our impetration? Our eager words have burst into flame before the very throne of God—and all in vain. We have cried like lost children seeking the kind and guiding hand, but no one came to wipe away our tears and speak words of comfort. We have prayed, but we have not been heard. We have cried to God, but He did not answer. We were speaking only into a gulf of silence. Indeed, our pleadings were saved from becoming ridiculous and absurd merely by the fact that they were voices from the depths of suffering and despair."

The case for the prosecution is complete: the accusations against the prayer of petition have been pleaded from every angle. But what is the verdict of the jury? There is a division into a convinced majority and an equally convinced minority, both sections, however, reaching the conclusion by different roads that prayer is useless against human misery. For the majority, there is no God Who hears our petitions. Either He does not exist at all, or He dwells in a remote glory far beyond the reach of our prayers. He allows His creation to work His glory, through its blood and its pain. His calm unconcern is like that of the gods "careless of mankind," who, as the poet says,

"smile in secret, looking over wasted lands,
   Blight and famine, plague and earthquake, roaring
      deeps and fiery sands,
   Clanging fights, and flaming towns, and sinking ships,
      and praying hands."

In moments of respite from pain, mankind may even indulge in some philosophising about the remoteness of God. Why should God stoop to an undignified meddling with the petty affairs of a petty world He has Himself created? At the outset, He must have set this clockwork world spinning with the utmost accuracy, to last as long as He willed. He must be now unaware even of its humming. The world was designed by Him to have its own complete meaning; it was not intended that He should perpetually stoop to it, to adjust and rearrange what He had already created adequate in itself. It is childish, therefore, to address petitions to God, for they are an insult to the omnipotence of God and a presumptuous overrating of our own importance. This is the line of reasoning taken by a person whose life is, for the moment, reasonably comfortable. Our salaries, our doctors, our police have their uses; but there is no need for the prayer of petition. But let things take a turn for the worse, and this same person is vehemently protesting that the prayer of petition is useless, because God has not rushed to anticipate his petition even before he had voiced it. Thus the mentality of the majority of the jury.

The minority hold a different opinion. They indeed tolerate prayers of petition, but only when such petition concerns the lofty needs of the soul. Our prayer to God must not degrade itself by becoming a concern for our daily bread, for bodily health, for long life, for protection from lightning and from catastrophes; nor should we pray to be shielded from pestilence, famine or other tribulations. We must pray only for purity of heart, for patience, for willingness to endure such sufferings as God may will to send us. Our prayers of petition are regarded as childish when they concern such protection and shielding from suffering, since they imply a lack of readiness to accept unconditionally the designs of God towards us. Rather than seek to have sufferings deflected from us, we should ask God for strength to bear the crosses He wills to send us. Apart from a few alleged miracles in answer to prayer—miracles of doubtful authenticity—the benefits reaped from the prayer of petition are of a spiritual kind, for this is the only type of largesse dispensed by God. The world pursues its inexorable course, the law of cause and effect functions ruthlessly in every age, and it is in vain that we hope to alter this by our tears or by our prayers.

Thus, then, the majority verdict and the minority verdict. According to the first, we are coldly alone on this earth, and cannot hope for any heavenly assistance; according to the second, we may indeed look to heaven for spiritual strength, but it is presumptuous of us to seek protection and material aid, since God does not listen to such pleas.

It is against God that this manifold indictment is drawn up. But He has preserved unbroken silence through age after age. Through His messengers, He has told mankind that He will not speak until the Day of Judgment; and meantime the accusations will pile up continually—accusations wrung from sorrow, accusations from those who "search into high matters", accusations on the lips of the cynical, accusations from those whose hearts lead their heads, accusations which reveal a spirit of infidelity.

Yet, despite this urgent plea against it, we feel a deep need to turn to God and lift pleading hands of prayer to Him. All these accusations are a source of distress to us, because we cherish a profound faith which cannot be shaken, despite what seem endless disappointments. We have been told: "When ye pray, ye shall say: Our Father . . . give us this day our daily bread." We have no wish to argue with God, to convince Him that our will is His glory; we are content to call humbly upon His mercy. Nor have we any desire to search into the secrets of life, to anatomise prayer, to question its *why* and its *wherefore*; we simply want to learn how to pray. It is not our aim to meet this case for the prosecution with a defence shattering in its greater logic and cogency. Suffice that we know we are suspended over the abyss of our nothingness by a thread of the mercy of God, and that we cling to that mercy. We seek only such light and strength as will enable us to persevere in prayer, lest our courage should fail us and our prayer turn to ashes in our mouth. We desire only the strength to persevere in the face of disappointment, while we await that Day wherein will be justified "the ways of God to men." In that Day, we shall be comforted and we shall understand all.

However, when we set aside for a moment our obsessive preoccupation with the pursuit of happiness on earth—which, after all, is not our purpose in life—we can listen to divine promptings which suggest a number of answers to those who would dismiss the prayer of petition as vain and useless. Why, our conscience whispers, do we suddenly demand God's assistance in disasters brought on us by our own sins? We cry out only when such disaster hits *us*, whereas we were perfectly contented and unmoved in face of the misfortunes of others. There is a certain hypocrisy in our attitude: while we thought we could get along quite nicely on our own, we ignored God; and now, when we find things getting too much for us, we call upon Him. He had no part in us when life smiled on us. But now our little nest of content is shaken by rough winds, and we expect the Kingdom of Heaven, so blissfully ignored, to be immediately concerned with setting things right again for us, in order that we may again be in the " happy " state of having no need of God. We have never really grasped that the glory of God in this world is the Cross of His Son.

We profess our belief in the everlasting happiness of heaven, but we want from this life as much comfort as is demanded by those whose thoughts do not reach beyond it. With a worldly shrewdness which is the very negation of the Christian spirit, we want our " bird in the hand " as well as our " birds in the bush "—happiness here as well as hereafter—in fact, the best of both worlds. We complacently regard our successes as the well-earned blessing and approval given by God to our work; and when He fails thus to bless with success our self-centred undertakings, we sternly ask what we have done to deserve such treatment. Childishly impatient, we are incapable of waiting for that Day wherein God will end His long silence by calling to the Great Reckoning the teeming generations of mankind. He has Eternity wherein to set right what appears to have gone astray in the course of Time. Do we really understand who God is, and who we are? Do we realise that, since He is the omniscient God, His ways and His judgments are beyond our powers of understanding? Do we understand that a creature cannot claim to be judge of the Creator? "Whom the Lord loveth, He chastiseth " seems blatant paradox to worldly wisdom, which cannot understand that the ways of God are so inscrutable that even His love and mercy must needs appear to us to be wrath and vengeance.

Let us repeat: all our suffering stems from our sins. We have refused to relinquish the cause, and now demand that God should deliver us from its effects, but leave us the cause. Which of us can honestly claim that he has not deserved this or that suffering? We are all sinners, and therefore we deserve greater suffering than any we are called upon to endure. Of course, a thousand excuses for sin are ready to hand: heredity, the pull of circumstances, the absence of the real malice of a desire to rebel against God. Surely God must understand that we are weak, that we want a bit of happiness in a grim world, that the fruit of the forbidden tree is sweet to the senses, that the tree of goodness has a somewhat ascetic taste. Besides, the fruit of that forbidden tree hangs down temptingly, while one is forced to reach up painfully for the fruit of the tree of good. Yes, surely God must make allowances.

Such are the sophistries with which we try to evade our guilt. Yet, sin is a crime against the Most Holy, and sin is our doing. Why do we not endeavour to minimise our sufferings by similar sophistries? In our own time, we have heard the theory propounded that it is good for the race that a certain section of mankind should go under periodically in the struggle for survival. Most of us have listened unmoved to eugenic theories and theories about racial purity, about the elimination of the "inferior" stock. On what grounds should we complain, if we happen to belong to a group marked for elimination? If the honour of God and the will of God are regarded as so unimportant, by what criterion do we set a value on our own wishes? God says to us "When you are angry and embittered, do not forget who *you* are and Who *I* am." Why, indeed, should we complain because God does not give to our prayers the answer demanded by our persistent selfishness?

It is not God Who must prove to us that He is good and holy: it is we who are called upon to show that we do not need the bait of constant reward to keep us faithful in our love. Sometimes the clouds gather and all seems impenetrably dark. It is then that we are called upon to love in faith—to nurse our firm belief in the stars of sweet reasonableness that continue to shine behind the darkness of events which seem to us sour and grim and beyond our understanding. That our limited sense-bound minds cannot fathom the ways of God, does not mean that He no longer exists. "O man, who are thou that repliest against God" (Rom. 9 : 20).

Let us now consider the evils from which we pray to be delivered. Are we so sure that, measured by the standards of God, they are really evils? They may indeed be so, and therefore God would have us ask Him to deliver us from them. But it is for Him to judge, and we must not anticipate His decision. We must realise how often the true meaning of our petition is: "Give us abundance, health, security and peace, and *then* we will love and serve you sincerely and faithfully." Yet, when we have all these, we are quick to forget our promise of love and service, with the result that these very blessings do us harm. That misfortunes are sent to us may then be put "shades of His Hand outstretched caressingly" to awaken us from our complacent torpor; the lash of stern compassion mercifully given. Our prayer was not a genuine lifting up of our real or imagined sorrows to God, but just a selfish whine to have things adjusted our way. We did not leave it to the inscrutable wisdom and infinite goodness of God to decide whether distress or prosperity, success or failure, life or death, was best in the interests of our eternal salvation. If, when we make our request, our intention is rather to force our own wishes on God than to abandon ourselves to His omniscient and merciful wisdom, then our petition is not a prayer but an act of arrogance and rebellion. We owe submission and adoration to God at all times; and most of all when we kneel to Him in our distress.

When we listen to the voice of conscience, we hear all these answers to our complaints about the inefficacy of the prayer of petition. But the essential reply to such complaints has been given us by God Himself, when He "emptied Himself, taking the form of a servant." Hanging on the cross, He too knew that moment of desolation when the Eternal Father seems to have left His human soul in desolation: "My God, my God, why hast thou forsaken me?" His coming among men "like unto them in all things, but without sin," was the answer to those ages of expectation wherein mankind had longed for Emmanuel, for God walking our ways. We have not, therefore, been harshly commanded to continue our prayer, with only the assurance that all will be righted on the Day of Judgment. Christ has come among us, to teach us how to pray, and to teach us the meaning of suffering. Through the Incarnation, the ecstatic prayer of the Son of God in the Bosom of His Father has become a human prayer on the lips of Christ, a prayer from the depths of the human misery and suffering of God made Man. In Christ, we find the true answer to the alleged inefficacy of prayer. He does not teach us the philosophy of prayer, nor does He discuss the conditions for prayer. We do not look to Him for the solution of those problems inherent in prayer: the readiness, for instance, we must show to accept God's answer to our petition, despite our longing that this answer should be the one we ourselves desire; the seeming paradox that, while prayer is efficacious, we cannot control the free decision of God in our regard; or, finally, the fact that, although we have been promised that prayers offered in the Name of Jesus will be heard, we find that so many of our prayers so offered go apparently unanswered. The great significant fact for us is that Christ taught us *how to ask* in prayer. Therefore, while we await in faith that Day of Judgment which will reveal all, we have Christ as our answer to all accusations against prayer. Our answer is that Christ of Whom the Scripture says: " In the day of his flesh, offering up prayers and supplications with a strong cry and tears to him that was able to save him from death, was heard for his reverence." (Heb. 5 : 7).

Christ has answered our questions by teaching us how to pray. He has taught us to pray in words of direct supplication, of holy confidence, of complete submission. His supplication was direct: " Remove this chalice from me." During His Agony in the Garden, He prayed with all the fervour of a man encompassed by terror and anguish. So earnest was His appeal that His sweat became as drops of blood. It pleased His infinite goodness to let us hear in His words the anguished cry of a *man*; for He did not ask for something sublime or heavenly, but for that mortal life to which we all cling so tenaciously. He shrank from the torture and disgrace He saw before Him, and asked His Heavenly Father to deliver Him from it. However, we know that He also spoke words which manifested complete confidence in His Father: "I know that thou hearest me always" (John, 11:42); and in the prayer of His agony, we are shown that complete submission which must animate all prayer: "Not my will but thine be done" (Luke 22:42). Apparently forsaken by His Father, tortured and crucified, He commended His soul into the Hands of His Father.

Let us consider how all this points to the great inner harmony in the Heart of Jesus. He wrestles with the Will of His Heavenly Father, and yet has entirely submitted to that Divine Will; He cries out in anguish, and yet is certain that He will be heard; He knows that He is heard always and in everything, and yet wishes to do nothing but the inscrutable Will of His Father; He begs for His life with the utmost urgency, and yet this prayer is an offering of His life to the Father. All these contrasts are harmonised in the prayer of Jesus, in a mysterious harmony wherein lies the secret of truly Christian prayer, because the prayer of God made Man is the model of Christian prayer. For as in Christ the Divinity and Humanity of Christ were united in one person, so human prayer and Divine prayer were united in the prayer of Christ.

A truly Christian prayer of petition is a prayer which is essentially human. We turn to God for His assistance in our fear of earthly distress, in our desire for protection, in our sorrows and sufferings. Such prayer is the cry of elementary self-preservation, a naked expression of our instinctive clinging to life, arising from the very depths of human life and human anguish. Yet, such prayer is also essentially divine. In the very act of, as it were, defending our earthly life against God, we adopt an attitude of complete submission to Him and to His inscrutable designs for us. We subordinate our instinctive self-preservation, wholly and unconditionally, to the Will of God, and we regard this Divine Will as the Source from which the final decision is to come. Thus, our prayer of petition is, in the ultimate analysis, not a plea for life and the things of this life, but a submission to the Will of God even when that Will points to deprivation and perhaps to death.

Such prayer is both human and divine. It is human,

in as much as it is a cry from the human heart in its misery and pain: it is divine in so far as it is an act of submission to the Divine Will. The more like our prayer is to that of Christ, the more vigorous, vital, and truly human it becomes. Thus transfused with the light and love of God, the earthly tribulations and desires which are the matter of our prayer are lifted to a higher plane, wherein they take on a higher significance as offerings of our submission to the Will of God. Such submission is a kind of divine alchemy by which both our failures and successes are transmuted to the pure currency that wins an eternal reward. By means of it, there is a mysterious fusion between the will of man and the Will of God—a fusion through which man is lifted to the heights of his true greatness. Christ has promised that all true prayer will be heard. He implements that promise always in the most exalted manner possible, by answering every prayer in accordance with the Will of God. The Divine Will of Christ is always at one with the Will of His Heavenly Father, and therefore the Father always hears Him. As children of the Father and brethren of Christ, we have been promised that our prayers too will be heard to the extent to which we identify our will with that of the Father. In other words, whatever our request, our ultimate wish must be that God may answer in such a way as to promote His own glory and increase His life in our souls. Such singlemindedness—" if thy eye be single," said Christ, " thy whole body will be lightsome "—casts out from our prayer of petition any shadow of selfish desire to make God's Will conform to ours, rather than ours to His; and thereby we become perfect children of God. While maintaining that freedom and autonomy of will which is our human prerogative, we yet establish with God a pure relationship of sympathy, a perfect harmony wherein we freely choose to submit our will to that of God. Thus, true to our nature, we may desire and pray for what we regard as conducive to our happiness; and yet know that we shall certainly receive the answer we desire, even in an apparent refusal of our request, because we desire only that the Will of God may be done.

We do not put all this forward as an explanation of the mystery of prayer, since it is simply a re-statement of the mystery of the Christian life in general. We explain the mystery of prayer by referring to the mystery of the whole Christian life; and though this may be to explain one mystery by another, nevertheless it is sufficient for one who has faith. Heaven and earth are realities. On the one hand, there is the Living, Free and Almighty God; on the other, there is the truly free nature of man, His creature. These two freedoms meet in prayer, wherein we find a cry of distress, a pleading for some good, coexisting with an attitude of complete submission to the inscrutable judgments of God. These two aspects—man's freedom to plead: man's submission to the free decision of God—are always found together in true prayer. "Unless you become as little children," said Christ—thereby pointing to the sublime virtue of Simplicity which is the essence of Christian perfection. To lead a truly Christian life is to place one's whole being into the Hands of God as confidently as a child takes the guiding hand of its father. The child's confidence is complete and without the slightest trace of reservation: the hand it grasps is of one who knows best, who loves, who will not lead it into any danger, who will shelter it from evil—but who certainly will not reach down that sharp knife or that poisonous liquid, however much the child, fascinated by the glitter or the colour, may clamour to have it. The profoundest secret of the Christian life and of Christian prayer is to become a child in our relations with God—a child whose quiet confidence and silent submission do not fail in moments of trial when God appears to have turned from us. Christ has given us the perfect example of this: "He went down to Nazareth and was subject" to Mary and Joseph, because it was the Will of His Father; He summed up His Public Life with the words —"I do not my own will, but the will of Him that has sent me"; and He ended His earthly life as One "obedient unto death, even unto the death of the cross." We have learnt from Him to plead with the the Father, but to find our peace of soul in the answer the Father mercifully gives.

This apology for prayer will be understood only by one who prays, for it is an understanding that can be reached only in the act itself of praying. We may indeed pray for material good—for necessities, for health; but always in such a way that our manner of asking redounds to our eternal glory, whatever the answer we receive. In asking, we must make an oblation of our will to that of God. We must pray with a constancy and perseverance which is a living proof of our trust in God's guidance of human affairs; of our hope in a world full of the shadows of death; of a true love for God which is not simply pious self-seeking and does not depend on incessant rewards. Since we are on this earth as " strangers and pilgrims " on a journey to eternity, we must not pray as though we had here " a lasting city." We know that it is through sickness and death that we shall enter into that life which is the final object of all our prayer. As long as we keep our minds raised to God in prayer, even when disappointments and misery crowd about us, we are sustained by the invisible and mysterious, yet true and real, power of God's grace and of participation in the life of God; and, when " this mind is in us," death loses its terrors and become a swallowing up in the abyss of God's everlasting love.

VI.

PRAYER OF DEDICATION.

PRAYERS of dedication play a great part in the private and public devotion of Catholics. Although this is not one of the oldest forms of prayer, it has now become so prevalent that it deserves some special consideration. We are familiar with the dedication of the world to the Sacred Heart pronounced in our churches e.g. on the Feasts of the Sacred Heart and of Christ the King. There is a similar dedication to the Immaculate Heart of Mary. We have the dedication of families to the Sacred Heart. Dioceses are dedicated by the bishops to a patron, or members of sodalities may dedicate themselves to their heavenly Patroness. The meaning and profundity of such dedications are subject to considerable variations according to the circumstances, the person to whom they are directed, the persons or communities who perform them, etc. However, we shall leave aside for the moment these differences; neither will we consider the official or liturgical aspects of some of these dedications. We shall confine ourselves to a consideration of the idea of dedication underlying such prayers, as found in the dedication of himself made by a person sincerely and on his own initiative.

Let us consider what exactly takes place in such a dedication. We know it is neither resolution nor vow. In the case of a resolution we resolve to do, or refrain from doing, something, in obedience to the commands or counsels given us by God. We put our own house in order; we are concerned with ourselves. In dedication, on the other hand, we do not primarily consider ourselves but the person to whom we dedicate ourselves. There is a transition from our heart to the heart of him to whom we dedicate ourselves.

In a vow we promise something specific to God, by imposing upon ourselves a new and strict obligation. This promise is certainly great and significant, since it is to result in a man's handing over of himself to the holy love of God. Thus, dedication to God is the ultimate aim of all vows. Yet, the immediate content of vows is certain clearly defined aims and efforts, while dedication goes straight from heart to heart. Dedication is not the choosing of a means of showing our love, a work in which love is to grow and to be tried, as in a resolution or a vow. Dedication is the free flow of love from person to person and heart to heart.

Is this something new? The Christian life should be always characterised by this flow of love, which extends not only to each single effort and good work, but to the whole of our existence. For this love is God's claim to our unconditional allegiance. Quite apart from the fact that many dedications are not directly addressed to God and Our Lord, do these dedications extend beyond a reiteration of what we already do, indeed what we are obliged to do, even without dedication? Dedication does not appear to be more than an echo of those quiet movements of the Holy Ghost which carry us gently and irresistibly unto God. Dedication cannot be a new obligation, because all old and all possible new obligations are always included in and anticipated by that love which, being higher than all duty, demands all from us. This love is fulfilled only when no boundaries are set to it: when, with our whole heart, we give our whole heart, a heart filled with love rather than with the idea of fulfilling a duty.

Yet, let us sound a warning at this point. Dedication concerns only what is always and everywhere our duty: I love Thee, my God. Does dedication add nothing to this? Is it of no added significance that these same words are now spoken earnestly from the heart, and with deliberation, where before they were perhaps lightly spoken without a deliberate conscious intention? In our spiritual life, there are surely prayers which are, as it were, its small talk. But dedication is seriously spoken: we put all that we are into our words, and see our future as bound by the dedication we are making. The current of our life goes on, apparently unchanged; but with a new, hidden, deeper significance.

It is through his spiritual life that a man strives for his ultimate goal, the perfection of his personality through the possession of God. This spiritual life is not a mere series of actions endlessly succeeding each other towards the attainment of a spiritual goal: the past exists mysteriously in every moment. Thus, as a spiritual being, man acts, or at least, can act, in every moment with the resoures of his entire past. His past is preserved in a concentrated form as the gathered experience of his life. The place from which a bullet was fired can be determined only by considering its whole path. Similarly a note sounded by a master violinist can be said to contain in essence that note as played by him up to the moment of its present perfection. In a far greater measure, the present action of a man embodies his whole past, his knowledge obtained through effort or through suffering, the depth of his experience, the revolutions of his life, his joys and his sorrows. Memory may modify these to some extent, but they are none the less present. By all these influences, the present action is given its direction, its depth and resonance. The past is preserved and carried forward in the present action. At least, that is how it ought to be. Into the present free decision, a person is called upon to gather up all the past, thus bringing to it all that he is and was—in other words the whole sum of his existence. Man must seize the successive possibilities offered to him, and in doing so, he realises what is eternal in him. Every moment is to be filled with his whole spiritual history, which to him is the ever more enriched possibility of present freedom.

It is still more mysterious, yet true, that in the grace of a present decision man can anticipate his future. This is not exclusive to such matters as resolution, planning, decision, premeditation, promise and vow, when man looks to the pattern of his future life. Besides, resolutions and similar spiritual and intellectual acts, remain in the present tense, however important they may be for the future of man: they become significant for the future only when actually carried

71

out, and this carrying out is subject to a subsequent rather than to a present decision. However, by saying that in a present action we can mysteriously anticipate the future, we mean something more than decisions which once taken cannot be altered, and therefore exercise an ineluctable influence on later conduct. There are such facts, and they vary in significance. Marriage and Holy Orders—indeed, even living through a certain unrepeatable period of our lives—create facts which exercise an influence on future actions and decisions. Any future action must take these facts into consideration, and a man can no longer act as if they did not exist. However, it is an equally important truth that a man can take these facts into consideration in very different ways. He can change the face of his decisions, e.g. he can either stand by his earlier decision to love a person, or he can betray this decision. His ordination to the priesthood can become more and more integrated into his life, or his life can be lived more and more outside his vocation, indeed he can become unfaithful to it. Thus the fact created in the past is not actually evaded, two opposite possibilities remaining after such facts have been created. For the future continues fundamentally undecided and undetermined. It is not this phenomenon to which we were referring when we said that the present moment can anticipate the future.

To explain what we mean, let us discuss an objection which might be put forward to disprove from the outset the possibility of such anticipation. Freedom seems to be incompatible with anticipation of the future. A man is always free. Therefore he is also free in the future moments of his life. Hence it is impossible that man should anticipate his future to such an extent that he decides it in the present moment, filling as it were the present moment with the import of the future and anticipating what is still in the future. The future cannot be realised in the present moment. It seems that at this point the words of Holy Scripture (Mat. 6:34) apply: "Sufficient for the day is the evil thereof."

One aspect of this objection is certainly to be maintained in our further considerations. Apart from exceptional cases to which we shall return later, the fact that in principle the entire life of man is free, means that in no case can the free decision of the moment decide the future in such a way that a man knows for certain and in a palpable manner that this decision has already shaped his future, and that thus the future has been decided here and now. If this were not so, the future would be an almost mechanical unfolding of what has happened in such a moment. Life would no longer be shadowed by the incalculable future, and would be no longer subject to the law of responsible initiative. Theology teaches us, and the history of the Saints bears out the truth, that there are cases in which a man can know, through a free and complete conviction reached in the sight of God, that his life has reached a stage where his salvation is already assured. This is what theologians term " confirmation in grace.' However, this is an exceptional case, which can be left aside at this stage, because it occurs but rarely and need not be considered with reference to our own life. In such confirmation in grace, man knows that, in a certain measure, his spiritual personality is already beyond the practical reach of sin.

As a general principle, such knowledge is not reconcilable with the freedom and uncertainty of our life on earth, where decisions are made in ignorance and in blind trust, due to the uncertainty of our insecure position in the face of God. Our question, therefore, is still unanswered. Is it possible to try to anticipate the future, even though the results of this venture may be uncertain? One reason for answering this question in the affirmative is that freedom is not essentially—as a common misconception would have it—the capacity to accomplish, at least by desire, whatever we wish to do here and now. The correct definition of freedom is a man's capacity to express his free personality completely, through decisions legitimately, freely and finally made. Freedom therefore does not deny the possibility of creating internal (as distinct from merely external) facts, which are definite and final. On the contrary, freedom has its ultimate meaning in this very possibility.

It is the very opposite of freedom to create conditions which are subject to alteration, change, reversion or revision. Freedom achieves unique and permanent finality. The ultimate, eternal destiny of the soul is not an accidental condition imposed on mankind as something which thwarts human freedom, as a foreign element which negates the very idea of that freedom. On the contrary, this destiny is the mature result of freedom itself. Therefore, at any moment a free decision can anticipate a man's entire life, since it can be decisive of his lot in eternity. Every moment of free decision exerts a shaping influence on the entire growth of human personality, since it is the complete expression of what a man really is within the depths of his own heart. There are many, of course, who make narrow decisions dictated by the expediency of the moment, rather than far-reaching decisions affecting their whole future and shaping their eternal destiny. Again, success often depends on external conditions outside the control of free will. A person may fail a thousand times in his attempts so to gather up all the possibilities of his spiritual life into one moment of decision, that all his future actions may receive a unifying significance from that decision. Yet the tendency to such decision is in us all, because it is part of the very essence of our freedom.

A truly free decision always reaches forward to the whole of our life and is decisive of our eternal destiny. In most cases, it will ultimately fail to sustain its effect, either because this free decision was too weak and therefore incapable of reaching down into the very springs of our being, or because external circumstances beyond our control were too much for us. It is scarcely possible to know with any degree of certainty whether our act of decision has completely succeeded in sustaining its effect. Nevertheless, in the moment of making such a decision, human freedom really expresses itself as a desire to influence our whole future, to shape that future to the image of our decision, and thus to reach its effect even into Eternity itself.

One such moment is inevitable. In death the thread of life is cut off, however much we might have liked to continue spinning the garment of our years. Although we never know how this can be done, and indeed although the appearances are inevitably against it, in death man completes his own pattern by dying his own death. In the moment of death he is what he has made of himself, freely and finally. The actual result of his life and what he wanted to be freely and finally, become as one. When exactly does death in the sense of this action of freedom, occur; and when does a man thus complete himself? What has been said of death is true in as much as, according to our faith, physical death is the free completion of man. However, we do not know whether this completion actually coincides in time with physical dissolution. What we know is that, apart from the exceptional cases to which we have referred, we can have no certainty that this moment of decision has been reached by us. Thus the moment of total decision lies always ahead of us, and we can only assume that it does not always coincide, and perhaps indeed very rarely coincides, with death in the physical sense. The approach of physical death is generally accompanied by a reduction of consciousness, and it is unlikely that in this state the total decision can be taken. Since any free action can in itself become an act of total decision, it is at least probable that such a moment of total decision takes place at a time other than that of physical death. Since this total decision is the basic aim of freedom, we should indeed prepare for it at any moment.

What has so far been theoretically deduced from the nature of freedom is confirmed by experience. In the history of our own soul, we remember moments which seemed indeed unforgettable. The experience, disposition and intention felt by us at that moment seemed to be destined to remain deeply rooted within us. We realised that we could never go back on what we had freely chosen in that moment, for the very reason that the choice was free. Advancing in age, we are sometimes overcome, gently and softly but with unspeakable rapture, by some awareness of the grace of God taking possession of us. The Divine Huntsman will see to it that His game does not escape Him. Our soul merely waits for the moment when His love will seize upon us finally. Let us not forget that such awareness of grace is an action involving our freedom, because it evokes a consent from the very depths of our being.

Even when such awareness proves to be an illusion, the very fact of this illusion seems to indicate our belief that there exists in reality what then appeared to us. When the mountaineer thinks he has reached the summit, a new stretch of the path opens up before his eyes, a stretch which was not yet visible when he estimated the distance he still had to cover. The illusion, in an individual case, merely proves that our soul has been created for such moments when everything is finally completed. Suddenly, unexpectedly and without any warning, there will come upon us what we had always hoped for, the fullness of life caught up in one moment of decision, the expression of freedom in its final perfection.

In freedom, we anticipate the whole unity of our life. Again and again, our anticipation will seize upon only a fraction of the whole, but we will not cease in our efforts to gather up past and future into that one decision of freedom from which our life will receive its final and definite truth and reality. Only God will hear when the hour of our glory strikes: unexpectedly and without knowing it ourselves, the fruits of our whole life will be in our hands. Whatever happens afterwards in our life is but an exultant Finale of a symphony, the final count in an election whose result is beyond doubt, the ripening of a fruit after it has been gathered.

Let us call this great hour of our freedom, the unique and undisguised presence of the moment of eternity in time, the moment of " temporal eternity ". The nature of this moment appears to us in a dark manner: indeed, being the fruit of freedom, the moment itself remains hidden. We know that it is of the nature of freedom to strive for this moment which is its fulfilment. Whether we are aware of it or not, we are always living in the attempt to reach this moment of fulfilment.

So far, we have endeavoured to determine the moment of " temporal eternity " in its abstract form as the act by which a man disposes of himself and of all the possibilities of his life. The content of this act, however, is still undetermined. This act of freedom can be one thing or another, Yes or No, ascent or descent, salvation or damnation, everlasting gain or eternal lose. Let us therefore try to determine the full content of this moment, if it is indeed to be everlasting salvation, pure and final affirmation. It is through the love of God that man succeeds in his attempt to secure his happiness in eternity. This definition is far from being self-evident. It is clear that not every act of the love of God is a moment of what we have called "temporal eternity". Every act of the love of God may be an attempt to achieve our unique moment of eternity in time; but only in very rare cases will we know with certainty whether we have succeeded in this attempt. In fact, except for one attempt, all these attempts are bound to fail. Needless to say, these failures are by no means insignificant in the eyes of God or for ourselves; they are important and indeed indispensible exercises leading up to the supreme effort.

The identification of the act of love and the moment of eternity in time cannot take place unless we enter into it with our whole heart, our whole soul, our whole mind and strength, that is to say, unless we entirely spend ourselves in this act of loving freedom, making it final and irrevocable. Such an act of love can be attained but rarely, indeed only once, and this for ever. When did we ever love God with our whole heart, our whole soul, our whole mind and all our strength (Mark 12:30)? If we could fully understand the terrifying meaning of the words "whole" and "all", we would see that the commandment to love God with our entire being amounts to a commandment to direct our entire life towards the achievement of that moment of eternity in time. Our life would then be a continuous effort, until this grace is given to us. To strive for this success, in the moment of eternity in time, is the commandment of love. Every act of love tends towards that moment, in which it finds its fulfilment; but not every act of love is yet that unique moment.

In still another respect, it is not immediately evident that an act of love or indeed any human act can indeed be the true moment of eternity in time. We have said that in this moment an integration of our whole life takes place. It is by no means self-evident how love, and love only, is able to bring about this integration. Indeed at this point we realise how little we really know about what we call Love. Which is the fundamental act into which a man can gather up his whole essence and his whole life? Which is the act that embraces everything, that comprehends everything and contains everything human, our laughter and tears, bliss and despair, mind and heart, everyday life and our moments of supreme happiness, compulsion and freedom, sin and redemption, past and future? We hesitate to answer this question: and yet, the answer is clear. The love of God, and only the love of God, embraces everything. It brings a man face to face with Him without Whom he could experience nothing but a terrifying consciousness of emptiness and negation. The love of God alone unites all powers in man—manifold, chaotic and contradictory as they are—and directs them to God. The One and Infinite God alone can create in man that unity which binds together what is manifold and contradictory without destroying it. Love alone makes man forget himself, and it would indeed be hell if such self-oblivion could never be achieved. Love alone can redeem even the darkest hours of the past, since love alone is brave enough to believe in the mercy of God. Love alone does not selfishly hold back: it is therefore able to dispose even of the future. Without love, man, anxiously guarding his finite Ego, would husband his future and yield it but grudgingly. Love alone can, as it were, draw God on to this earth, thus integrating all earthly love in the moment of eternity. To love alone, therefore, is given that persistency of courage which loves Him Who sees, through guilt, failure and death, the bravery of His creature. The love of God is really the only total integration of human existence. Its sublime dignity and all-embracing greatness become clear to us when we understand this point. The full content of the moment of " temporal eternity " cannot be anything else, because without the love of God that moment would be nothing more than the secret judgment (John 3 : 18) and because conversely, only in that moment can the love of God be what it desires to be and what it must be.

78

Much more could be said of this act of love in the moment of eternity in time. Above all, we must bear in mind that this act is grace, although it is the most sublime act of freedom. This moment is grace, because we can love God only in His strength and power, because our love is only the response to His love, and because there is no love in us other than that which His Holy Spirit has poured out into our hearts. This moment is pure grace as such, because it transcends all the general grace of the love of God. It is given only to the Angels to be free at any moment to surrender entirely, to seize the very depth of all possibilities, and to smelt the core of life that it may be used without dross for the casting of a true image of God. Men are given this possibility only in those supreme moments of their lives granted to them by grace, when this possibility is given to them in such a way that they can really fulfil it. It is by grace that this moment is given to them, and it is by the super-abundance of grace that this moment is given to them in such a way that they can fill it with the love of God. Thus the highest moment of freedom is essentially both grace and freedom; in that moment, freedom determines itself in the everlasting integration of an entire life.

We seem to have strayed far away from our initial question concerning the nature of dedication. Yet, our goal is at hand. We can now define dedication as the earnest attempt to reach the moment of eternity in time through an act of love. We will readily see that this definition is true when we consider our definition of the moment of eternity in time as the act of total and final integration of our whole life, and when we compare this definition with our experience of what is done in dedication. It requires no further proof that dedication is fundamentally an act of love. The very externals of dedication reveal its nature as a pure and recollected act involving the whole strength of our being, uniting all the powers of the mind and the heart, deliberately and earnestly. What else is the preparation, the solemnity, and the explicit and deliberate form of dedication?

It will have now become clear that such an act of love strives by its very nature to bring about the moment of eternity in time, because only in that moment does love well up from the very depths of the heart. Dedication as such implies that there is the possibility of success in this effort. Such success means that the moment of eternity in time occurs, as, in the eyes of God, the decisive event in our life, the act to which our previous life was the mysterious prelude. That moment is the object, goal and end; what follows is but the working out of the theme irrevocably adopted. This attempt will frequently end in failure or at least only in partial success, and we will never know whether and how far it has been successful. After our dedication, therefore, we will have to continue to strive earnestly for our salvation, conscious of the fact that we are not yet what we are to be and what we are called to be. The pilgrimage will continue, perhaps for a long time, and it will hold many surprises. Yet, even as an attempt, dedication is holy and great. No one knows but the attempt may have been successful. Perhaps the decisive word has been spoken—the word in which we have borne witness to what we are. *We* do not know, but *He* knows. Let it suffice. It is in the nature of love to seek ever for new words, more intimate, more sincere and more earnest still, until the word is found that really expresses everything and for ever.

We may wish to consider the manner in which dedications should be performed. It cannot be an everyday event in our spiritual life. It requires preparation. It needs some consideration of the intellectual, mental and spiritual properties of him who dedicates himself, so that his heart is really in the words of dedication. It would be wrong to multiply dedications, since dedication must be the result of an earnest and realistic representaion of our whole life. We must pray for true dedication as a gift of grace. However, we cannot consider these aspects more fully here.

This chapter started with the question of what takes place in dedication, and we can now attempt to answer this question. Dedication is the attempt to consecrate in some way the whole of life. If this attempt is successful, it is not just an achievement, but the totality of all achievement. If this attempt is not completely succccessful, something of supreme importance has nevertheless been achieved: a part of that love has been realised which in any case is the task of this life and the meaning of eternity. Someone may say that this is done every day of the Christian life, because the monotony and bitterness of everyday life is the true theatre of love. Quite true, if everyday life is really love. As everyday life is not, by nature, love, it is wholesome and good that what *should* be done always, *is* actually, expressed and deliberately done on certain occasions. Such occasions are dedication, even where we do not succeed in bringing the fullness of love into the moment of eternity in time. In dedication, therefore, everything, or at least something very important, is achieved.

So far we have looked upon dedication from the point of view of man. Let us now ask whether in dedication something is done by God. Let us consider His answer to the word of love spoken in dedication. This answer given by God is indeed the very essence of what is done in dedication. The Scripture says: " Draw nigh to God and He will draw nigh to you " (James 4:8). We should say more of the nearness of God and His splendour as experienced in dedication. Yet, the decisive point has already been made: He approaches to us by giving us the grace to approach to Him. The meaning of this approach to and by God has been discussed throughout this chapter.

So far, our considerations have been based on the assumption that we treat of dedications to God the Father, the Holy Trinity, to the Love of God made-Man and to His Sacred Heart. We have spoken of the highest moments of the love of God when it is directed to God Himself. Let us briefly consider dedications to the saints, especially to the Blessed Virgin, rather than to God directly. If we have rightly understood the meaning of dedication, it will be obvious to us that such indirect dedications to God are covered by our definition. Such dedications, as acts of love to a human being now assumed into the community of God in heaven, are essentially acts of the love of God. Love of our neighbour—and one eternally united to God is in a special way our neighbour —is directed towards God, since it is an expression of the theological virtue of Charity. Why this is so and how this can be so, requires no explanation, but has been extensively discussed by theologians. In dedication to a human being in heaven, our heart does not centre on him, but we unite ourselves with that purity of soul through which he has won eternal bliss. By this means, we sanctify our prayers and our actions, giving them a power more than their own. This concerns in particular dedications to the Blessed Mother of God and to her Immaculate Heart, the living symbol of her love of God, the symbol of the totality of her purity and her complete surrender to the Will of God in eternal love. He who dedicates himself to this love and really understands what he is doing, will be irresistibly drawn into the eternal movement of love in the Immaculate Heart of Mary. In this act of love, he loves God; and his dedication is to God through Mary.

Many different prayers of dedication have been said on our behalf and by us. Sometimes they may have appeared to us all too frequent. We may feel uncomfortable at the way in which they use the loftiest words, since such words seem so far in excess of our real feelings. There may be cases in which he who truly loves God prefers to remain silent, content with offering to God his sincere desire of that love of which his cold heart comes short. We may feel that there is no need to declare our love to Him who reads our hearts. Still, we must reassure ourselves of this love, and God in His love knows the weakness of our heart. His Divine Love accepts from us even that love which is not worthy of Him. He loves in us that diffidence which makes us distrust our love and our ability to love. It is perhaps part of our unredeemed pride that, although we know how God loves us, we remain silent in modesty and fear rather than speak like children. This pride implies fundamentally that our love could be worthy of Him, and that He loves us truly only when our love is as it should be. Let us abandon this pride. Let us speak to Him as children, confidently and earnestly: " My Father, I dare to tell Thee that I love Thee." All prayers of dedication are but expositions and variations of this one inexhaustible theme.

VII.

PRAYER FOR FORGIVENESS.

"WHEN thou shalt pray, pray in this manner: Our Father, . . . forgive us our trespasses." (Matth. 6:6 and 9). Having thus learned how to pray, a Christian prays every day for the forgiveness of his sins. Let us pray for this intention every day and with renewed fervour. Let us not pray merely for the forgiveness of former sins, of sins committed at the time prior to our conversion, when we had not yet repented and when perhaps we were not yet sanctified by the forgiveness of sins through our re-birth by water and the Holy Ghost. Let us pray ceaselessly for the forgiveness of that guilt of sin which is ours here and now.

However, we do not really feel our guilt to such an extent that every day we could strike our breast in the spirit of true repentance, saying with a contrite heart: "Lord, have mercy upon me, a poor sinner." Moreover, we are redeemed children of God, whose very countenance should be suffused with the glory of redemption. We are the joyful heirs of the saints in light, the re-born children of the Father, shining like stars in a world of darkness. We are the children of mercy, the new people, the heirs of His promise.

In general, Christians nowadays become conscious of their faith only many years after their Baptism. Baptism marks the beginning of a man's spiritual life. In Baptism the mercy of God appears at the beginning of his pilgrimage, before that pilgrimage has properly started. This position of Baptism is justified when we consider what is the part played by God in our life, and what the part left to ourselves. Still, Baptism does not exempt us from running our course, from fighting against the powers of darkness and the onslaughts of temptation. We cannot evade the great and decisive task laid on us by our Baptism: to become Christians, that is, to accept God by a free decision of our innermost being, with our whole heart and mind.

83

We must go forward to meet the majesty and the incomprehensible mercy and grace of God, Who appeared to us in Christ, was revealed on the Cross, and shone forth in the Ascension and in the Descent of the Holy Ghost. In this encounter between God and man, which, beginning with our Baptism, will decide our fate in life everlasting, there is a phase in which man strays away from God in the vanity of his heart as if the flesh and the earth were his ultimates. In this situation, a man may appear to be a perfectly normal and decent individual, who never gets into trouble with the police or transgresses the easy code of accepted day-to-day social conduct. However, in this situation, he remains unaware of the consuming holiness of God. Partly guilty, partly innocent, he trespasses against the commandments of the Lord which decide life and death. He does not realise how seriously he should regard the life of man, the waywardness of youth, and the concessions which advanced age makes to the demands of life, concessions between what ought to be and what is considered as unfortunately inevitable. There are the years in which he turns away from his Church, saying that he does not know how he slipped into this retrogression. Shrugging his shoulders, he contents himself with a bare statement of the fact that faith no longer exists for him.

In this situation he may be overtaken, as in olden times some men were overtaken before their Baptism, by the grace of God. The judgment of God may come upon him, tearing down the mask he has assumed, showing him what he is. Despite his denial, he has always known in the depths of his heart what he really is: a sinner loving darkness more than light, and easily accommodating his standards of conduct to the demands of his own wishes. He admits that he consented to his retrogression, even if he did not actually bring it about. It was not his fault if he unwittingly turned off the alarm clock of conscience that he might sleep out his life without a feeling of guilt. Imperceptibly, he had moved away from God. He could not stand the presence of God, a fact which seemed to prove to him that God does not exist, or at least no longer exists in the way he first envisaged Him. His complacency had appeared to him as a sign of a good conscience, though he admitted the theoretical possibility that his conscience might be wrong. Overtaken by the judgment of God, this idea collapses. He realises that his so-called good conscience proves the depth to which free and therefore truly guilty sin has affected him to the very core. Sin had so taken possession of him that in his heart there was no longer any voice warning him.

That this internal light of true conscience was extinguished is then no longer an excuse, but on the contrary is the clearest proof of his love of darkness. He no longer sees the light that enlightens every man, and is the result of the incomprehensible grace of God. Perhaps, for some time, he will fight the new light, defending his former " good conscience " or even turning the new light into a reproach against God. He will say that God should have shown him the light earlier, and he will not admit that it was he himself that refused to see, perhaps in order to avoid a real break with and full condemnation of his former life. Though he has now received a new and better understanding, he still wishes to maintain an unbroken continuity in his life. He will try to shelter in excuses by saying that he always meant well, though he did not always succeed too well. He will claim that his road followed a straight line as laid out for him from the beginning, and that he really remained true to this line.

However, when the sweet and burning light of God, the truth of God rather than of man, and the love of God, continue their inexorable and divinely inscrutable persistence, he will yield. In thus yielding, he finds his strength. He is given courage to relinquish his false freedom, and accept the dictates of a true conscience. In these dictates, he recognises the judgment of a merciful God. He admits that he is a sinner. He admits his guilt, and no longer excuses himself by saying that he did not know. He no longer claims that it was by a natural development that he found his way back to God, and that fundamentally he had never lost his innocence. No, he sincerely admits his guilt. He realises that in the depths of his heart there had been evil, and that he had deliberately evaded the whole issue by cultivating a false conscience which he knew would give him the answers he wished to hear. He had forgotten God, and he no longer claims that he had forgotten "accidentally". His corrupted heart had suggested "good" reasons to his mind, misnaming them "intellectual difficulties". He had been overcome by his inclination to evil because fundamentally he had sided with it long before it had made any specific demands on him. He was a sinner, fighting a continuous rear guard moral action, to prevent the cowardice of the final capitulation from becoming all too apparent. He had only too readily permitted the birds of passage of this age to steal the seed of God from the soil of his heart, because he wanted to escape the effort of bringing forth good fruit. He had been very clever in inventing ingenious moral principles of his own, dictated by the need of the moment or coming to him as veritable "inspirations", and enabling him to do with an easy conscience whatever he wished. He had been a man who said to God: "Give me good advice, as long as this advice falls in with my wishes. Let me have a good conscience such as will enable me to yield peacefully to temptation."

Now, a splendid transformation has taken place. Enlightened by God, he admits that he had nourished in his heart wickedness masked as light. He no longer asks how this could have come about in his heart, but confesses that he is himself its author. Speaking to God, he no longer tries to cloak his guilt like the Samaritan woman at Jacob's well. He does not shelter any longer behind a delusion of impersonal guilt. By the grace of God, he renounces himself. Nothing remains in him, when once he has renounced his former way of thinking, that would deserve the punishment of hell. God has saved him for the sake of that last spark of goodness that remained alive. In this transformation, man flees from himself rather than from God. He witnesses against himself where before he put up a defence; and thus he promotes the glory of God. Carried over the abyss by Divine grace, he is at one with God. The judgment of God is His mercy. He begins to love God, and because of this love he need not hate himself any longer. The miracle of grace has occurred: he is enamoured of the love of God, because he now recognizes that his very denial of that love was the dark prison of self to which he had been condemned by his own insincerity. Thus, he really comes to pray:

" Father, I have sinned against Thee. Forgive my sins."

This transformation, however, does not yet answer our initial question whether he who is honest and is redeemed can recite every day a prayer for the forgiveness of his sins. We still want an answer which applies to all of us and to every day. It will be said that one redeemed from the darkness of his own guilt into the Light of God will again and again confess his guilt, this confession being the profession of love by a sinner redeemed, liberated and restored to happiness. Though given to us by God, grace remains His property. He who has truly received grace, who is pure in himself, and who has been restored to the liberty of love, never claims the Divine glory of his new life as his own achievement. He never claims it as his well-deserved right. Grace remains grace, depending on the ever renewed miracle of the love God bears to us. It can never be regarded as something that has an existence independent of the generosity of God. Only as so dependent, is it man's new life. It is grace only as long as it is received as the ever renewed embrace by which the prodigal is forgiven. Is it in fact renewed or is it continuous and permanent? The sequence of time disappears in this act that covers a man's whole life. By grace, man is lifted from the most profound depths of his guilt to an equally profound union with God. Man must always say: " I am a sinner," because God always says: " Thou art the child of my love." But, through the creative love of God, the human truth that a man is a sinner, is reversed by God's truth that he is a child of God, and therefore cannot be fundamentally a sinner. This transformation can take place, however, only through God and through mans' prayer for His mercy.

Those who have but a superficial knowledge of general practice might be inclined to say that a good Christian indeed prays every day for the forgiveness of his daily faults and weaknesses. These venial sins do not separate him from God, and in spite of them he remains a child of God. Still, they are sins. Despite the miracle of grace, he will fall seven times daily, as the Scripture warns us; and therefore it is not as supererogation, but as a necessity, that even the saints ask for the forgiveness of their sins. All this is true, but it is not the whole truth.

Venial sins must, of course, be taken seriously, and must not be considered too trivial to require forgiveness. We must understand the meaning of the word "slight" applied by moral theologians to venial sin, and we shall have more to say later on the seriousness of these sins. Yet, the daily prayer of a good Christian, of a Christian in the state of grace, is not solely concerned with actual venial sin. It is not conducive to praying for forgiveness from the bottom of our heart, to consider only our venial sins. In fact, we have here one of the great sources of spiritual dishonesty, abhorrent to the Lord in our prayers. Confining ourselves to the consideration of actual venial sins and assuming, as taught by the Church, that they are but slight sins, we are not brought to that deep heart, that profundity of conviction, wherein a man really grapples with himself and wherein his eternal destiny is decided. The consideration of venial sins only touches the fringe, however revealing these sins may be as regards our true spiritual state and however voluntary they may have been in the strict sense of freedom. Accordingly, such sins cannot be the subject of a contrition deeper than their own nature. Contrition as the reaction of the heart to venial sin, cannot plumb the depths of a man, because it cannot be more serious than the venial sins themselves. An attempt to take them more seriously leads to dishonesty and is a dangerous strain on our spiritual potentialities. It may result in narrowing down the difference between venial and grievous sin, and, since venial sins cannot be avoided altogether but must be accepted to some extent as inevitable, we are in danger of losing the proper perspective also with regard to mortal sin. Experienced confessors know that the indiscriminate confession of mortal and venial sins shows this to be a very real danger. Venial sins can be the subject of regret. We can and should strive to avoid them. They show us how little we are fundamentally directed towards God and how little we have 'put on the new man'. We may be terrified at the possible developments of our character as adumbrated by our venial sins, which make us fear for our salvation. We may measure by them how far we are from that inner harmony of spirit effected in us by the love of God our Saviour. We must reject venial sins, because they cannot be positively reconciled with the perfect keeping of the commandments of God bidding us to strive for our only and eternal goal. They keep us in opposition to—or, as Aquinas said, at a distance from— the will of God. They reveal a deficiency in zealous love of God, and we must overcome this deficiency by a new effort of the heart. All this, however, does not stir hearts to their depths in realization of the words of God: " Thou art a sinner." We are not pierced by the sword separating body and soul, entering right into the centre of our heart. By confining ourselves to venial sins, we make these words apply where the real sin is not, and we thus escape the necessity of passing judgment upon our innermost intentions.

When said by those redeemed in the spirit, and by the saints, the words: " Forgive us our trespasses " have a totally different significance. Spoken in tears, in fear and terror, these words apply to something other than venial sins alone. Precise and correct though it is in moral theology, the term "venial sin " becomes fraught with danger when not considered in direct relationship to the sinner's entire personality.

What, then, is the meaning of the prayer for forgiveness as literally intended even by the saints, but not restricted merely to daily faults and negligence, nor to those venial sins due to our imperfect union with God?

Let us consider this point in the light of the teaching of Catholic theology. We have said that a man can be convicted by God of being a sinner. A man is made to realise that he personally, rather than men in general and everywhere, has sinned and has decided against God. Deceiving himself, he may not admit that it was he himself, unique, irreplaceable and fully responsible as he is, that trespassed. The realization of this fact is of overwhelming terror to the Ego. At last, a man can no longer claim to be other than a sinner. He cannot flee from himself, unless he tries to escape from God. He must condemn himself. He tries to save himself by sophistry: to minimise his sin, he magnifies the sin to a disease affecting all men, and of which he is the unfortunate victim. He does not say: " I have sinned against God," without hiding behind the thought that others have done likewise; but he says: "Truly, man everywhere and always is a sinner, always and in everything; he is fundamentally evil in Thy sight, O God. Man is a sinner by the very fact that, being man, he is different from Thee. Even before he begins to think, he finds he has decided against God. Man cannot escape from his guilt, and it remains his personal guilt; to try to escape is mere useless pride, attempting to justify itself in the eyes of God rather than confess its universal guilt." Thus, actual and concrete sin, committed in a definite set of circumstances, with full advertance and full consent, is impersonalised and made to appear as sin in its abstract essence. Actual sin seeks shelter behind original sin, by claiming to be an accidental and inevitable manifestation of original sin.

In this way, the nature of sin seems to be understood in a more radical sense. It is generalised. Its beginning is seen as prior to the actual trespass. Actual sin is dissolved into the past. It becomes quite natural to issue a decree to everyone: "Confess that you are a sinner." However, the individual tries to hide in the multitude, so that the confession of personal sin is swallowed up in the general intoning of the sombre *Miserere* of all men.

This condition is far from the truth. Catholic teaching is that my guilt is due to my individual action and is a new fall of Adam—however much, as a son of Adam, I may plead that I bear my father's burden; each time I must reckon with the possibility that others have had no part in my personal sin. Each one of us must confess that he was not compelled to commit this sin, that he could have avoided it and that, when he had committed it, it was his sole responsibility. There can be no deeper explanation than the personal admission that I have sinned, rather than the abstract admission that I am a sinner. This admission must not be the beginning of a flight from the sophistry of evil in my own heart. Our sin is scaled down to its real proportions by our admission that it was we who have committed it. Not even in the eyes of God, is everyone "fundamentally" like ourselves; others did not sin, where we have sinned; we alone have sinned and that sin is ours alone. Nothing else can be included by a man in such confession except sin, his own sin; and this he must radically reject. Only in this way will he attain to truth.

In this specific and personal confession, we understand anew what it means to be a creature. This confession, leading to the abandoning of ourselves, is indeed impregnated by the love of God. Where no personal and actual sin is committed and the white garment of baptismal grace has been kept unstained unto the judgment seat of Christ, there is still nothing but grace, pure grace, and indeed grace in more than usual abundance. The grace of Divine life is given to the creature as an unmerited gift. It is even more unmerited since we share in the sin of our first parents. It is solely due to our redemption through Christ. Moreover, any decision in which the grace of God might have been lost had it not been taken in such a way that we did not after all forfeit our inheritance, is in itself grace, as is every right and inspired action resulting from our free will. Those who have never sinned are nevertheless saved purely by grace. It was not they themselves that avoided falling into the abyss of guilt, but it was God who prevented them from falling. He holds us in our freedom. Our freedom is not such that the Almighty cannot act until it has vanished.

St. Irenaeus says that he who remains from the beginning in the love of God is a hymn of praise to the inscrutable grace of God. Like the worst sinner, he remains with God only by continual fleeing from himself and from his occasions of sin. There is nothing that we have not received. The more we have, the more we are indebted to God. The purest innocence leaves us the greatest debtors of God, and this debt is paid only in praising Him for His ineffable grace, and in confessing that everything is His work.

Thus there is the theoretical possibility of being free of sin, though we do not know, except in the case of the Handmaid and Mother of the Redeemer, whether any have been preserved from sin, and if so, how many. God alone knows what redemption is, and the redemption of each of us is His secret. How truly then can we say: "I am a sinner," since no one may say he is free from sin.

St. John writes: "If we say that we have not sinned, we make him a liar and his word is not in us" (I. John 1:10). Whatever may be the meaning of these words, if no one may claim to be free of sin, must each one admit that he has committed sin, even though he cannot remember having ever done so? Or if he does not admit to sin, is he necessarily a stubborn liar refusing to confess and to surrender to God? Is he always inspired by a cowardice and a pride which refuses to admit that God is in the right? Or is there something savouring of presumption in an excessive readiness to admit that I have sinned, and this merely to be at peace with Him Who is always right?

A point can be reached where the words: " I confess that I am a sinner " are equivalent to: " I do not say that I am not a sinner." In the latter case the judgment is left to God; in the former, it is assumed by man. The latter is possible, but the former is not always possible. A man may be genuinely unaware that he has committed any sin, and yet not be justified by this knowledge; and God can have mercy as He wills, keeping us from sin or snatching us from sin, preserving us or raising us. Of course, there are cases, indeed innumerable cases, in which a man, while leaving the final judgment to God Who alone knows our hearts, must say simply and honestly: " I have sinned." This confession, then, is something we can make both in the eyes of God and of the Church. It is made from the conviction of a conscience which honestly states the facts and admits the truth. This confession, made in strict sincerity before God and his Church, is a man's only honest expression of the glory of Divine grace. If, however, this confession is not possible owing to the fact that the person is genuinely unaware of any sin, the rejection of such a confession, out of respect for human sincerity and truth, does not amount to the claim that one is not a sinner. " For if I am not conscious to myself of anything: indeed in this I am not justified: but he that judgeth me is the Lord " (I. Cor. 4:4). If in thanksgiving for the grace of God, I dare to say, in fear and awe, that I am not conscious to myself of anything, I do not necessarily presume to be justified in the eyes of God. Regarding himself, a man can say, soberly and realistically, that he has fought a good fight and that he has kept faith and charity. Lifting up his eyes to God and kneeling down before Him, he will add: " If thou wilt mark iniquities, Lord, who shall stand it." (Ps. 129:3).

God alone knows what is in man. No man knows, with a certainty that requires nothing but Divine confirmation, whether his unselfishness is merely a refined form of egotism, whether his meekness is merely weak cowardice, whether his purity is mere physical impotence, whether his faith is escape into facile security and cheap sentimentality, and whether his general conduct is merely "decorum". We have become aware of the dark powers hidden in the depths of our soul. Our daily sins assume a new complexion and a greater weight when they reveal to us that everything *is* in us and everything is *possible* in us and through us. Thus we cannot assert that our Ego, acting, deciding and bearing the ultimate responsibility in the eyes of God, is to be located in that inextricable maze of contradictory forces, at the precise place where it can be identified with that force which testifies in us against darkness and for God. Standing before God rather than in the marketplace of life, we cannot say with ultimate certainty whether what is good in us is merely the mask concealing evil, and whether the evil in us has really been conquered. No one knows what really to make of himself in his poor distracted heart; whether his real self lives in his longing for a greater love of God, or in his unacknowledged and unrepentant grumbling at the immeasurable demands of this love. We long for simplicity: to see our twisted and tortuous selves with that clear directness with which God sees us. But this is impossible for us.

The most exalted goodness can pervert itself to the grimmest evil with the speed of lightning. Paradise was the scene of the most abominable fall. Even the elected messengers of God may be deluded by the belief that they can promote the glory of God by obeying the guidance of their own light rather than the testimony of the Son of God. "I saw Satan fall like lightning from heaven," was Christ's solemn warning to the Apostles when He heard them presuming on their own fitness for the Kingdom of Heaven. No man can claim that he is justified before God: his daily sins rise up to testify against him; and though these may be but venial, he must recognise them as pointers to the deep insubordination of his heart. Radical wickedness need not always reveal its presence conspicuously and outwardly. Should a man say, though he is not aware of having committed any sin: "I am a sinner"? How else can he express concisely and plainly the truth about himself and about what he is apart from the grace of God, which is always present as the active principle of goodness? It is by God that a man is upheld and saved; it is through himself that a man is lost; it is to himself that a man is a mystery. He can be judged only by God, and in this judgment there is but one confession, that contained in the word "sinner". O Lord, Thou knowest everything. Thou knowest me, a sinner, and Thou knowest the love that Thou workest in me.

What man really is, he is already in this life. In spite of his miserable inadequacies and in spite of all future possibilities from new decisions, he is what he really is in the eyes of God: for all things concerning him are "naked and open" to the eyes of God, even though they may be a tangled confusion to the man himself. How is it that we do not know ourselves, although we are clearly aware of the actions we freely do, and of how they must appear to God? In order to preserve the ambiguity of our present state, do we attempt to hide in a twilight which blurs the definite lines of free responsible action, although our salvation clearly depends on such action and indeed is decided by it?

To answer this question, we must know what "certain knowledge" about ourselves we have excluded, and what "lack of knowledge" we have cultivated, before we can decide whether we deserve love or wrath. We have ruled out reflection and introspection, because we have recognised once and for all that these do not give us certain knowledge of ourselves. In this field, we cannot allow simplification in accordance with theories that achieve clarity at the expense of completeness. In the spiritual, as in every other sphere, introspection is of little value to us in establishing the precise condition of our interior state. We cannot observe a thing or an action without immediately beginning to reflect upon it; and in so doing, we change the thing itself or the action itself, because such reflection is not a passive process of objective examination, but adds a foreign element of significant judgment. It is then no longer the thing or the action which is being considered, but the thing or the action as coloured by our own minds. This in turn demands further analysis, and so the process of endless reflection goes on. It has been suggested that this process is like that of a self-conscious golfer trying *not* to see himself posing to hit the ball; an attempt which immediately involves him in the problem of *not seeing* himself *not seeing* himself posing to hit the ball . . . and so on endlessly. However accessible, necessary and useful introspection may be, it cannot give us a complete prelogical, *objective* verdict on our actions. One process of introspection must necessarily lead to another, and we can have no guarantee that each process is not vitiated by a desire to hoodwink ourselves—by a manipulation of the figures, so to speak, that the answer may come out as we ourselves wish. The more elaborate the introspection, the less lucid is the result yielded likely to be; and there is no degree of reflection which can guarantee us certain knowledge of ourselves. A man realizes himself only through union with something outside himself, but he cannot *become* that "something." We can therefore have no clear and self-evident knowledge of ourselves. To some extent, the explanatory springs of our conduct remain hidden in the unconscious. Hence the Council of Trent specifically declared that no one can say with absolute certainty that he is in the state of grace.

Yet there is some sort of knowledge—or whatever name we give to the light that is compatible with action—by which we can distinguish what we are now doing from what we have done in the past, and by which we recognise our responsibility towards God. It may be expressed by a man's saying that he *knows* provided he is not asked how he knows. The judgment of God will uncover the hidden recesses of our heart and will confound mere introspection; while our heart will admit that at bottom it always knew what now comes to light. This knowledge was indeed knowledge of myself, and therefore could not be clarified by subjective reflection. It is only when a man has turned to God that this clear knowledge, which eludes all introspection, emerges clearly and compellingly. It cannot be translated in terms of what we usually call knowledge. Man can judge himself only in his actions.

Nevertheless, there is that peculiar knowledge which may be described as the voice of inexpressible fundamental existence, the mysterious knowledge of the *anima* (in contrast to the daylight knowledge of the *animus*), conscience (exceeding all knowledge and reflection) or the spark of light in the human soul. This knowledge is where freedom, knowledge and the Ego are as yet fused within that common root which must put forth its shoots to form the human personality. As a result of this light in the heart of our darkness, we always know who we are, but are unable to express it in words, even when confessing to God what we know of ourselves. Therefore, apart from the testimony of the Holy Ghost pleading within us " with unspeakable groanings," a man can only confess from the heart of his own darkness: " I am a sinner, O God. Have mercy on me." A man would cease to have any part of human existence were he to try to turn impatiently from his suffering, never knowing properly, never able to express his knowledge, never clearly realising what he is. He would cease to be himself did he try to observe and pass judgment on the actions of his life, like an impartial referee. For a man is himself involved in the actions he is attempting to judge. He can do nothing but run his race, and provided the direction of this race is away from self and towards God, he will soon cease to torture himself about the nature of that race. We are still on the course, and we must therefore forget what is behind us, even if the outcome of the race appears to have been already decided. Therefore the prayer which we must say concerning ourselves is never: " I am in Thy grace " but always: " Have mercy on me, a sinner." We can say these words in truth and in humility, because justification comes only through grace and because we never know whether we are justified, but only that justification is something beyond our unaided powers. The prayer of confession does not, of course, take on its full significance in isolation, any more than the fifth petition of the *Our Father* has a context other than that which places it in vital relation to the other petitions in that prayer. It is as united with the prayer of praise for the gift of God's love; with the prayer of thanksgiving for the living power of grace; with the prayer of hope; with the prayer for our necessities, and with unselfish prayer for our neighbour—that our prayer for forgiveness attains to the fulness of Christian prayer, in praise and glorification of God. Such a blending of prayer cannot be achieved by any process of reasoning. It is the free gift of the Holy Ghost.

VIII.

THE PRAYER OF DECISION.

" TIME travels in divers paces with divers people," says Shakespeare's Rosalind, and she goes on to list those " who Time ambles withal, who Time trots withal, who Time gallops withal, and who he stands still withal." Measured by the clock, one moment ticks over just as evenly as another; but as measured by the mind, an hour can live a minute, and a minute can seem like an hour. So, too, moments vary greatly in significance. There are dull moments when life just continues its monotonous flow, and there are burningly acute moments into which we feel that our whole past and all that we are is crowded, and which stand out in our lives as our moments of decision. Something is created in such a moment which shapes the course of our life irrevocably, or at least for a considerable period of time to come. Such moments do not begin and end in themselves; they, as it were, " look before and after," since the decision reached in them may well be determined by all that has gone before, and will certainly be made with a view to, or in defiance of, the future as thus determined. Thus, a whole life, and indeed eternity, may hang in the balance of such a moment. Hence, in the most literal sense they are the moments of decision.

The moment of choosing a career is an example of this; or that moment wherein we decide to link our life and destiny irrevocably with that of another person in Holy Matrimony. A marriage vow or a vow made to God is such a decision; and whoever takes it does so with a clear knowledge that, in the eyes of God, it is irrevocable, and may even be so too in the eyes of the law of the land. These, however, are the moments of public decision, announced with a certain amount of pomp and ceremony. Far more frequent, however, are those moments of decision which pass within a man's own mind, which no one witnesses. The straight path of one's years suddenly takes a bend, and, in the very heart of a routine existence, we are presented with a vital decision to be made—vital because on it depends the whole structure of our developing character, and because it is never likely to occur in the same way and with the same significance again. Life, or God, makes demands of us whether we will adhere to truth or take refuge in a cowardly falsehood; whether we will act justly or with unjust greed; whether we will choose the ennobling way of marital fidelity, or degrade our vow brutishly at the instigation of lust. The importance of such moments are to be measured, of course, by the importance and the consequences of the matter to be decided. There are some decisions which, as it were, just glance off the surface of a man's character; but there are others which reach down into his very foundations, so that, whether he shirks the decision or bravely meets it, one thing is certain—his character has been fundamentally affected for ill or for good.

It is to this latter kind that we especially refer when we speak about "moments of decision", for in them a man comes face to face with God. In such moments, a man is clearly aware of the answer demanded of him. He feels that the Hand of God has, as it were, been laid on him, and that the eyes of God are upon him asking whether the decision is to be that of selfishness or that dictated by the Will of God. It is God Who puts the question, and asks for His own reply on the lips and in the heart of a man. Thus the answer becomes a courageous crushing of the human will, an answer to the demands of Divine Love, a proof of a man's boundless confidences in the Will of God. On such decisions depends the very foundation of our relationship with God, for this relationship is essentially that of the loving oblation of the human will to the Divine Will. Hence the great significance for time and eternity of these moments of decision. They become moments of lived prayer, when a man chooses to make God's decision. They cannot be other than the very essence of prayer, since they are practical answers to the sweet insistence of Divine Love. Hence when we speak of the "prayer of decision," we mean that lived prayer in every decision made in accordance with the Will of God.

Let us consider three types of the prayer of decision:

prayer in temptation; the prayer of decision in our age; and the prayer of decision in the hour of death.

"Man's life on earth is a warfare," says Job; and no amount of wailing protest can alter that fact. We must accept temptation as part of human life, varying in matter and in intensity from man to man, but something very real for all of us. Temptation steals upon us unawares; we have no immunity for it, since it possesses as its powerful allies our own fallen nature, our thirst for human happiness, the eagerness of our senses to seek a glut of pleasure, or trust in the things of this world, our lack of living faith in the hereafter, and our amazing powers of self-deception in matters where a moral decision must be made. We can "sugar o'er the devil himself" by the ingenuity with which we put a face of goodness on our wickedness, so as to deceive not only others but even ourselves. This ingenuity reaches to the very principles of moral judgment, which we either blissfully ignore altogether, or set aside in favour of more "enlightened" standards of conduct formulated by ourselves. A stage is quickly reached when our conscience devises a kind of personal alchemy by which sin and perverse behaviour are transformed into virtue and righteousness.

Temptation, in the full sense of the word, is not a daily phenomenon in our lives, although, since the Scripture says that even the just man sins daily, each day will have its quota of minor temptations. However, as we use the term in this context, we mean that strong and decided temptation which assails us personally, and which seeks out the weak place in our spiritual defences. This does not mean, of course, that we must necessarily succumb, but it does mean that such temptations are a definite personal challenge to us which we must meet and answer as we should, if we are to grow in moral strength through conquering them. It would be deluded conceit for a man to imagine that his moral strength is all sufficient, or that he can marshal all his powers of resistance at any and every moment. He must, of course, have sufficient moral stamina to meet the sudden thrust of temptation; but he must also keep in mind that such stamina is not always at its best. Every man has troughs of weariness and depression, wherein even such vital considerations as God, life everlasting, virtue, truth, purity, and so forth, lose their lustre and their appeal and seem luxuries belonging to his happier states of mind. In such moods, pleasure, success, wealth and bodily comfort, take on an alluring appearance of palpable solidity; while the higher urges and the things of the spirit fade to a shadowy unreality, and concern about them seems but an elusive playing with shadows. This condition may be part of the temptation, in the sense it represents the gradual preparation for the assault.

Before openly attacking, temptation has infiltrated, after the manner of a fifth column, into the fortress of the soul, undermining its power of resistance. A condition is thus created in which it is possible for temptation to become very real and very dangerous for us. There will be no victory then, unless there is an increment of new moral strength in the very act of resisting. He who relies on his moral strength at the moment of being attacked, is bound to be eventually defeated. For he has already been cornered into a position of weakness by his love of comfort, his self-complacency and moral sloth. He is himself in league with the temptation. What, then, must he do? The spiritual significance of every great temptation is that by conquering it a man can add cubits to his moral stature; and he will arouse himself to do so, only by a vivid realisation through faith that his battle is on the plane of the eternal, not the temporal, and that eternity is the matter at stake. He must look up from his petty preoccupations, that strong spiritual winds may sweep his soul to strength. Faith must be his armour, and an intense love of God his spear and his shield. He must lift up the Divine Law in his own heart as a challenge to himself. Grace must sweep to the aid of free will, so that these two become a united strength wherein a man learns to brush from him with contempt the selfishness and love of pleasure, the weakness and the cowardice which have proved such insidious allies of the temptation. He must feel the strong surge of manly anger within him against that sophistry which attempts to falsify standards of conduct when they become awkward. He must scorn a heart which preferred comfort to constancy, fortune to fortitude, and its own will to the Will of its Creator. Only when he possesses such moral weapons is a man a true and efficient soldier of Christ, a warrior worthy of victory, standing prepared for the onslaught of any temptation. Thus armed, indeed, his victory is a foregone conclusion.

How are we to explain that moral miracle which occurs when a man whose inner spirit has been drab and slattern, is converted to God? Now a victim of his own crass presumption, and now a dupe of his own deluded conscience, such a man had ceased to know himself; and suddenly an Angel has placed a fiery sword in his hand, and the light and sweetness of God have taken possession of him. Such a sublime transformation will not take place, however, in one who meets a temptation languidly, who seeks to come to terms with temptation and is secretly resigned to defeat. Nor will it occur in one who seeks to delude himself into believing that there is some legitimate ground on which he and the temptation can come to an amicable settlement. The secret of such transformation is prayer, and prayer *only*. Suddenly beset with temptations to lust, weakness, cowardice, envy or despair, a man must summon all his strength of resistance, and must protest, with a strong cry to God, against his rebellious flesh and his temporising mind. He must not seek to fight unaided, but must turn with all the urgency of his heart to God. He must fly from his own weakness to the strength of God; from his own wavering infidelity to the eternal changelessness of God. He must beg for love, plead for the gift of the Holy Ghost, thirst for the strength that comes from Christ dying on the Cross. The grace given in answer to such prayer will alone give courage to relinquish his hunger for the pleasures of this world, and choose the way of justice and of Divine Truth. He must not parley and reason with the temptation, but must plead with God; and in making this plea, he must not concern himself with the temptation, but only with the Grace, the Life, the Love, of which he knows himself to be so vitally in need.

Nothing pleases the tempting serpent so much as a man's willingness to discuss the whole matter with him, for the serpent knows that a man's poor brain is no match for his own cunning. To get a man to consider nicely the law against which he is tempted, to make a subtle distinction about its application in this or that particular set of circumstances, is already a victory for the tempter. A man must therefore turn from all this, and fix his mind on God, the only sure and everlasting foundation, the adorable First Principle of all moral principles. Only through prayer can we overcome temptation, because only through prayer can a man regain that holy innocence of the children of God which instinctively rejects and despises the enticement of sin. Real temptation always finds us weaker than we should be; otherwise, our inclinations and the lower cravings of our nature would not be so ready to ally themselves with the temptation. The conquest of temptation is, therefore, the conquest of these inclinations and cravings, through a returning of our hearts to a full allegiance to God and through pleading for His assistance.

We must pray in temptation, and we must learn how really to pray. Let us never say in temptation: " I cannot resist "; let us rather turn with renewed faith and revived love to God, and say: " I know that Thou canst save me." Let us not say despairingly to ourselves: " I cannot live without this pleasure or that posssession "; let us rather lift our voice in an earnest, persistent, reiterated prayer: " Lord, without *Thee* I cannot live." Let us not say to our dark oppressive weakness: " You are my death "; but: " You are the dawn of my true life which must begin in a realisation of my own weakness." Remember the warning of Saint Augustine: " Do not darken thy darkness; God doth not darken it, but rather enlighteneth it." We must cry for that enlightenment which will prevent us from being deceived by a temper disguised as an angel of light. We must not listen to a thousand specious reasons why, in this particular case, the law of God does not apply, nor to flattering arguments about the law's being designed for people less enlightened than we are. Let us pray for protection against what has been called " the mysticism of sin," to which Saint Paul was referring when he said: " Should we continue in sin that grace may abound? God forbid." (*Romans* 6:1). The grace of God can raise a poor sinner from his fall; but woe to him who, having fallen, does not believe that God is greater than his sin, and to the even less enlightened person who permits himself to fall in order that God may have the opportunity of raising him again! He is guilty of presumption in taking for granted beforehand that God will do so. There are sins against the Holy Ghost which are forgiven neither in this life nor in the next. A person who deliberately wishes to be redeemed by sinning and being raised from his sin, is dangerously close to the sin against the Holy Ghost; and, at the present time, it is to be feared that this temptation lays hold of many. Let us always pray for enlightenment in our temptations.

We must cultivate a sensitivity to the first signs of internal weakness and loss of spiritual vigour. That inner feeling of well-being which is associated with spiritual and mental health, begins to give place to ill-humour, to irritability, and to a distaste for spiritual things (*acedia*). The love of God grows weak in us, and His yoke becomes bitter where before it was sweet. Our sensitivity of conscience must sound the warning, and we must immediately set about retrieving the spiritual ground we have lost. Calmly and without anxiety, we must attempt to reestablish that interior harmony which has become disrupted. It is even more imperative that we should do so when it was a temptation which first drew our attention to the weakened state of our spiritual life. More than ever, it is then our duty to turn earnestly to God.

Only by keeping close to God can we escape the pervasive power of evil, which would otherwise slowly poison heart, mind and soul. There can be no victory for him who, while he does not actually accept defeat, is yet unwilling to shake off the sluggishness of his heart. He fails to recognise the true nature of temptation as an invitation to take a more firm grasp on the love of God. The answer to this invitation is prayer—prayer in all its forms.

If a person is subjected to a continuous onslaught of evil thoughts and desires, it may be as well for him to refrain from praying explicitly for deliverance from this temptation. To pray explicitly for this, might result in fixing his mind all the more on the temptation, thus aggravating his condition. His prayer should be characterised by a cheerful trust in God, and by quiet perseverance; for this will enable him to ignore the obsessive thoughts and desires by bravely throwing himself into the business of his daily life. Such strategy of spiritual warfare means looking to God for strength; and this is prayer.

Temptation is a moment of decision, and victory is dependent on prayer. Our Lord said: "Watch ye and pray that ye enter not into temptation" (*Math.* 26:41). Prayer in temptation is the prayer of decision.

Let us briefly consider the second type of prayer of decision: that in our own age, which age is a moment of decision to a far greater degree than were other periods in human history. Many things have already been decided. Europe, once chosen by God to bring the Name of Christ to the nations of the whole earth, has lost the leadership of the world. Its strength has been undermined by its own infidelity. Having rent the seamless garment of Christian unity, it went on to adore the golden calf of material progress, adopted rationalism as its new faith, and was abandoned to the horrors of its own blind tyranny, the swastika taking the place of the Cross. Europe has forfeited its right to lead, and therefore God's command and the honour attaching to that command seem about to be transferred to other nations and other races, who will one day bring forth fruits more worthy of the Kingdom of God—though, indeed, at the present moment, it would be difficult to point out any nation which would seem to qualify for this great destiny.

Decisions have been taken, in which is revealed, through what seem the iron laws of history, the bitter-sweet severity of Divine Love guiding the course of mankind. We have witnessed developments which have taken place in accordance with their own inexorable laws. In the course of these developments and these decisions, certain opportunities have occurred, either to be seized upon or ignored; and such opportunity may recur. Europe may be given a breathing space in which to realise how it has failed in its God-given mission, and how possibilities of further evil or new blessing depend on whether it awakens to a sense of its new responsibilities. If indeed it does so, God may give it a new soul to work for the spread of His Kingdom—may reinvest it with its ancient dignity as His ambassadors, His special family of nations. On this depends not only the happiness of Europe itself, but the personal happiness of each and every European.

As yet, it is impossible to say whether Europe, like the precious box of alabaster (Mark, 14:3) is destined to be broken in order that the fragrance of its faith, its spirit and its history may pervade the whole world; or whether it will simply be broken as a vessel gone sour and useless, and its shards flung aside by the potter as worthy only of the dustbin. It is yet an open question whether God will give the nations of Europe, beloved by Him from the dawn of Christianity, another period of peace so that they may regain their lost sense of a Christian vocation to the whole world; or whether, having failed in that mission, these nations may degenerate into physical and spiritual paupers. Must Europe become again the battlefield of the world, and collapse in a final ruin of blood and tears, before a new era is ushered in? But who can read the Mind of God? Or who can be His counsellor?

Yet, there is one thing which emerges quite clearly. Despite the alleged dictates of so-called historical determinism, by whose laws God is not bound, God can still say to the nations of Europe what He said to the people of His Old Dispensation: Behold, today I place before you life and happiness, or death and misfortune. I call upon the heavens and the earth to witness that today I have put before you life or death, blessing or a curse. Choose therefore life, that life may remain with you and with your seed. Love the Lord your God; obey Him and remain true to Him. Your life depends on the choice you make . . . That choice we have still to make, and there are many false roads to which we are being beckoned. But the decision is ours to make.

We stand among the ruined years, but we can still claim our right. We can still find courage to pray for the happiness and the true greatness of Europe. Through His Blessed Mother, the Lord has urged us to pray for this intention; and such prayer will be a real force in determining the story of Europe today; and the future of the world. Are we going to obey Him? Are we going to become a great family of praying Christian nations—each earnestly imploring a renaissance of grace, each pleading for the rebirth of Europe as the continent of God, however desperate that plea may seem? Will our prayer be the prayer of our faith in God's omnipotence, or our hope when, humanly speaking, hope seems dead? Or will we remain hardened and disillusioned, indifferent and selfish, concerned only with rescuing our own few sticks from the general conflagration, and callous about what happens to our neighbours—obedient to that dictum of Hell that " now is it every man for himself "? The general obligation of prayer in this crisis is laid upon all alike, and there will be no prayer if every man waits for his neighbour to begin, in accordance with that other principle one hears so much nowadays that " it is as much his duty as mine." Are we going to become victims of that herd instinct by which the individual recognises his duty only when that duty has become socially accepted in practice, and no longer demands anything of him except to take the direction of the herd? Our age is one of vital historical decisions affecting the whole of mankind: it is unique in that every such decision has its repercussions from pole to pole. Does this situation bring us to our knees in ardent prayer that these decisions may in accordance with the infinitely merciful Will of God?

The third type of prayer of decision we have listed above, is that in the hour of death. The whole life of a man is gathered into that hour, and his past appears clear, solid and final at that moment when for him time is to be swallowed up in eternity. In the hour of death, both God and the dying person speak their last word—a word which is final and decisive for all eternity. The important question for us is whether we shall obtain the grace to make our last conscious moment a moment filled with the prayer of decision, by which we mean such a prayer as will lift up all that we were and are, all we have done and suffered, in oblation to the mercy of God; whether, as the shades of death darken in our minds, we shall turn a last glance of faith on Him Who has crossed the bar of death and yet behold He lives. Shall we say to Him at that moment: " Come, Lord Jesus "; and will that prayer be strengthened by the prayer of the *Sponsa Christi*, the " prayer of faith " (James 5 : 15) spoken by the minister of His Church anointing us to appear before the King of Everlasting Life? Shall we be able to pray in that hour of decision, to commend our souls into the hands of God? May God mercifully grant us the grace to depart from this world in prayer, so that the last thought in our minds may fit us for life everlasting. Blessed is he who can utter a prayer of decision when the hour comes which is for him the most decisive of all.

We do not know whether we shall be given the grace to meet death with full consciousness, greeting it with prayer and resignation as the messenger of God. For death comes like a thief in the night. We have no assurance that our last word of decision on time and eternity will not be spoken at a moment when we do not think that death is at hand. Therefore we must begin in time to tend the lamp of our faith and our love, that it may always be filled with the oil of good works. Let us watch and pray, so that the Lord at His coming may not find us asleep. That prayer of decision which we wish to say in the hour of our death must be said by us again and again during our life. We must pray now for the decision of that future hour, and we must pray for the grace of fortitude. Let us pray that God may prevent us from being separated from Him, and that even when we are about to leave Him, He will not leave us, but lovingly compel our wayward heart back into His service, through His almighty and mysteriously gentle grace. To think of one's death is prayer indeed, a prayer of decision. The uncertainty of the hour of death compels us to anticipate in our everyday prayer, the prayer for the hour of death. Our everyday prayer thus becomes an intimate preparation for the ultimate prayer of decision. Let us pray unceasingly.

We have said much—perhaps in too many words—about the subject of prayer. And yet, we have said almost nothing, and many points of importance have scarcely been touched. One point above all should have been made in and for our age. The prophet Isaias stated an essential prerequisite for true prayer when he said (58:7 and 9): "Deal thy bread to the hungry and bring the needy and the harbourless into thy house, then thou shalt call and the Lord shall hear. Thou shall cry and he shall say: I am here." What we can say *about* prayer is of little consequence: what matters is what we say *in* prayer. These words we find for ourselves. They may be shy, weak and poor; they may rise on silver wings to the heavens from a cheerful heart; or they may be drawn with pain from the deep wells of sorrow. They may have in them a resonance like thunder among the hills; or they have in them the softness of summer rain. What matters only is that they come from our heart, and that we desire our hearts to be raised to God with them.

What matters is that the spirit of God lives in our prayer. Such prayer is heard by God. No word of such prayer will be forgotten. For God will give an answer of love to prayers which come to him in words of warm sincerity. That answer will be the giving of Himself to us at every moment of our lives, and most of all in that last hour of decision, when " the shadows lengthen, and the evening comes, and the busy world is hushed, and the fever of life is over, and our work is done. Then in His mercy may He give us a safe lodging and a holy rest, and peace at last! " (Cardinal Newman).

This " safe lodging," this " holy rest," this " peace at last," will be the reward of our fidelity in prayer.

CONFLICT OF SCIENCE
AND RELIGION

The Age of Reason, edited by the outstanding teacher and author, Stuart Hampshire, presents selections from the basic writings of such great 17th century philosophers as Descartes, Leibniz, Spinoza and others, with a penetrating introduction and interpretive commentary illuminating their works.

The 17th century was the great formative era of modern philosophy, marked by the decline of medieval conceptions of knowledge, by the rise of the physical sciences and by the gradual transition from Latin to French and English as instruments of philosophical thought. In this "age of reason," philosophers began to explain natural processes in mathematical terms. They also developed vital concepts of knowledge and certainty, appearance and reality, freedom and necessity, mind and matter, deduction and experiment.

STUART HAMPSHIRE is a Fellow of All Souls College, Oxford. Author of many articles on logical theory and on ethics, he has published a book on Spinoza. A lecturer in philosophy at Oxford since 1936, he has been a visiting professor at Columbia University.

". . . a very important and interesting series of philosophical writings . . ." is what Gilbert Highet, of the Department of Greek and Latin of Columbia University, said about The Mentor Philosophers series which traces, in six volumes, the course of philosophy from medieval times to the present.

Other MENTOR Books of Special Interest

THE ORIGINS OF SCIENTIFIC THOUGHT
Edited by Giorgio de Santillana

This collection of the basic writings of the ancient philosophers of science from Anaximander to Proclus (600 B.C. to 500 A.D.), with commentaries by the editor, is the first book in the new series, *The Mentor History of Scientific Thought.*   (#MQ336—95¢)

PHILOSOPHY IN A NEW KEY *by Susanne K. Langer*

A study of the symbolism of reason, rite and art, in clear, readable style.   (#MD101—50¢)

THE PRINCE *by Niccolo Machiavelli*

The classic work on statesmanship and power, the techniques and strategy of gaining and keeping political control.   (#MD69—50¢)

ADVENTURES OF IDEAS *by Alfred North Whitehead*

A history of man's great thoughts, tracing the development of crucial ideas from ancient times to the present.   (#MD141—50¢)

TO OUR READERS: We welcome your request for our free catalog of SIGNET and MENTOR books. If your dealer does not have the books you want, you may order them by mail, enclosing the list price plus 5¢ a copy to cover mailing. The New American Library of World Literature, Inc., P. O. Box 2310, Grand Central Station, New York 17, N. Y.

The Mentor Philosophers

THE AGE OF REASON

The 17th Century Philosophers

SELECTED, WITH INTRODUCTION AND INTERPRETIVE COMMENTARY.

by

STUART HAMPSHIRE

A MENTOR BOOK

Published by The New American Library

190
H A

© 1956 BY STUART HAMPSHIRE

All rights reserved

FIRST PRINTING, FEBRUARY, 1956
SECOND PRINTING, APRIL, 1957
THIRD PRINTING, MAY, 1958
FOURTH PRINTING, AUGUST, 1959
FIFTH PRINTING, JUNE, 1960
SIXTH PRINTING, NOVEMBER, 1961

A cloth-bound edition of *The Age of Reason*
is published by Houghton Mifflin Company

MENTOR TRADEMARK REG. U.S. PAT. OFF. AND FOREIGN COUNTRIES
REGISTERED TRADEMARK—MARCA REGISTRADA
HECHO EN CHICAGO, U.S.A.

MENTOR BOOKS are published by
The New American Library of World Literature, Inc.
501 Madison Avenue, New York 22, New York

PRINTED IN THE UNITED STATES OF AMERICA

Foreword

GREAT PHILOSOPHERS MUST BE READ WHOLE IF THEY ARE to be fully understood. This is particularly true of systematic thinkers like Spinoza. This book is designed solely as an introduction to the philosophy of the seventeenth century. It may encourage readers to turn to the original works themselves.

The following works need to be read in their entirety by anyone who wishes to go further in understanding the permanent contribution of that century to philosophy:

Hobbes's *Leviathan;* of Descartes, the *Discourse on Method,* the *Six Meditations,* the *Replies to Objections;* of Spinoza, the *Ethics, On the Correction of the Understanding, Letters;* of Leibniz, the *Discourse on Metaphysics,* the *Letters to Arnauld,* the *New Essays on the Human Understanding,* the Clarke-Leibniz *Correspondence,* the *Monadology, Of the Ultimate Origin of Things.*

Of the great commentators, Bertrand Russell's *The Philosophy of Leibniz* should also be read, together with the early chapters of A. N. Whitehead's *Science and the Modern World.*

These are the still-living classics which every student of philosophy needs to read before he speculates on philosophy himself. Some of the following extracts—but not many—illustrate rather the development of thought than surviving problems; most of them illustrate issues which are still discussed, even if the problems would no longer be stated in the same way. Much has been omitted, particularly from the works named above, which is still of living philosophical importance and omitted solely for reasons of space.

The translations of Descartes, Pascal, Spinoza and Leibniz are the responsibility of the editor. Several existing translations have been used for comparison. The following have been found particularly useful: the Everyman

(Dent) edition of Descartes; the Hale White and Amelia Stirling translation of Spinoza's *Ethics* (Oxford University Press); *Selections from Leibniz,* edited by Professor Philip Wiener (Scribner). Acknowledgment is also due to Mr. A. C. Crombie for the selection from Galileo, which is taken from his *From Augustine to Galileo* (The Cresset Press).

I am indebted for help in the preparation of this book to Mr. Isaiah Berlin of All Souls College, Oxford, and to Mr. B. A. O. Williams, of New College, Oxford.

Contents

conceive is in us now, called another IMAGINATION, therefore is nothing but decaying sense, and is found in men, and many other living creatures, as well sleeping as waking.

The decay of sense [in] men waking, is not the decay of the motion made in sense, but an obscuring of it, in such

THE AGE OF REASON

Introduction

PHILOSOPHY IS A CONTINUOUS ACTIVITY OF THE HUMAN mind, and the divisions between historical periods are always to some extent arbitrary and unreal. But the phase which can be constructed by beginning with Galileo (1564-1642) and ending with Leibniz (1646-1716) has a certain unity; it is the great formative period of modern philosophy. It marks the rise of the physical sciences and the continuing, and almost final, decline of medieval conceptions of knowledge, based upon Aristotelian methods. Throughout the sixteenth century human reason had, in different places and in different subjects, asserted its independence of authority and challenged scholastic methods of thought. But in the sixteenth century the idiom—the style, the way in which men's minds moved and expressed themselves—was still that of the old world, and not of our own; even in reading Machiavelli, Erasmus and Montaigne, one is aware always of a certain quaintness, as it seems to us now, which constitutes a barrier between us and them. Their canons of relevance, their constant appeals to the authority of ancient Greece or Rome, are not natural to us; their sense of literalness, and their manner of argument, are not ours. Most important of all, the national languages had not yet established themselves, in any form familiar to us, as the natural instruments of abstract thought. All through the seventeenth century one can observe the gradual transition from Latin to French and English as the natural instruments of philosophical thought. At the beginning of the century Latin is still the unavoidable vernacular of the learned world; individuals even of genius, such as Bacon and later Hobbes, seem to be struggling against the poetical and concrete temperament of their language when they turn to abstract argument in English; the path of argument

11

from one expression to another has not yet been made smooth by centuries of use, as it has when they fall back into Latin. It is for this reason, among others, that Descartes (1596-1650) is normally and properly taken as the first great modern philosopher, the first of the line which continues unbroken until the present day. He invented a style of abstract argument which was clear and simple and largely free from the technicalities of scholastic Latin. Philosophy became a proper part of French literature, and the French language itself was to become the focus of European civilization.

Philosophy is a free inquiry into the limits of human knowledge and into the most general categories applicable to experience and reality. The condition of philosophy at any time depends in the main upon two related, but distinguishable, activities of the human mind: religious and moral belief, on the one hand, and the search for positive knowledge, on the other. When religious belief is firmly established and largely unchallenged, narrow limits will be set to the free inquiry which is philosophy; where there is insecurity or conflict of religious and moral belief, philosophical problems will present themselves with particular urgency and be left more open to free inquiry. The seventeenth century was an age of religious conflict, in which Christian theology had often to be defended, in one of its many forms, with savage desperation; the doctrinal unity of Western Europe had disappeared, and every thinking man was aware of this change. At the same time the search for positive knowledge seemed to be entering on a new phase with a new vitality; great new areas of natural knowledge had been opened up by Galileo, Copernicus, Kepler, and many others. It gradually became clear that natural processes must be explained by laws of nature expressed in quantitative terms; the key to the understanding of nature seemed to be found in the application of mathematics and in precise methods of measurement. The Aristotelian conception of nature as a system or hierarchy of natural kinds, distinguished by essential qualitative differences, began to seem inadequate; and yet the logic which had for centuries been taught in all the schools of Europe still depended on this conception of nature. It was the logic of the syllogism, which made classification seem the typical subject of argument and the standard expression of knowledge. "All Xs are Ys; this is an X; therefore this is a Y"—this scheme of argument had for centuries been taken as the model of rational inference in the sciences. The sciences were required to arrive at definitions which state the essence and essential properties of things of different kinds. Definition and essence, substance and attribute, essential properties and accidental properties—these are the central notions of scholastic philosophy, ultimately derived from Aristotle.

If the natural order is to be understood as God's museum of things and creatures, eternally divided into their kinds, these are indeed the notions appropriate to the organization of natural knowledge. But if nature is to be understood as the manifestation of mathematically precise natural laws, this logic becomes inappropriate and too narrow; the divisions into kinds by perceived qualitative differences become irrelevant and have no important place in the organization of scientific knowledge. A logic is needed which shows the forms of mathematical argument, since natural knowledge must, as far as possible, assume the form of mathematical demonstration. Natural science must, as far as possible, be abstract and general and indifferent to qualitative distinctions. Laws of motion and change provide a rational explanation of phenomena only if they are stated in the most general terms possible; ideally, they should apply not merely to things of a particular kind, qualitatively distinguished, but throughout the physical realm without restriction. Therefore metaphysicians are led to represent the subject to which natural laws apply as a single, qualitatively undifferentiated substance, called Matter or Extension; all qualitative changes are to be explained as fundamentally changes of state within the single system of material or extended things; the qualitative differences apparent to the human senses are irrelevant to the true understanding of the motions of material things.

Some variant of this view of nature, and of natural knowledge, will be found in Descartes, Spinoza, and Leibniz, who are the great philosophers of the century. All of them agreed in rejecting much of the Aristotelian logic still taught in the schools as being irrelevant to modern scientific conceptions of the world. All of them agreed in rejecting our ordinary judgments of perception, and the vocabulary in which they are expressed, as inadequate to the representation of reality. They all agreed that the propositions of the new mathematical physics more nearly correspond to the ultimate constituents of nature. But they differed among themselves in the positive account which they gave of the ultimate constitution of reality.

It must be remembered that, until the death of Newton and even later, there was no generally recognized, clear line of distinction between philosophy and the natural sciences; "natural philosophy" was the common term which could embrace both what we would call metaphysics and what we would call physics. Descartes and Leibniz were not only philosophers in the narrow, modern sense; they were also distinguished figures in the history of mathematics and of science. It was part of the function of metaphysical philosophy to suggest the forms of explanation and system of concepts which scientific investigators of nature should use. Particularly in the works of Descartes and Leibniz, the problems of theoretical physics, as we should describe them, are intertwined with perennial philosophical problems. Descartes, Spinoza and Leibniz each made his own suggestions about the nature of space and the fundamental constitution of bodies. Reading them now, we may choose to disregard those parts of their theories which now fall within the domain of the experimental sciences; at least in part, their theories will seem outmoded science, and we shall be interested only in their treatment of the perennial philosophical problems; these are the problems which cannot be treated as experimental problems and cannot fall under any of the special sciences. But we must allow for, and understand, their motives in constructing a natural philosophy which was largely speculative but which was not at that time useless.

Philosophy has always been wider than natural philosophy and more than the philosophy of science. All great philosophers have tried to provide an account, not only of the natural order, but of man's place in nature. A theory of human knowledge and its limits must also carry implications about human purposes and human ends; and a theory of the natural order must also suggest some answer to the problems of creation, and therefore carry some implications about the existence and nature of God. It was in the seventeenth century that the modern conflict, or apparent conflict, between science and religion had its beginning. Galileo was condemned by the Church for disproving the official Aristotelian theories of the motion of bodies. Copernicus and Kepler had discovered the true nature of the solar system, and the whole medieval Christian cosmology was left without a basis. The earth had been shown not to be the center of creation, but, in terms of physical space, an utterly insignificant part of it. This discovery did not immediately become known to educated people in general; it was at first confined to a narrow circle of natural philosophers, many of whom, including Bacon, rejected it. But it was clear that if it did become known, and if it could not be rejected on any rational grounds, popular Christian thought, and the imagery and conception of the world that everyone took for granted, would finally be undermined. The effects would pass far beyond the learned world and would be felt by every educated man, however little he might be interested in science. He would have to think about the place of man in creation in a quite different way. Copernicus' result, like Galileo's, was condemned by the Church, but it was plain that the truth could not be suppressed for long. Two great Christian thinkers had some more or less permanently effective answer to the challenge: Pascal and Descartes. Pascal was not, in the strict sense of the word, a philosopher, and is therefore represented only by two short fragments in this book. He did not try to give a coherent account of the possible range of human knowledge or of the natural order, or even of the moral duties of man. Rather he showed in his *Lettres Provinciales* and in the *Pensées,* what the attitude of Christian faith must be, when men realize, as they should, that none of the ultimate philosophical questions can be answered by human reason; as Mon-

taigne had suggested, there can be no reasonable certainty
in human knowledge; Pascal had looked for, and found, a
desperate moral certainty of the truth of the Christian reve-
lation. The universe is vast and men are physically insignificant within it. Their greatness is that they alone have souls
and can recognize their own insufficiency and their dependence on God. Pascal was a skeptic about philosophical
questions, and abandoned, almost to the point of heresy,
the rational arguments which were supposed to prove or
justify Christian theology. But with great psychological insight he showed how a Christian might regard all mundane
knowledge as in the last resort vain and as equally irrelevant
to his true spiritual needs.

Descartes was a loyal Catholic and at the same time a
systematic philosopher who found a place for the truths
of Christian theology and of mathematical physics in his
scheme. The necessity of God's existence had to be proved
before the certainty of any of our natural knowledge could
be guaranteed; and he accepted some of the traditional
proofs of the existence of God. The realm of extended things
is wholly separated from the realm of souls who think, and
the causes which operate in one realm have no directly deducible effects in the other. Human beings are composite
beings, and are the meeting point of the two realms; they
are partly minds which think, partly bodies which are
governed by the universal laws of physics. Descartes, unlike Spinoza, was not in his published works primarily concerned with moral problems; his interest was in natural
philosophy. And even in natural philosophy he was prepared not to publish the conclusions which he had reached
if they would be disagreeable to the Church. His whole
philosophy, however incoherent it might be as an account
of man's position in nature, seemed an acceptable com-
promise between the claims of mathematical physics and
the claims of Christian theology. It was immediately acceptable therefore as the advanced thought of the time, and
dominated its century until Locke's *Essay* was published.
Clear thought and rational argument were increasingly
identified with the Cartesian method of analyzing complex
ideas into their simple components and of deducing con-

sequences from the most simple, self-evident propositions, in the manner of pure mathematics.

The conditions of thought in England, following the Reformation, were largely different from France, and the seventeenth century was the age of French predominance both in thought and in manners. With the publication of Locke's *Essay* English thought, and specifically English empiricism, spread across the Channel and formed the basis of radical thought throughout Europe in the eighteenth century. Bacon at the beginning of the century was equally a European figure, a point of reference for every philosopher of the time, but he was rather the last philosopher of the Renaissance than the first philosopher of the seventeenth century. He did not allow for the all-important place of mathematics in the organization of natural knowledge. And the seventeenth century can properly be called, in the history of philosophy, the Age of Reason, because almost all the great philosophers of the period were trying to introduce the rigor of mathematical demonstration into all departments of knowledge, including philosophy itself. The form of philosophical argument in Descartes, Spinoza and Leibniz is largely deductive and a priori; their intention was to prove their conclusions about the ultimate constituents of reality, and the limits of human knowledge, as a mathematical theorem is proved. Hume and Kant have long ago convinced most philosophers, particularly English and American philosophers, that deductive metaphysics of this kind must be empty and without content, and that no conclusions about the ultimate nature of things can be established by purely a priori argument. And in the last thirty years the possibility of any systematic construction in philosophy has been called in question again, on the ground that philosophy must be concerned with the analysis of concepts and of the meanings of words, and not with assertions or denials of existence. Perhaps some change in the nature of scientific problems, or in the conception of physical theory, or in the study of language itself, will at some time re-create the need for systematic philosophy; there may come a time when, as in the seventeenth century, some speculative synthesis seems the only way of understanding new forms of knowledge and of making their relationships clear. In the meantime, Descartes, Leibniz and Spinoza are read, not only as formative figures in European thought, but also for the richness and variety of their analyses of the concepts upon which our thought depends—for their analyses of knowledge and certainty, appearance and reality, existence and identity, freedom and necessity, mind and matter, deduction and experiment. These, among others, are the continuing problems of philosophy which present themselves in new forms in every age; and the best way of approaching them is to see how they have presented themselves to the greatest thinkers of the past.

CHAPTER I

Bacon

FRANCIS BACON WAS BORN IN LONDON IN 1561 INTO A family connected on both sides with the Court and government, and he was always destined for great offices. He studied law at Gray's Inn and sought office and promotion from his uncle, William Cecil. Failing to obtain from Cecil the advancement he wanted, he attached himself to the Earl of Essex, who, in 1593, nominated him as attorney general. But, after long hesitation, Queen Elizabeth refused to accept him for that post.

When Essex's armed rebellion failed, Bacon was one of his accusers. After the accession of James I, Bacon's advance to power began. In 1603 he was knighted; in 1606 he married a rich heiress, and in 1607 he was made solicitor general and in 1613 attorney general. As a friend of James's favorite, George Villiers, he became a privy councilor in 1616, lord keeper in 1617, and, finally, lord chancellor and Baron Verulam in 1617. In 1621 he was made Viscount St. Albans. But, falling from favor, he was accused of accepting bribes, deprived of all his offices, and, after a short imprisonment, he retired to the country. He died in 1626.

Bacon stands outside the circle of the great philosophers of the seventeenth century; in spirit and outlook he belongs rather to the sixteenth century than to the age of the new mathematical physics and of rationalism in philosophy. Unlike Descartes, he had no vision of the application of mathematics in the study of nature and he made no lasting contribution to the analysis of concepts or of the different categories of thought. But his great works, the *Novum Organum* (1620) and the *Advancement of Learning* (1605), had an immense influence throughout Europe and

19

his name became a symbol of the inductive method in science. He was a subtle, many-sided, prolific thinker, half medieval in his conceptions and half modern. There is a magnificence and disorder in his writing as in his life. His mind was full of projects and various learning, and he had a sharp appetite for new sensations and curiosities. His famous essays show his subtlety and sophistication. But he had not the hard sense of relevance in abstract argument, the love of logic, which we find in the great philosophers, and, above all, in Descartes, Spinoza and Leibniz. His eye was always caught by the color and variety of concrete things in nature before he had followed an argument far enough among generalities. In short, he had the temperament of a naturalist rather than a philosopher.

Bacon, like Descartes, proclaimed a new method in the sciences; but his method, unlike Descartes's, was not to involve a priori reasoning to indubitable truths. He advocated a purely empirical, experimental method which, starting from observations of particular things and events, would move towards wider and wider generalization. These general statements, unlike those of mathematics, would be capable of being proved false by experiment. His interest is thus primarily in an *inductive* method, by which one arrives from observation of fact at generalizations which are merely probable. It is as a contributor to "inductive logic" and experimental method that he has a permanent place in the history of philosophy. Hume and Mill were to carry further the investigation which Bacon began. He turns his attention to topics wider than the methods of empirical observation, to the function of scientific generalization and the design of fruitful experiment. He is concerned also with the "notions" used in empirical inquiries, and suggests that philosophers must analyze the language of science. By gaining a clear idea of the concepts employed, they would eradicate those confusions of language which hamper empirical investigations from the beginning. He has also a theory of classification, of the principles which should guide us in natural history and in making an inventory of the natural objects around us. We should not classify things simply on the basis of superficial resemblances, but should turn our attention to those divisions of kind in nature which are the most far-reaching and systematic. It was such a fundamental method of classification that Linnaeus (1735) introduced into the science of botany, so providing new foundations for natural knowledge.

The following extracts include examples both of his criticisms of the scholastic logic of science and of his positive recommendations. He attacks Aristotelian logic from several points of view. First, being based on the syllogism, it concentrated attention on the valid deductions of particular statements from more general statements, and ignored the problem of how these general statements are reached. Secondly, he showed that the generalization from particulars, as it is represented in scholastic logic, is hasty and superficial (see Aphorisms 1, 19, 22, 25). Traditional logic is equally inadequate in its account of the formation of "notions" and classes (see Aphorism 14). Thirdly, it suffers from the more fundamental disadvantage of being merely a method of recording knowledge already obtained (Aphorism 12); it is not a method of discovery, suggesting further research, and it cannot lead either to practical control over nature (Aphorisms 3, 4, 8), or to the discovery of new sciences (Aphorism 5).

In the place of this concentration on the orderly arrangement of general statements and of their particular instances in the syllogism, Bacon suggests a method of discovering more and more new and true statements of fact. The method of induction by simple enumeration—that is the mere listing of what is seen to occur together in nature—is to be replaced by a method of systematic experiment, which will rely on "proper rejections and exclusions." Thus, to take a very simple example, if some conjunction of features $a, b, c,$ is observed, it is not enough merely to record it and to go on recording similar particular matters of fact indefinitely; one must make experiments which will leave out systematically each one of the features in turn, and so enable us to discover, for instance, that only a or only b is necessary for the production of $c,$ and not both a and b together; or, if they are found to be jointly necessary, to find some more general, common feature of them in virtue of which they are always followed by *c*. Here we see the need for the analysis and classification of notions which Bacon demands; for, if the scientist relies on a fund of common language which has some confused term serving as the name of *a* and *b*, taken together, he will not be able to separate them in his mind and so will never think of the experiment which is needed.

Perhaps Bacon's most profound observation was that the scientist must recognize the superior power of negative instances (Aphorism 46). If he has made a generalization of the form "whenever *a* happens *b* happens," he must always look for a case of *a* happening without *b*. If this negative instance is found, he must look for the most fruitful way of amending his law, and not be content with introducing some "frivolous distinction" (Aphorism 25). It is the essence of superstition to pay attention only to the positive instances which support one's beliefs and not to look for counter examples. Lastly, generalization must be as wide and embracing as is possible compatibly with the known facts and with the structure of existing science, and not merely wild, arbitrary or isolated (Aphorism 106). If we do not observe these principles, generalizations will be merely designed to fit the facts already known and will lead to no new discoveries. They are useless unless they have greater logical power than the particular statements on which they are based, that is, unless they imply that certain observations will be made outside the domain from which the generalization was derived. Here Bacon notices the truth that it is the broadness of its application that gives a scientific theory its power and usefulness.

Bacon's remarks on the logic of induction are tentative and often veiled in obscure terminology. But there are glimpses of that logic of experiment which was later fully expounded by John Stuart Mill. Bacon correctly stresses the importance of "putting nature to the question" systematically and in pursuit of a general hypothesis, rather than of merely recording observed facts on no constant principle. Perhaps he was too simply empirical, and his logic is still more easily applicable to the sciences of classification than to physics. He was inferior to Galileo and Descartes in his vision of the future. He did not foresee the physics of differential equations.

The extracts that follow are from the edition of James Spedding; the first is from the Preface to the *Novum Organum*.

[Now my method, though hard to practise, is easy to explain, and it is this. I propose to establish progressive stages of certainty. The evidence of the sense, helped and guarded by a certain process of correction, I retain. But the mental operation which follows the act of sense I for the most part reject; and instead of it I open and lay out a new and certain path for the mind to proceed in, starting directly from the simple sensuous perception. The necessity of this was felt no doubt by those who attributed so much importance to Logic, showing thereby that they were in search of helps for the understanding, and had no confidence in the native and spontaneous process of the mind. But this remedy comes too late to do any good, when the mind is already, through the daily intercourse and conversation of life, occupied with unsound doctrines and beset on all sides by vain imaginations. And therefore that art of Logic, coming (as I said) too late to the rescue, and no way able to set matters right again, has had the effect of fixing errors rather than disclosing truth. . . . There remains but one course for the recovery of a sound and healthy condition,— namely, that the entire work of the understanding be commenced afresh, and the mind itself be from the very outset not left to take its own course, but guided at every step; and the business be done as if by machinery. Certainly if in things mechanical men had set to work with their naked hands, without help or force of instruments, just as in things intellectual they have set to work with little else than the naked forces of the understanding, very small would the matters have been which, even with their best efforts applied in conjunction, they could have attempted or accomplished. . . .]

The following is from the *First Book of Aphorisms*.

III

Human knowledge and human power meet in one; for where the cause is not known the effect cannot be produced. Nature to be commanded must be obeyed; and that which in contemplation is as the cause is in operation as the rule.

IV

Towards the effecting of works, all that man can do is to put together or put asunder natural bodies. The rest is done by nature working within.

VII

The productions of the mind and hand seem very numerous in books and manufactures. But all this variety lies in an exquisite subtlety and derivations from a few things already known; not in the number of axioms.

VIII

Moreover the works already known are due to chance and experiment rather than to science; for the sciences we now possess are merely systems for the nice ordering and setting forth of things already invented; not methods of invention or directions for new works.

XI

As the sciences which we now have do not help us in finding out new works, so neither does the logic which we now have help us in finding out new sciences.

XII

The logic now in use serves rather to fix and give stability to the errors which have their foundation in commonly received notions than to help the search after truth. So it does more harm than good.

XIV

The syllogism consists of propositions, propositions consists of words, words are symbols of notions. Therefore if the notions themselves (which is the root of the matter) are confused and over-hastily abstracted from the facts, there can be no firmness in the superstructure. Our only hope therefore lies in a true induction.

XIX

There are and can be only two ways of searching into and discovering truth. The one flies from the senses and particulars to the most general axioms, and from these principles, the truth of which it takes for settled and immovable, proceeds to judgment and to the discovery of middle axioms. And this way is now in fashion. The other derives axioms from the senses and particulars, rising by a gradual and unbroken ascent, so that it arrives at the most general axioms last of all. This is the true way, but as yet untried.

XXII

Both ways set out from the senses and particulars, and rest in the highest generalities; but the difference between them is infinite. For the one just glances at experiment and particulars in passing, the other dwells duly and orderly among them. The one, again, begins at once by establishing certain abstract and useless generalities, the other rises by gradual steps to that which is prior and better known in the order of nature.

XXIV

It cannot be that axioms established by argumentation should avail for the discovery of new works; since the subtlety of nature is greater many times over than the subtlety of argument. But axioms duly and orderly formed from particulars easily discover the way to new particulars, and thus render sciences active.

XXV

The axioms now in use, having been suggested by a scanty and manipular experience and a few particulars of most general occurrence, are made for the most part just large enough to fit and take these in: and therefore it is no wonder if they do not lead to new particulars. And if some opposite instance, not observed or not known before, chance to come in the way, the axiom is rescued and preserved by some frivolous distinction; whereas the truer course would be to correct the axiom itself.

XXXI

It is idle to expect any great advancement in science from the superinducing and engrafting of new things upon old. We must begin anew from the very foundations, unless we would revolve for ever in a circle with mean and contemptible progress.

XXXVI

One method of delivery alone remains to us; which is simply this: We must lead men to the particulars themselves, and their series and order; while men on their side must force themselves for awhile to lay their notions by and begin to familiarise themselves with facts.

XLVI

The human understanding when it has once adopted an opinion (either as being the received opinion or as being agreeable to itself) draws all things else to support and agree with it. And though there be a greater number and weight of instances to be found on the other side, yet these it either neglects and despises, or else by some distinction sets aside and rejects; in order that by this great and pernicious predetermination the authority of its former conclusions may remain inviolate. And therefore it was a good answer that was made by one who when they showed him hanging in a temple a picture of those who had paid their vows as having escaped shipwreck, and would have him say whether he did not now acknowledge the power of the gods,—"Aye," asked he again, "but where are they painted that were drowned, after their vows?" And such is the way of all superstition, whether in astrology, dreams, omens, divine judgments, or the like; wherein men, having a delight in such vanities, mark the events where they are fulfilled, but where they fail, though this happen much oftener, neglect and pass them by. But with far more subtlety does this mischief insinuate itself into philosophy and the sciences; in which the first conclusion colours and brings into conformity with itself all that come after, though far sounder and better. Besides, independently of that delight and vanity which I have described, it is the peculiar and perpetual error of human intellect to be more moved and excited by affirmatives than by negatives; whereas it ought properly to hold itself indifferently disposed towards both alike. Indeed in the establishment of any true axiom, the negative instance is the more forcible of the two.

C

But not only is a greater abundance of experiments to be sought for and procured, and that too of a different kind from those hitherto tried; an entirely different method, order, and process for carrying on and advancing experience must also be introduced. For experience, when it wanders in its own track, is, as I have already remarked, mere groping in the dark, and confounds men rather than instructs them. But when it shall proceed in accordance with a fixed law, in regular order, and without interruption, then may better things be hoped of knowledge.

CIV

The understanding must not however be allowed to jump and fly from particulars to remote axioms and of almost the highest generality (such as the first principles, as they are called, of arts and things), and taking stand upon them as truths that cannot be shaken, proceed to prove and frame the middle axioms by reference to them; which has been the practice hitherto; the understanding being not only carried that way by a natural impulse, but also by the use of syllogistic demonstration trained and inured to it. But then, and then only, may we hope well of the sciences, when in a just scale of ascent, and by successive steps not interrupted or broken, we rise from particulars to lesser axioms; and then to middle axioms, one above the other; and last of all to the most general. For the lowest axioms differ but slightly from bare experience, while the highest and most general (which we now have) are notional and abstract and without solidity. But the middle are the true and solid and living axioms, on which depend the affairs and fortunes of men; and above them again, last of all, those which are indeed the most general; such I mean as are not abstract, but of which those intermediate axioms are really limitations.

The understanding must not therefore be supplied with wings, but rather hung with weights, to keep it from leaping and flying. Now this has never been done; when it is done, we may entertain better hopes of the sciences.

CV

In establishing axioms, another form of induction must be devised than has hitherto been employed; and it must be used for proving and discovering not first principles (as they are called) only, but also the lesser axioms, and the middle, and indeed all. For the induction which proceeds by simple enumeration is childish; its conclusions are precarious, and exposed to peril from a contradictory instance; and it generally decides on too small a number of facts, and on those only which are at hand. But the induction which is to be available for the discovery and demonstration of sciences and arts, must analyse nature by proper rejections and exclusions; and then, after a sufficient number of negatives, come to a conclusion on the affirmative instances; which has not yet been done or even attempted, save only by Plato, who does indeed employ this form of induction to a certain extent for the purpose of discussing definitions and ideas. But in order to furnish this induction or demon-

stration well and duly for its work, very many things are
to be provided which no mortal has yet thought of: insomuch that greater labour will have to be spent in it than
has hitherto been spent on the syllogism. And this induction
must be used not only to discover axioms, but also in the
formation of notions. And it is in this induction that our
chief hope lies.

CVI

But in establishing axioms by this kind of induction, we
must also examine and try whether the axiom so established be framed to the measure of those particulars only
from which it is derived, or whether it be larger and wider.
And if it be larger and wider, we must observe whether by
indicating to us new particulars it confirm that wideness
and largeness as by a collateral security; that we may not
either stick fast in things already known, or loosely grasp
at shadows and abstract forms; not at things solid and realised in matter. And when the process shall have come
into use, then at last shall we see the dawn of a solid hope.]

The following is Aphorism X from the *Second Book of
Aphorisms*.

[Now my directions for the interpretation of nature embrace two generic divisions; the one how to educe and
form axioms from experience; the other how to deduce
and derive new experiments from axioms. The former again
is divided into three ministrations; a ministration to the
sense, a ministration to the memory, and a ministration
to the mind or reason.

For first of all we must prepare a *Natural and Experimental History,* sufficient and good; and this is the foundation of all; for we are not to imagine or suppose, but to
discover, what nature does or may be made to do.

But natural and experimental history is so various and
diffuse, that it confounds and distracts the understanding,
unless it be ranged and presented to view in a suitable order. We must therefore form *Tables and Arrangements of*

Instances, in such a method and order that the understanding may be able to deal with them.

And even when this is done, still the understanding, if
left to itself and its own spontaneous movements, is in-
competent and unfit to form axioms, unless it be directed
and guarded. Therefore in the third place we must use
Induction, true and legitimate induction, which is the very
key of interpretation.]

CHAPTER II

Galileo

GALILEO GALILEI (1564-1642), THE GREAT ASTRONOMER, was born at Pisa. He was both a brilliant experimental scientist and a mathematician, and became professor of mathematics at the University of Pisa. At the age of nineteen he had already observed the equality of oscillation of a simple pendulum; he later arrived at the proposition that all bodies, whatever their weight, descend with equal velocity. He proceeded to demonstrate his generalization experimentally, in spite of the fact that it removed the basis of the orthodox Aristotelian physics. He became famous throughout Europe, and, at Padua, and under the protection of the Medici family in Florence, he went on to make further revolutionary discoveries. Perhaps the greatest of them was the design for a refracting telescope. Using this telescope, he made a series of observations which seemed to him to confirm Copernicus's hypothesis that the sun is the center of the system of the heavens. He also arrived at the conclusion that the Milky Way is a vast path of separate stars. These deductions from observation were gradually to transform man's conception of his place in the universe and particularly his conception of the size of the universe in relation to man himself. The tidy Aristotelian universe, with man on earth as its physical, as well as its moral, center, was destroyed. We shall see how the great philosophers of the century, particularly Spinoza and Leibniz, tried to represent the immensities of the universe in their conceptual scheme.

The Catholic church condemned Galileo's discoveries as incompatible with doctrine, and ultimately attacked Galileo in person. When he was seventy years old and in bad health he was called before the Inquisition and, after a prolonged trial, compelled to disclaim his true opinions. He was reprieved by outside intervention from the dungeons of the Inquisition and retired to Florence to make further discoveries in physics. The Church had hoped to crush the statement of truth, based on observation of fact, by an exercise of power. It failed, with ignomiry.

Galileo's magnificent achievements were based on two principles which have become the guiding principles of modern science: first, that ir. making statements and hypotheses about nature one must always appeal to observation and not to authority; secondly, that natural processes can best be understood if they are represented in mathematical terms. These principles are stated in his "Dialogue Concerning the Two Great Systems of the World."

The second of these prir.ciples is stated in the first of the two extracts from *Il Saggiatore* given below (Question 6): by "philosophy" is meant "natural philosophy," which includes the whole of science. The second extract (Question 48) states that physical nature is to be understood, and represented in science, solely in terms of its directly measurable properties, "shape, quantity and motion." This distinction between what came to be called Primary Qualities, which are the directly measurable qualities of things, and Secondary Qualities (odors, tastes, sounds, colors) runs all through the philosophy of the century following Galileo.

Secondary qualities are represented as in some way subjective and unreal, being mere ideas produced in us by the action of physical realities on our sense organs. Physical nature itself, apart from our perception of it, is exactly as it is described in the laws of physics and mechanics, and not as it is described in our ordinary language. It was left to Bishop Berkeley in the next century to question this assumption that the primary qualities can intelligibly be said to exist without secondary qualities. The distinction which Galileo is here making was assumed to be valid and necessary by Descartes and is the foundation of his philosophy of nature.

[Philosophy is written in that vast book which stands forever open before our eyes, I mean the universe; but it cannot be read until we have learnt the language and become familiar with the characters in which it is written. It is written in mathematical language, and the letters are triangles, circles and other geometrical figures, without which means it is humanly impossible to understand a single word.

No sooner do I form a conception of a material or corporeal substance, than I feel the need of conceiving that it has boundaries and shape; that relative to others it is great or small; that it is in this or that place and in this or that time; that it is moving or still; that it touches or does not touch another body; that it is one, few or many; nor can I, by any effort of imagination, dissociate it from these properties. On the other hand, I find no need to apprehend it as accompanied by such properties as to be white or red, bitter or sweet, sounding or silent, pleasant or evil smelling. Perhaps, if the senses had not informed us of these qualities, the reason and imagination alone would never have arrived at them. Therefore I hold that these tastes, odors, colors, etc., of the object in which they seem to reside, are nothing more than pure names, and exist only in the sensitive being; so that if the latter were removed these qualities would themselves vanish. But having given them special names different from those of the other primary and real qualities, we would persuade ourselves that they also exist just as truly and really as the latter. . . . But I hold that there exists nothing in external bodies for exciting in us tastes, odors and sounds but size, shape, quantity and slow or swift motion. And I conclude that if the ears, tongue and nose were removed, shape, quantity and motion would remain but there would be no odors, tastes or sounds, which apart from living creatures I believe to be mere words.]

CHAPTER III

Hobbes

THOMAS HOBBES WAS BORN IN 1588 AND DIED IN 1679. HE was known for his remarkable memory and his wit. He became a private tutor attached to the Cavendish family, and traveled in France and Italy. He worked with Francis Bacon, whom he did not respect as a philosopher, and he was deeply impressed by the physics of Galileo, whom he later visited in Italy. He became interested in optics, one of the developing sciences of the time. He read Descartes with great excitement. In 1640 he wrote *The Elements of Law* as a defense of absolutism, but thought it necessary to take refuge in France when he foresaw the coming triumph of the parliamentarians. He remained there until 1651. The Latin adaptation of his work on law, published in Paris under the title of *De Cive,* was put on the index of prohibited books by the Church. In Paris he followed English politics during the Revolution with passionate interest, and he had foreseen Cromwell's success. He wrote his great work, the *Leviathan,* to recommend a powerful secular state, whether republican or royalist, to act independently of the Church, and shocked the Stuart Court at St. Germain, at which he had been living. In 1651 he returned to London, and even worked for Cromwell, while remaining friendly with Royalists. In 1655 the first part of his *De Corpore* was published, which again contained attacks on the influence of priests. He had been tutor to Charles II while in France, and welcomed him in London at the Restoration. But his militant atheism was unpopular and he could not republish his earlier works. He was still writing at the age of ninety.

He was a man of strong personality, witty, sharp, brilliant, and of powerful physique; he admired strength, authority and lucidity of mind. He despised superstition and feared the influence of sects and churches. He was a famous figure of his age and a symbol of independence of mind, often feared and execrated.

Hobbes was a materialist and skeptic, who attacked scholastic philosophy as being a meaningless play with meaningless words—"absurd speeches . . . without any significance at all." Words have meaning only when they are associated, directly or indirectly, with qualities of sense or feeling. Qualities of sense or feeling are produced by the motions of bodies acting on our body; these motions leave traces, and associations are set up. This engenders memory and imagination, which is "nothing but decaying sense." But men have the capacity to attach names to their imaginations, and to use signs; and some names are universal names, which stand for a "similitude in some quality." "Truth consists in the right ordering of names in our affirmation," and we are apt to be "entangled in words" unless we attend carefully to the definitions of words. Philosophers, unlike geometers, have written nonsense, because they have not followed the geometrical method of beginning with clear definitions; by this method the conclusions of geometry have been made indispensable, and philosophy should imitate it. Spinoza was later to follow in his *Ethics* this suggestion that philosophical arguments should be set out in geometrical form. Hobbes himself tries to base the argument of the *Leviathan* on clear definitions; the reading of Euclid's *Elements* was a determining influence in his philosophy. He tried to build a philosophy of mind, and to account for the workings of the mind, using solely the facts of memory and imagination. Reasoning is mere calculation, the manipulation of signs, and the reasoning is correct if the same signs are constantly attached to the same images. The science of mechanics shows the pattern which human reasoning should follow; for in mechanics we calculate the movements of bodies according to the law of cause and effect, and the movements of the human mind can be calculated in the same way. From this mechanistic philosophy of the human mind he deduced the simple theory of sentiment and appetite, on which his political philosophy was based.

His political philosophy was of greater originality and of more permanent importance than his theory of knowledge. But the following extracts illustrate, first, his rejection of scholastic abstractions and, secondly, his doctrine of words as signs, and of the necessity of clear definitions. In his attempt to prove, by appeal to clear definitions and scientific method, that traditional metaphysics was meaningless, he may be compared with the logical positivists of the twentieth century. He deliberately formed a style which was coarse, direct, unpedantic and shocking; he wanted to make the philosophy of the schools ridiculous, and to bring the argument down to brass tacks—the brass tacks of materialism and cool, common sense. His abrupt, mocking, eccentric personality can be felt in his paragraphs, very much as it is described by Aubrey in his *Brief Lives*.

The extracts that follow, from the first three chapters of the *Leviathan*, illustrate the tough materialist basis of Hobbes's philosophy of mind. He starts from a simple causal notion of perception, which pictures it as a transaction between external objects and the sense organs, which sets up a train of motion in the "brain and heart"; these motions, reverberating later, give rise to "imagination." Hobbes uses the term "imagination" for any experience of having mental images (as he himself calls them); and classifies memory merely as a particular way of speaking of imagination, when we wish to emphasize the past origin of the images.

In giving this account of perceptions, Hobbes is influenced almost entirely by what we should call physical or physiological considerations. He is not really alive, as Descartes was, to the *philosophical* questions that arise about perception, the problems of how we know what external objects are really like, whether they exist as we perceive them, questions which were later in the English tradition to be the main concern of Locke and Berkeley. But he does hold the then current doctrine that the only qualities that are really "in" objects are those of extension, shape, and motion: it is the "motions" in objects that produce in us a sensation of the other qualities of color, hardness, heat and so on, which we wrongly suppose to be qualities of the objects themselves. This doctrine was elaborated by Locke in his distinction between "primary" and "secondary" qualities; it was subjected to radical criticism by Berkeley, who argued that there could be no more reason for saying that the so-called primary qualities were "in" objects, independently of an observer, than for saying that the secondary qualities were.

Hobbes next turns to the "train of imagination," as he calls it. Here we find that Hobbes did not, as is sometimes said, suppose that all thinking is conducted in words; he clearly has in mind thinking by means of mental images. But it is hardly thinking in a distinctively rational sense. He discusses prediction and retrodiction, that is, inferences to the future and to the past, considering them (appropriately in the present context) in terms of *expectation*, a nonrational state of mind brought about by past experience and habit. Prudence, the ability to be right about the future, he considers merely as a matter of conditioning; and indeed remarks that animals can sometimes in this respect be superior to human beings.

[CHAPTER I. Of Sense

Concerning the thoughts of man, I will consider them first singly and afterwards in train, or dependence upon one another. Singly, they are every one a representation or appearance, of some quality, or other accident of a body without us; which is commonly called an object. Which object works on the eyes, ears and other parts of a man's body; and by diversity of working, produces diversity of appearances.

The original of them all is that which we call sense; (For there is no conception in a man's mind, which has not at first, totally, or by parts, been begotten upon the organs of sense.) The rest are derived from that original. . . .

The cause of sense, is the external body, or object, which presses the organ proper to each sense, either immediately, as in the taste and touch; or mediately, as in seeing, hearing, and smelling; which pressure, by the mediation of nerves, and other strings and membranes of the body, continued inwards to the brain and heart, causes there a resistance, or counter pressure, or endeavour of the heart, to deliver itself: which endeavour because *outward*, seems to be some matter without. And this *seeming*, or *fancy*, is that which men call sense; and consists, as to the eye, in a *light*, or *colour figured;* to the ear, in a *sound;* to the nostril, in an *odour;* to the tongue and palate, in a *savour;* and to the rest of the body, in *heat, cold, hardness, softness*, and such other qualities, as we discern by *feeling.* All which qualities called *sensible*, are in the object which causes them, but so many several motions of the matter, by which it presses our organs diversely. Neither in us that are pressed, are they any thing else, but divers motions; (for motion produces nothing but motion.) But their appearance to us is fancy, the same waking, that dreaming. And as pressing, rubbing, or striking the eye, makes us fancy a light; and pressing the ear produces a din; so do the bodies also that we see or hear produce the same by their strong, though unobserved actions. For if those colours and sounds were in the bodies or objects that cause them, they could not be severed from them, as by glasses, and in echoes by reflection, we see they are; where we know the thing we see is in one place; the appearance in another. And though at some certain distance, the real, the very object seems invested with the fancy it begets in us; yet still the object is one thing, the image or fancy is another. So that sense in all cases, is nothing else but original fancy, caused (as I have said) by the pressure, that is, by the motion, of external things upon our eyes, ears, and other organs thereunto ordained.

But the Philosophy schools through all the Universities of Christendom, grounded upon certain texts of Aristotle, teach another doctrine; and say, for the cause of *vision* that the thing seen sendeth forth on every side a *visible species* (in English) a *visible show, apparition*, or *aspect*, or a *being seen*, the receiving of which into the eye is *seeing.* And for the cause of *hearing*, that the thing heard sends forth an *audible species*, that is an *audible aspect*, or *audible being seen;* which entering at the ear, makes *hearing.* For the cause of *understanding* also, they say the thing understood sends forth *intelligible species*, that is, an *intel-*

ligible being seen; which coming into the understanding, makes us understand. I do not say this as disapproving the use of Universities; but because I am to speak hereafter of their office in a Commonwealth I must let you see on all occasions by the way, what things would be amended in them; amongst which the frequency of insignificant speech is one.

Chapter II. Of Imagination

That when a thing lies still, unless something else stir it, it will lie still for ever, is a truth that no man doubts. But that when a thing is in motion it will eternally be in motion, unless something else stop it, though the reason be the same, (namely, that nothing can change itself,) is not so easily assented to. For men measure, not only other men, but all other things, by themselves: and because they find themselves subject after motion to pain, and lassitude, think every thing else grows weary of motion, and seeks repose of its own accord; little considering whether it may not be some other motion, in which that desire of rest they find in themselves consists. From hence it is that the Schools say, heavy bodies fall downward, out of an appetite to rest, and to conserve their nature in that place which is most proper to them; ascribing appetite and knowledge of what is good for their conservation, (which is more than man has,) to inanimate things, absurdly.

When a body is once in motion it moves (unless something else hinder it) eternally; and whatsoever hinders it, cannot in an instant, but in time, and by degrees, quite extinguish it: and as we see in the water, though the wind cease, the waves do not give over rolling for a long time after; so also it happens in that motion, which is made in the internal parts of a man, then, when he sees, dreams, etc. For after the object is removed, or the eye shut, we still retain an image of the thing seen, though more obscure than when we see it. And this is what the Latins call *Imagination,* from the image made in seeing; and apply the same, though improperly, to all the other senses. But the Greeks call it *Fancy;* which signifies *appearance,* and is as proper to one sense as to another IMAGINATION therefore is nothing but *decaying sense;* and is found in men, and many other living creatures, as well sleeping as waking.

The decay of sense in men waking, is not the decay of the motion made in sense; but an obscuring of it, in such manner, as the light of the sun obscures the light of the stars; which stars do no less exercise their virtue, by which they are visible, in the day, than in the night. But because amongst many strokes, which our eyes, ears, and other organs receive from external bodies, the predominant only is sensible; therefore the light of the sun being predominant, we are not affected with the action of the stars. And any object being removed from our eyes, though the impression it made in us remain; yet other objects more present succeeding, and working on us, the imagination of the past is obscured, and made weak; as the voice of a man is in the noise of the day. From which it follows that the longer the time is, after the sight, or sense of any object, the weaker is the imagination. For the continual change of man's body destroys in time the parts which in sense were moved: so that distance of time, and of place, has one and the same effect in us. For as at a great distance of place, that which we look at appears dim, and without distinction of the smaller parts; and as voices grow weak and inarticulate: so also after great distance of time, our imagination of the past is weak; and we lose (for example) of cities we have seen, many particular streets; and of actions, many particular circumstances. This *decaying sense,* when we would express the thing itself, (I mean *fancy* itself,) we call *Imagination,* as I said before: but when we would express the *decay,* and signify that the sense is fading, old, and past, it is called *Memory.* So that *Imagination* and *Memory* are but one thing, which for divers considerations has divers names.

Much memory, or memory of many things, is called *Experience.* Again, Imagination being only of those things which have been formerly perceived by Sense, either all at once, or by parts at several times; the former, (which is the imagining the whole object, as it was presented to the sense) is *simple Imagination;* as when one imagines a man, or horse, which he has seen before. The other is *compounded;* as when from the sight of a man at one time, and of a horse at another, we conceive in our mind a Centaur. So when a man compounds the image of his own person, with the image of the actions of another man; as when a man imagines himself a Hercules, or an Alexander, (which happens often to those who are much taken with reading of Romances) it is a compound imagination, and properly but a fiction of the mind. There are also other imaginations that rise in men, (though waking) from the great impression made in sense: as from gazing upon the sun, the impression leaves an image of the sun before our eyes a long time after; and from being long and vehemently intent upon geometrical figures, a man shall in the dark, (though awake) have the images of lines, and angles before his eyes: which kind of fancy has no particular name; as being a thing that does not commonly fall into men's discourse.

The imaginations of them that sleep, are those we call *Dreams.* And these also (as all other imaginations) have been before, either totally, or by parcels in the sense. And because in sense, the brain, and nerves, which are the necessary organs of sense, are so benumbed in sleep as not easily to be moved by the action of external objects, there can happen in sleep, no imagination; and therefore no dream, but what proceeds from the agitation of the inward parts of man's body; which inward parts, for the connection they have with the brain and other organs, when they are distempered, keep the same in motion; whereby the imaginations formerly made there appear as if a man were waking; saving that the organs of sense being now benumbed, so that there is no new object which can master and obscure them with a more vigorous impression, a dream must necessarily be more clear, in this silence of sense, than are our waking thoughts. And so it comes to pass that it is a hard matter, and by many thought impossible to distinguish exactly between sense and dreaming. For my part, when I consider that in dreams I do not often, nor constantly, think of the same persons, places, objects and actions that I do waking; nor remember so long a train of coherent thoughts, dreaming, as at other times; and because waking I often observe the absurdity of dreams, but never dream of the absurdity of my waking thoughts; I am well satisfied that, being awake, I know I dream not; though when I dream, I think myself awake. . . .

The imagination that is raised in man (or any other creature indued with the faculty of imagining) by words, or other voluntary signs, is what we generally call *Understanding;* and is common to man and beast. For a dog will understand by custom the call, or the rating of his master; and so will many other beasts. That understanding which is peculiar to man, is the understanding not only of his will; but his conceptions and thought, by the sequel and contexture of the names of things into affirmations, negations and other forms of speech. . . .

CHAPTER III. Of the Consequence or Train of Imaginations

By *Consequence,* or TRAIN of thoughts, I understand the succession of one thought to another, which is called (to distinguish it from discourse in words) *Mental Discourse.*

When a man thinks on anything whatsoever, his next thought after is not altogether so casual as it seems to be. Not every thought to every thought succeeds indifferently. But as we have no imagination, whereof we have not formerly had sense, in whole or in parts; so we have no transition from one imagination to another, whereof we never had the like before in our senses. The reason for which is this. All fancies are motions within us, relics of those made in the sense: and those motions that immediately succeeded one another in the sense, continue also together after sense: in so much as the former coming again to take place, and be predominant, the latter follows, by coherence of the matter moved, in such manner as water upon a plain table is drawn which way any one part of it is guided by the finger. But because in sense, to one and the same thing perceived, sometimes one thing, sometimes another succeeds, it comes to pass in time that in the imagining of any thing there is no certainty as to what we shall imagine next; only this is certain, it shall be something that succeeded the same before, at one time or another.

This train of thoughts, or mental discourse, is of two sorts. The first is *unguided, without design,* and inconstant; wherein there is no passionate thought, to govern and direct those that follow to itself, as the end and scope of some desire, or other passion: in which case the thoughts are said to wander, and seem impertinent one to another as in a dream. Such are commonly the thoughts of men that are not only without company, but also without care of anything; though even then their thoughts are as busy as at other times, but without harmony; as the sound which a lute out of tune would yield to any man; or in tune, to one who could not play. And yet in this wild ranging of the mind, a man may often perceive the way of it, and the dependance of one thought upon another. For in a discourse of our present civil war, what could seem more impertinent than to ask (as one did) what was the value of a Roman Penny? Yet the coherence to me was manifest enough. For the thought of the war introduced the thought of the delivering up the king to his enemies, the thought of that brought in the thought of the delivering up of Christ; and that again the thought of the 30 pence, which was the price of that treason: and from this easily followed that malicious question; and all this in a moment of time; for thought is quick.

The second is more constant; as being *regulated* by some desire, and design. For the impression made by such things as we desire, or fear, is strong and permanent, or, (if it cease for a time) of quick return: so strong it is sometimes as to hinder and break our sleep. From desire arises the thought of some means we have seen produce the like of that which we aim at; and from the thought of that, the thought of means to that mean; and so continually, till we come to some beginning within our own power. And because the end, by the greatness of the impression, comes often to mind, in case our thoughts begin to wander, they are quickly again reduced into the way: which observed by one of the seven wise men, made him give this precept, which is now worn out, *Respice finem;* that is to say, in all your actions, look often upon what you would have, as the thing that directs all your thoughts in the way to attain it. . . .

Sometimes a man desires to know the event of an action; and then he thinks of some like action past, and the events thereof one after another; supposing like events will follow like actions. As he that foresees what will become of a criminal, re-cons what he has seen follow on the like crime before; having this order of thoughts, the crime, the officer, the prison, the judge, and the gallows. Which kind of thoughts is called *Foresight,* and *Prudence,* or *Providence;* and sometimes *Wisdom;* though such conjecture, through the difficulty of observing all circumstances, is very fallacious. But this is certain; by how much one man has more experience of things past, than another; by so much also he is more prudent, and his expectations the seldomer fail him. The *Present* only has a being in Nature; things *Past* have a being in the memory only, but things *to come* have no being at all; the *Future* being but a fiction of the mind, applying the sequels of actions past to the actions that are present; which with most certainty is done by him that has most experience; but not with certainty enough. And though it be called prudence, when the event answers our expectation; yet in its own nature, it is but presumption. For the foresight of things to come, which is Providence, belongs only to him by whose will they are to come. From him only, and supernaturally, proceeds prophecy. The best prophet naturally is the best guesser; and the best guesser, he that is most versed and studied in the matters he guesses at: for he has most *signs* to guess by.

A *sign* is the event antecedent of the consequence; and contrarily, the consequence of the antecedent, when the like consequences have been observed before: and the oftener they have been observed, the less uncertain is the sign. And therefore he that has most experience in any kind of business, has most signs, whereby to guess at the future time; and consequently is the most prudent: and so much more prudent than he that is new in that kind of business, as not to be equalled by any advantage of natural and extemporary wit: though perhaps many young men think the contrary.

Nevertheless it is not prudence that distinguishes man from beast. There are beasts that, at a year old, observe more, and pursue that which is for their good, more prudently, than a child can do at ten.

As prudence is a *Presumption* of the *Future,* contracted from the *Experience* of time *Past*: so there is a presumption of things past taken from other things (not future but) past also. For he that has seen by what courses and degrees a flourishing State has first come into civil war, and then to ruin; upon the sight of the ruins of any other State, will guess, the like war and the like courses have been there also. But this conjecture has the same uncertainty almost as the conjecture of the Future; both being grounded only upon experience.

There is no other act of man's mind, that I can remember, naturally planted in him, so as to need no other thing, to the exercise of it, but to be born a man, and live with the use of his five senses. Those other faculties, of which I shall speak by and by, and which seem proper to man only, are acquired, and increased by study and industry; and of most men learned by instruction and discipline; and all proceed from the invention of words, and speech. For besides sense and thoughts, and the train of thoughts, the mind of man has no other motion; though by the help of speech, and method, the same faculties may be improved to such a height, as to distinguish men from all other living creatures.

Whatsoever we imagine, is *Finite*. Therefore there is no Idea, or conception of any thing we call *Infinite*. No man can have in his mind an Image of infinite magnitude; nor conceive infinite swiftness, infinite time, or infinite force, or infinite power. When we say any thing is infinite, we signify only that we are not able to conceive the ends, and bounds of the thing named; having no conception of the thing, but of our own inability. And therefore the Name of *God* is used, not to make us conceive him; (for he is *Incomprehensible;* and his greatness and power are unconceivable;) but that we may honour him. Also because whatsoever (as I said before,) we conceive, has been perceived first by sense, either all at once, or by parts; a man can have no thought, representing any thing, not subject to sense. No man therefore can conceive any thing, but he must conceive it in some place; and imbued with some determinate magnitude; and which may be divided into parts; nor that any thing is all in this place, and all in another place at the same time; nor that two, or more things can be in one and the same place at once: for none of these things ever have, or can be, incident to sense; but are absurd speeches, taken upon credit (without any significance at all,) from deceived Philosophers, and deceived, or deceiving, School men.]

THE DISTINCTION BETWEEN MEN AND ANIMALS LIES, FOR Hobbes, in the possession of language; what he has to say about language will be seen in his second group of extracts.

About language, and the uses of it, Hobbes has many extremely interesting and valuable ideas; and he was remarkably sensitive to the philosophical dangers of falling into nonsense. His accusations of this failing are liberally and somewhat hastily distributed; but the unfairness and superficiality of many of his criticisms, and the sketchiness of his own doctrines, are compensated by his great shrewdness and originality, and by the unfailing verve and humor with which he lays about him.

The "marks" or "notes" that make up language, when they are used as names of things, he calls "signs." Signs can be the names of objects, either of single objects (proper names), or of many (common names). Not all names, however, refer directly to things in nature; there are also the names of names, terms which (in the modern phrase) "refer intra-linguistically." Hobbes thinks that the assumption that all words—e.g. abstract nouns—refer to some independently existent entities is a fruitful source of philosophical errors; there is general agreement on this today, and the sorts of consideration which he sketches have been widely developed and refined by analytic philosophers in the last thirty years. He also rightly observes that language is not always used to make statements, but also, for instance, to express our intentions and emotions. In his idea that we use language about God not to describe, but to honor Him, we see a brilliant foreshadowing of the theories of emotive, and of other nondescriptive, uses of language which are constantly under discussion among philosophers now.

About the old philosophical question of how common, or general, terms get their meaning—the so-called problem of universals—Hobbes is intransigently radical. The problem turned in part on the questions "What have all the things that fall under a general term in common?" or "What binds the indefinitely large class of such things together?"; and to this Hobbes answers: "Nothing, except the possession of the common name which we attach to them." This position of extreme nominalism, like any other simple answer to such an involved question, is an exaggeration, but many would now agree that it was at least an exaggeration in the right direction. Hobbes gives no consideration to the difficulties involved, and dismisses the various theories which supposed that there must be some common property to hold the class together.

The possession of language enables man's thinking to take the form, not just of a train of mental images, but of a reckoning of "the consequences of terms." Hobbes regards these as two different ways of thinking about *things*: with his usual common sense, he says that words stand directly for things, and not, as Locke and his successors later misleadingly insisted, for ideas. He seems to consider that the advantage of verbal thinking over image thinking lies in the greater generality given by the use of general terms; he gives the example of a man without knowledge of language who, he claims, could *in a particular case* "see" that the angles of a triangle were equal to two right angles from mere inspection of the figures. How the man's success in this feat is to be accomplished, or to be recognized by others, Hobbes does not explain; nor does he explain how this is to be reconciled with what he elsewhere says, that all deductions consist in the working out of the "consequences of terms." In general he rightly regards the necessary truth of a deductive inference as lying in the logical interrelations of the meanings of the terms employed.

When he comes to consider the statements of science, Hobbes's usual empiricism deserts him. For he thinks *all*

scientific thinking is just the following out of the "consequences of terms," and that any statement made must be
true, if it is true at all, in virtue of the meanings of the
terms employed in it. Truth, he says, consists in "the right
ordering of names in our affirmations"; and falsehood consequently must be the same as absurdity in the application
and use of terms. In modern terms, Hobbes regards all true
statements as "analytic," and all false ones as self-contradictory. All science, then, will be like a geometrical deductive system: that is, on Hobbes's own view, it will be
a linguistic calculus and the validity of the inferences in it
will be guaranteed by the definitions adopted. But such a
system could not possibly, by itself, give us an empirical
science: for no provision is made for observations of what
actually happens, or for predictions of future events.

In his view of science, the rationalist model of geometry
as the ideal form of knowledge—"the only Science that it
has pleased God hitherto to bestow on mankind"—has over-
ridden the natural tendency of his thought. Had he merely
re-expressed, in terms of prediction and hypothesis, what
he had already said about prudence and "presumption of
the future," he could have given a more accurate account
of the falsifiable inductive conclusions with which science
works.

The last extract from Hobbes, which comes from the
fourth book of the *Leviathan,* is highly characteristic of
him. In attacking the theory of separate essences, which he
inaccurately attributes to Aristotle, he makes the valuable
observation that one must not base philosophical theories
merely on the grammatical forms of one's own language,
and suggests that there could easily be a language which had
no equivalent of "is" to provide the copula in such predi-
cations as "a man is a living body." (He got this idea, it
seems, from some knowledge about Chinese.) This is a
valuable philosophical remark, even though it is combined
with the inadequate theory that all predication consists in
joining together two names of the same thing. Certainly
there is no such quick way with metaphysical theories, and
Hobbes has no time to linger over the arguments. The reasons for his haste emerge in the last paragraph of this

extract. Hobbes was not primarily concerned with the problems of metaphysics and theory of knowledge at all. His interest was in political theory, and in the philosophical foundations of strong government; everything else is incidental. Yet in considering these incidentals he shows very great insight and power of mind; for all his crudities, he was an original genius who contributed much to the rise of British empiricism and who has been, in this respect, unduly neglected. He has also a claim, which these extracts can only inadequately illustrate, to be considered the most amusing philosopher of his time. His scathing humor enlivens the *Leviathan* from end to end.

[CHAPTER IV. Of Speech

.   .   .   .

The general use of speech is to transfer our mental discourse into verbal; or the train of our thoughts into a train of words; and that for two commodities; whereof one is the registering of the consequences of our thoughts; which being apt to slip out of our memory, and put us to a new labour, may again be recalled, by such words as they were marked by. So that the first use of names, is to serve for *Marks,* or *Notes* of remembrance. Another is, when many use the same words to signify (by their connection and order) one to another, what they conceive, or think of each matter; and also what they desire, fear, or have any other passion for. And for this use they are called *Signs*. Special uses of speech are these; first, to register, what by cogitation, we find to be the cause of anything present or past; and what we find things present or past may produce, or effect: which in sum, is acquiring of Arts. Secondly, to show to others that knowledge which we have attained; which is, to counsel and teach one another. Thirdly, to make known to others our wills and purposes, that we may have the mutual help of one another. Fourthly, to please and delight ourselves and others, by playing with our words, for pleasure or ornament, innocently.

To these uses, there are also four correspondent abuses. First, when men register their thoughts wrong, by the inconstancy of the signification of their words; by which they register for their conceptions, that which they never conceived; and so deceive themselves. Secondly, when they use words metaphorically; that is, in other sense than that they are ordained for; and thereby deceive others. Thirdly, when by words they declare that to be their will which is not. Fourthly, when they use them to grieve one another: for seeing nature has armed living creatures, some with teeth, some with horns, and some with hands to grieve an enemy, it is but an abuse of speech to grieve him with the tongue, unless it be one whom we are obliged to govern; and then it is not to grieve, but to correct and amend.

The manner how speech serves to the remembrance of the consequence of causes and effects, consists in the imposing of *Names,* and the *Connection* of them. Of names, some are *Proper,* and singular to one thing only; as *Peter, John, this man, this tree*: and some are *Common* to many things: as *Man, Horse, Tree;* each of which though but one Name, is nevertheless the name of divers particular things; in respect of all which together, it is called a *Universal;* there being nothing in the world universal but names; for the things named are every one of them individual and singular.

One universal name is imposed on many things, for their similitude in some quality, or other accident: and whereas a Proper Name brings to mind one thing only, universals recall any one of those many.

And of universal names, some are of more, and some of less extent; the larger comprehending the less large; and some again of equal extent, comprehending each other reciprocally. As for example, the name *Body* is of larger signification than the word *Man,* and comprehends it; and the names *Man* and *Rational* are of equal extent, comprehending one another mutually. But here we must take notice, that by a name is not always understood, as in Grammar, one word only; but sometimes by circumlocution many words together. For all these words, *He that in his actions observes the Laws of his Country,* makes but one name, equivalent to this one word, *Just.*

By this imposition of names, some of larger, some of stricter signification, we turn the reckoning of the consequences of things imagined in the mind, into a reckoning of the consequences of appellations. For example, a man that has no use of speech at all, (such, as is born and remains perfectly deaf and dumb) if he set before his eyes a triangle, and by it two right angles, (such as are the corners of a square figure) he may by meditation compare and find, that the three angles of a triangle, are equal to those two right angles that stand by it. But if another triangle be shown him different in shape from the former, he cannot know without a new labour, whether the three angles of that also be equal to the same. But he that has the use of words, when he observes that such equality was consequent, not to the length of the sides, nor to any other particular thing in his triangle; but only to this, that the sides were straight, and the angles three; and that that was all, for which he named it a Triangle; will boldly conclude universally, that such equality of angles is in all triangles whatsoever; and register his invention in these general terms, *Every triangle has its three angles equal to two right angles.* And thus the consequence found in one particular, comes to be registered and remembered as a universal rule; and discharges our mental reckoning, of time and place; and delivers us from all labour of the mind, saving the first; and makes that which was found true *here,* and *now,* to be true in *all times and places.*

．　．　．　．　．　．　．　．　．　．

When two names are joined together into a consequence, or affirmation; as thus, *A man is a living creature;* or thus, *if he be a man, he is a living creature,* if the latter name *living creature,* signify all that the former name *Man* signifies, then the affirmation, or consequence is *true;* otherwise *false.* For *True* and *False* are attributes of speech, not of things. And where speech is not, there is neither *Truth* nor *Falsehood. Error* there may be, as when we expect that which shall not be; or suspect what has not been: but in neither case can a man be charged with Untruth.

Seeing then that *Truth* consists in the right ordering of names in our affirmations, a man that seeks precise *truth,* needs to remember what every name he uses stands for; and to place it accordingly; or else he will find himself entangled in words, as a bird in lime-twigs; the more he struggles, the more belimed. And therefore in Geometry, (which is the only Science that it has pleased God hitherto to bestow on mankind) men begin at settling the signification of their words; which settling of significations they call *Definitions;* and place them in the beginning of their reckoning.

By this it appears how necessary it is for any man that aspires to true Knowledge, to examine the definitions of former authors; and either to correct them, where they are negligently set down; or to make them himself. For the errors of definitions multiply themselves, according as the reckoning proceeds; and lead men into absurdities, which at last they see, but cannot avoid, without reckoning anew from the beginning; in which lies the foundation of their errors. From whence it happens, that they that trust to their books do as they that cast up many little sums into a greater, without considering whether those little sums were rightly cast up or not; and at last finding the error visible, and not mistrusting their first grounds, do not know which way to clear themselves; but spend time in fluttering over their books; as birds that entering by the chimney, and finding themselves enclosed in a chamber, flutter at the false light of a glass window, for want of wit to consider which way they came in. So that in the right definition of names, lies the first use of speech; which is the acquisition of science; and in wrong, or no definition, lies the first abuse; from which proceed all false and senseless tenets; which make those men that take their instruction from the authority of books, and not from their own meditation, to be as much below the condition of ignorant men, as men endued with true Science are above it. For between true science, and erroneous doctrines, ignorance is in the middle. Natural sense and imagination are not subject to absurdity. Nature itself cannot err: and as men abound in copiousness of language; so they become more wise, or more mad than ordinary. Nor is it possible without Letters for any man to become either excellently wise, or (unless his memory be hurt by disease, or ill constitution of organs) excellently foolish. For words are wise men's counters, they do but reckon by them; but they are the money of fools, that value them by the authority of an Aristotle, a Cicero, or a Thomas, or any other Doctor whatsoever, if but a man.

CHAPTER V. Of Reason, and Science

When a man reckons without the use of words, which may be done in particular things, (as when upon the sight of any one thing, we conjecture what was likely to have preceded, or is likely to follow upon it;) if that which he thought likely to follow, follows not; or that which he thought likely to have preceded it, has not preceded it, this is called ERROR; to which even the most prudent men are subject. But when we reason in words of general signification, and fall upon a general inference which is false; though it be commonly called *Error*, it is indeed an ABSURDITY, or senseless speech. For error is but a deception, in presuming that something is past, or to come; of which, though it were not past, or not to come; yet there was no impossibility discoverable. But when we make a general assertion, unless it be a true one, the possibility of it is unconceivable. And words whereby we conceive nothing but the sound, are those we call *Absurd, Insignificant,* and *Nonsense*. And therefore if a man should talk to me of a *round Quadrangle;* or *accidents of Bread in Cheese;* or *immaterial Substances;* or *a free Subject; a free-Will;* or any *Free,* but free from being hindered by opposition, I should not say he were in an Error; but that his words were without meaning; that is to say, absurd.

I have said before, (in the second chapter) that a Man excelled all other animals in this faculty, that when he conceived any thing whatsoever, he was apt to enquire the consequences of it, and what effects he could do with it. And now I add this other degree of the same excellence, that he can by words reduce the consequences he finds to general rules, called *Theoremes,* or *Aphorisms;* that is, he can reason, or reckon, not only in number; but in all other things, in which one may be added to, or subtracted from another.

But this privilege is allayed by another; and that is by the privilege of absurdity; to which no living creature is subject, but man only. And of men, those are of all most subject to it that profess Philosophy. For it is most true that *Cicero* says of them somewhere; that there can be nothing so absurd, but may be found in the books of Philosophers. And the reason is manifest. For there is not one of them that begins his ratiocination from the definitions, or explications of the names they are to use; which is a method that has been used only in Geometry; whose conclusions have thereby been made indisputable.

The first cause of absurd conclusions I ascribe to the want of method; in that they do not begin their ratiocination from definitions; that is, from settled significations of their words: as if they could cast account, without knowing the value of the numerical words, *one, two,* and *three.*

And whereas all bodies enter into account upon divers considerations, (which I have mentioned in the precedent chapter;) these considerations being diversely named, divers absurdities proceed from the confusion, and unfit connection of their names into assertions. And therefore

The second cause of absurd assertions, I ascribe to the giving of names of *bodies, to accidents;* or of *accidents* to *bodies;* as they do that say, *Faith is infused,* or *inspired;* when nothing can be *poured,* or *breathed* into any thing, but body; and that, *extension* is *body;* that *phantoms* are *spirits,* etc.

The third I ascribe to the giving of the names of the *accidents* of *bodies without us,* to the *accidents* of our own *bodies;* as they do that say, the *colour is in the body; the sound is in the air,* etc.

The fourth, to the giving of the names of *bodies,* to *names,* or *speeches;* as they do that say, that *there be things universal;* that *a living creature is Genus,* or *a general thing,* etc.

The fifth, to the giving of the names of *accidents,* to *names* and *speeches;* as they do that say, *the nature of a thing is its definition; a man's command is his will;* and the like.

The sixth, to the use of Metaphors, Tropes, and other rhetorical figures, instead of words proper. For though it be lawful to say (for example) in common speech, *the way goes, or leads hither, or thither, The Proverb says this or that* (whereas ways cannot go, nor Proverbs speak) yet in reckoning, and seeking of truth, such speeches are not to be admitted.

The seventh, to names that signify nothing; but are taken up, and learned by rote from the Schools, as *hypostatical, transubstantiate, consubstantiate, eternal-Now,* and the like canting of School men.

To him that can avoid these things, it is not easy to fall into any absurdity, unless it be by the length of an account; in which he may perhaps forget what went before. For all men by nature reason alike, and well, when they have good principles. For who is so stupid, as both to mistake in Geometry, and also to persist in it, when another detects his error to him? .   .   .   .]

The following is from Chapter 46, "Of the darkness from vain philosophy and fabulous traditions," *Leviathan,* Part IV, "The Kingdom of Darkness."

[Now to descend to the particular tenets of vain philosophy derived to the Universities, and thence into the church, partly from Aristotle, partly from blindness of understanding; I shall first consider their principles. There is a certain *Philosophia Prima,* on which all other philosophy ought to depend; and consisteth principally, in right limiting of the significations of such appellations, or names, as are of all others the most universal: which limitations serve to avoid ambiguity, and equivocation in reasoning; and are commonly called definitions; such as are the definitions of body, time, place, matter, form, essence, subject, substance, accident, power, act, finite, infinite, quantity, quality, motion, action, passion, and divers others, necessary to the explaining of a man's conceptions concerning the nature and generation of bodies. The explication (that is, the settling of the meaning) of which, and the like terms, is commonly in the Schools called *Metaphysics;* as being a part of the philosophy of Aristotle, which hath that for title; but it is in another sense: for there it signifieth as much, as *Books written, or placed after his natural philosophy*: But the Schools take them for *Books of supernatural philosophy*: for the word *metaphysics* will bear both these senses. And indeed that which is there written, is for the most part so far repugnant to natural reason, that whosoever thinketh that there is anything to be understood by it, must needs think it supernatural.

From these metaphysics, which are mingled with the scripture to make School divinity, we are told, there be in the world certain essences separated from bodies, which they call *abstract essences, and substantial forms*: for the interpreting of which *jargon,* there is need of somewhat more than ordinary attention in this place. Also I ask pardon of those who are not used to this kind of discourse, for applying myself to those that are. The world (I mean not the earth only, that denominates the lovers of it *worldly men,* but the *universe* that is, the whole mass of all things that are) is corporeal, that is to say, body; and hath the dimensions of magnitude, namely, length, breadth, and depth: also every part of body, is likewise body, and hath the like dimensions; and consequently every part of the universe, is body; and that which is not body, is not part of the universe: and because the universe is all, that which is not part of it, is *nothing;* and consequently *no where.* Nor does it follow from hence, that spirits are *nothing;* for they have dimensions, and are therefore really *bodies;* though that name in common speech be given to such bodies only, as are visible, or palpable; that is, that have some degree of opacity: but for spirits, they call them incorporeal; which is a name of more honour, and may therefore with more piety be attributed to God himself; in whom we consider not what attribute expresseth best his nature, which is incomprehensible; but what best expresseth our desire to honour him.

To know now upon what grounds they say there be

essences abstract, or *substantial forms,* we are to consider what those words do properly signify. The use of words is to register to ourselves, and make manifest to others, the thoughts and conceptions of our minds. Of which words, some are the names of the things conceived; as the names of all sorts of bodies, that work upon the senses, and leave an impression in the imagination: others are the names of the imaginations themselves; that is to say, of those ideals, or mental images we have of all things we see, or remember: and others again are names of names; or of different sorts of speech: as *universal, plural, singular,* are the names of names; and *definition, affirmation, negation, true, false, syllogism, interrogation, promise, covenant,* are the names of certain forms of speech. Others serve to show the consequence, or repugnance of one name to another; as when one saith, *a man is a body,* he intendeth that the name of *body* is necessarily consequent to the name of *man;* as being but several names of the same thing, *man;* which consequence is signified by coupling them together with the word *is.* And as we use the verb *is;* so the Latins use their verb *est,* and the Greeks their ἐστι, through all its declinations. Whether all other nations of the world have in their several languages a word that answereth to it, or not, I cannot tell; but I am sure they have not need of it; for the placing of two names in order may serve to signify their consequence, if it were the custom, (for custom is it, that gives words their force) as well as the words *is,* or *be,* or *are,* and the like.

And if it were so, that there were a language without any verb answerable to *est,* or *is,* or *be;* yet the men who used it would be not a jot the less capable of inferring, concluding, and of all kind of reasoning, than were the Greeks, and Latins. But what then would become of these terms, of *entity, essence, essential, essentiality,* that are derived from it, and of many more that depend on these, applied as most commonly they are? They are therefore no names of things; but signs, by which we make known, that we conceive the consequence of one name or attribute to another: as when we say, *a man, is, a living body,* we mean not that the *man* is one thing, the *living body* another, and the *is,* or *being*

a third; but that the *man,* and the *living body,* is the same
thing; because the consequence, *if he be a man, he is a
living body,* is a true consequence, signified by that word
Is. Therefore, *to be a body, to walk, to be speaking, to live,
to see,* and like infinitives; also *corporeity, walking, life,
sight,* and the like that signify just the same, are the names
of *nothing;* as I have elsewhere more amply expressed.

But to what purpose (may some man say) is such sub-
tility in a work of this nature, where I pretend to nothing
but what is necessary to the doctrine of government and
obedience? It is to this purpose, that men may no longer
suffer themselves to be abused, by them, that by this doctrine of *separated essences,* built on the vain philosophy of
Aristotle, would fright them from obeying the laws of their
country, with empty names; as men fright birds from the
corn with an empty doublet, a hat, and a crooked stick. For
it is upon this ground, that when a man is dead and buried,
they say his soul (that is his life) can walk separated from
his body, and is seen by night amongst the graves. Upon
the same ground they say, that the figure, and colour, and
taste of a piece of bread, has a being, there, where they say
there is no bread: and upon the same ground they say, that
faith, and wisdom, and other virtues are sometimes *poured*
into a man, sometimes *blown* into him from Heaven; as if
the virtuous, and their virtues could be asunder; and a great
many other things that serve to lessen the dependence of
subjects on the sovereign power of their country. For who
will endeavour to obey the laws, if he expect obedience to be
poured or blown into him? Or who will not obey a priest,
that can make God, rather than his sovereign; nay than
God himself? Or who, that is in fear of ghosts, will not
bear great respect to those that can make the holy water,
that drives them from him? And this shall suffice for an
example of the errors, which are brought into the church,
from the *entities,* and *essences* of Aristotle; which it may
be he knew to be false philosophy; but writ it as a thing
consonant to, and corroborative of their religion; and fear-
ing the fate of Socrates.   .   .   .   .   .   .]

CHAPTER IV

Descartes

RENÉ DESCARTES WAS BORN IN 1596. HIS MOTHER DIED A year later, and he was brought up in the country by a tutor. He was educated by the Jesuits at La Flèche, and he was later to praise their teaching in the *Discourse on Method*. He studied law at Poitiers, but decided to travel and to study by himself in Paris. He was particularly interested in music and in fencing and he even wrote treatises on these subjects. He joined, as a volunteer, a force under Maurice of Nassau, which was fighting on the Protestant side in the Thirty Years' War; Descartes was always a loyal Catholic, but it was not unusual at the time for gentlemen to become soldiers of fortune, even though they were indifferent to the cause which they were defending in that confused war. Descartes's motive simply was to travel and to have leisure to think. While at Breda in Holland he decided to write a general treatise on mathematics and the mathematical sciences. While serving in Germany in 1620, he experienced at least two moments of illumination, or visions, in which his philosophy, or some parts of it, seemed to be revealed to him. In 1624 he went from France to Italy to render thanks for his visions to the Virgin Mary at Loretto. In 1629 he settled in Holland, determined to protect his privacy and independence. In 1637 the *Discourse on Method* was published at Leyden, and he was immediately recognized as the foremost philosopher of his age. He left Holland for Stockholm in 1649 at the invitation of Queen Christina, partly because he was increasingly involved in religious controversy in Holland; throughout his life he had tried to avoid polemics. He died of pneumonia in Stockholm in 1650.

He had published his *Meditations on the First Philosophy* in Paris in 1641, *Principia Philosophiae* in Amsterdam in 1644, the *Passions of the Soul* in Paris in 1649. A number of works, including the *Regulae Ad Directionem Ingenii* and *Traité du Monde,* remained to be published after his death.

Descartes is the type of the philosopher who avoids any entanglements or attachments, particularly in politics and public affairs. He was a solitary and entirely original thinker who had moments of pure inspiration, and the power to express his visions later with exquisite clarity. He was fascinated by mathematics and corresponded with Fermat, the great mathematician of his time. He had an extraordinary pride of intellect, and a visionary confidence in his own powers of mind. He did not acknowledge the necessity of a conflict between religion and modern science, and he thought that he had found the true adjustment between them in his philosophy. Withdrawn and quiet by temperament, he became one of the great revolutionaries of European thought by the compelling clarity and the subtle simplicity of his thought and language.

Mathematics is for Descartes the model of clear and certain knowledge, which advances step by step from one indisputable conclusion to another. Outside mathematics all claims to knowledge seem, when one pauses to reflect, uncertain, unsystematic, and unsupported by any common method of proof. The first step therefore is to introduce into the chaos of philosophy and physical science the clear and uniform deductive method of mathematics; only by system and method can knowledge be built upon sure foundations. The proper order in philosophy is to start from the most simple and clear truths, containing only the most simple notions, and to advance step by step towards more complex truths, making sure that each step of the argument is indisputable. In restarting philosophy from the beginning, one must reject every statement which can possibly be doubted, until one arrives at simple and self-evident truths which cannot possibly be doubted. These are the sure foundations of knowledge.

Descartes shows his method in action in the *Discourse* and *Meditations,* applying his method of doubt until he arrives at the indubitable proposition "I think, therefore I am." He also shows that he cannot doubt the existence of God. Using these two indubitable truths, he proceeds to show that we have reason to believe in the existence of the external world, although our ordinary judgments of perception are in themselves fallible and our senses may deceive us. When we have proved the existence of God, we have reason to trust that account of the world of spatial beings, called by Descartes Extension, which alone commends itself to our reason. Descartes distinguishes ideas in the mind from the external reality which, in the process of perception, imprints ideas on the mind. He then distinguishes the different kinds or types of idea in the mind. Only ideas which are entirely clear and distinct can be accepted into the structure of knowledge. And only the ideas which represent the true nature of external things, as this nature is made intelligible in mathematical physics, can be accepted as genuine knowledge.

The following extracts show only Descartes's method of criticizing claims to knowledge, his method of doubt, and his standard of certainty; for it is this critical investigation, rather than his constructive metaphysics, that has been permanently important. He may be called the founder of the modern theory of knowledge, since he made the questions "How do I know?" and "Can I be certain?" the first questions of philosophy. He was to be followed by the English empiricists in the next century, and by Bertrand Russell and others in this century, in looking for the foundations of knowledge in some propositions which are certain and indubitable. But he had also a positive philosophy of mind and a positive philosophy of physics. He conceived the realm of mind as wholly distinct from the realm of extended things; and he expressed this distinction in the traditional terms of substance and cause, with their medieval connotations. He believed also that there were certain ideas that are innate in the mind, and in no manner derived from experience. All these doctrines had presented themselves to him as parts of a single system, together with the conception of human personality as an immaterial substance, the mind, lodged in a mechanical system, the body. He was convinced that all the problems of science, mathematics and practical life are soluble by "the natural light" of reason, following its own natural order. This unlimited claim for "the natural light," and for the clear style and method of thought which went with it, became the foundation of French civilization up till the French revolution. The Encyclopedists and radicals of the next century were his direct heirs in style and method, in spite of their difference of aim. He taught men to reject scholastic obscurities and to think for themselves, confident that whatever seems self-evident in the clear light of reason must be true. And he invented a style which for nearly two centuries remained the natural vehicle of French thought.

In the following passages of the *Discourse on Method* (1637) Descartes explains how, by using the method of systematic doubt, he arrives at the foundations of his system: knowledge of his own existence and of the existence of God. His demonstration of his own existence as one unshakable fact, immune from the process of doubt, is of an extreme and elegant simplicity. We are often deceived by our senses, or suppose something to be true which is not true, and obviously we do not know, at such moments, that we are being deceived. Thus it is possible at *any* moment to suppose that we are being deceived, for instance, that we are dreaming, and we can sensibly doubt the genuine existence of what seems to exist around us in the world. But one thing we cannot doubt is that we are doubting; for if we were to doubt that, we should still, once more, be doubting. The self, Descartes argues, must be immune from the doubt, for the self always re-enters with any doubt that one has—it is always the self that doubts. But doubting is only a sort of thinking, and it is in virtue of its power to think that the self is seen to exist. Hence Descartes's fundamental proposition, *cogito ergo sum*, "I think, therefor I am."

Descartes next asks what it is about this proposition

that makes it so certainly true, and finds the answer in the "clarity and distinctness" with which it appears to be true. This does not mean, as it might at first seem, that Descartes will just be satisfied with any proposition that seems, psychologically, to be obviously true. No philosophy could go very deep which did not examine critically many beliefs which, from unreflective habit, we do in fact feel to be certainly true. What Descartes is looking for as the foundations of his system are propositions which it is not just difficult to doubt, but nonsensical or contradictory to doubt. To think that one was not thinking (and thus to doubt the existence of one's own mind) seems to be, in a peculiar way, self-contradictory. Other propositions have this peculiar kind of self-evidence, and are such that it would be nonsensical to doubt their truth. In particular, there are the propositions of mathematics, which Descartes constantly takes as his model of how thought should proceed.

Descartes mentions various features of these indubitable propositions which help to explain what he means by their "clarity and distinctness." Their truth, unlike that of propositions about the external world, is independent of the conditions in which they are conceived: "If a geometer should conceive some new demonstration (when dreaming), the circumstance of his being asleep would not militate against its truth"; whereas if he had some empirical belief, for instance that he was flying or seeing the stars, it might well be false. Hence Descartes emphasizes that it is only on the evidence of our *reason,* and not on that of our imagination or senses, that we ought to be persuaded of the truth of anything. His fundamental thought is that the truth of an indubitable proposition must be *intrinsic* to it, not dependent on any external circumstances.

A proposition of the required kind must be, to use the scholastic term, a statement of *essence.* The essence of a thing, roughly, consists of those features of it which it must have, if it is to be that thing at all. Many features of a thing can be "thought away" without self-contradiction—it would be possible, for instance, for a table to have some color different from that which in fact it has—but there are some characteristics which that thing must have if it is to be a table at all, and these are its essential characteristics. The second extract from Galileo in Chapter II shows him applying this idea, in a special way, to the notion of a material body in physics; he names those qualities which it seems to him are of the essence of such a body, without which it cannot be conceived at all.

The statement of the essence of something fits admirably the Cartesian requirements for a necessarily true proposition; it contains intrinsically the marks of its own truth, ar.d we cannot conceive that the opposite should be true. Thus Descartes, having arrived at the statement *"cogito ergo sum,"* is able to say that the essence of his personal identity, his "selfhood," must lie in his mind. He could conceive of himself as not having a body, but not as not having a mind; therefore the existence of his mind is seen as what is essential to his existence as a person, while the existence of his body, on the other hand, is "accidental," not essentially connected in this way with his existence.

This notion of essence Descartes applies also in the second step of the construction of his system, his proof of the existence of God. For just as he found that in the idea of a triangle is contained "the equality of its three angles to two right angles"–this is part of its essence–so he found, or claimed to find, that in the idea of a Perfect Being is contained the idea of existence. Although he could make various statements about the essence of a triangle, none of them was to the effect that there in fact existed such a thing as a triangle; but in the case of a Perfect Being, its "existence is included in its essence"–one has only to gain a clear idea of what a Perfect Being is, to see that such a Being must exist.

This argument–which is similar to the famous "ontological proof" of the existence of God, invented by Anselm–is only one of Descartes's proofs of this conclusion. Starting, again, from the concept he in fact has of a Perfect Being, he reasons that such an idea could not have arisen merely from himself: for he himself is imperfect (as is shown, for instance, by the fact that he doubts, a state of mind inferior to pure knowledge), and it is evidently contrary to reason that the less perfect should give rise to the more perfect. Thus he claims to see contained in his own imperfection, and in that of anything else that may exist, a state of dependence on a Perfect Being; such a Being must therefore exist. This argument is highly characteristic of Descartes's position in the history of philosophy; it is very similar in form and terminology to a famed scholastic proof of the existence of God, the argument *"ex contingentia mundi,"* yet it is based, in a typically Cartesian way, on what is evident to the light of natural reason, to anyone who reflects on his own internal experience.

Having thus proved the existence of God, Descartes finds himself in a position to reconstruct those things the existence and truth of which he had previously doubted. For, he argues, the Perfect Being, whom we now know to exist, could not allow us to be completely and systematically deceived in the way we had supposed, and hence some reliance — with due allowance for the imperfection of any human observer — can be placed on the existence of those things that we normally suppose to be in the world about us. The nature of the things, and the laws that govern their behavior, can be discovered by application of those analytical and mathematical methods which, at the metaphysical level, Descartes has already been using. He admits elsewhere in the *Discourse* that not all can be done by pure a priori reasoning; the limitations of the human mind are such that experiments will be necessary to show the way. Ideally, however, an organized science will know the essence of each thing and so be able to deduce from that knowledge the whole body of mathematical laws that will explain the world.

In considering the foundations of Descartes's system, one is bound to ask what kind of peculiar self-evident necessity *does* characterize the propositions he establishes; and when we ask this, his reliance on the self-evident is seen to be less satisfactory than it seems at first. It is agreed that more is required than a mere psychological obviousness; reliance on this, as has been seen, could only lead to the perpetuation of error. The alternative, then, is a *logical* necessity; a proposition will in this sense be necessarily true if its opposite is self-contradictory. Yet if this is Descartes's sense, his fundamental conclusions are not of the right type. His whole system is based on propositions that assert *existence* — of his own mind, and of God. But philosophers since Kant are generally agreed that no proposition that asserts existence in this way can be logically necessary; and this now seems obvious. The logical relations of our language do not determine the contents of the universe.

Both Descartes's fundamental premises can be seen on closer inspection not to have the necessity he claims for them. The proposition "I am thinking," if necessary, should have an opposite which is self-contradictory; but "I am not thinking," which is its opposite, is not self-contradictory. Certainly, if anyone thinks it, it is false, but it is not self-contradictory, as is, for instance, "I am a married bachelor." We might, for example, imagine a man under an anaesthetic who made various remarks, and if one of these remarks were "I am not thinking," we could say that in that case it was true. A proper self-contradiction, however uttered or produced, must always be necessarily false. "I am thinking" is a proposition which can carry with it, in the circumstances of its consideration, the facts that make it true. There are other propositions of the same kind: such as "I am writing," when written, or "I am saying something in English," when spoken. "I am thinking" is one of the most general cases of this phenomenon.

Descartes is not justified in drawing from this proposition the more far-reaching conclusions of the kind he embraces, concerning the individual, substantial, noncorporeal and eternal nature of the mind that is doing the thinking. In the sense in which "I am thinking" is made true by thinking it, the "I" can have none of this content — it is a mere mark of reference. Alternatively, if "I" is supposed to have some content, and to contain the notions of individual personal existence, then the most that Descartes can properly conclude is *"cogitatur,"* "there is some thinking going on." Kant, in the *Critique of Pure Reason,* showed, with the greatest care and subtlety, how the whole program of "rational psychology"–the Cartesian attempt to pass from necessarily true premises to informative and substantial conclusions about the self–must be invalid.

Kant was also responsible for the final demolition of the "ontological proof" of the existence of God. That argument depended on the idea that the existence of a Perfect Being must be included in his essence, that it must be a necessary property of such a being that he should exist. But how could existence be connected by logical necessity with a set of properties, however perfect? Existence, Kant showed, is not a property, like largeness or redness— rather a thing must exist before it can have any properties at all.

It now seems that Descartes, in his search for a certainty on which to base science, had turned his attention in the wrong direction. He was fascinated by the necessary truths of mathematics, and erected the mathematical kind of certainty into the canon for all statements that were to be considered reputable. But certainty of this kind, by itself, is insufficient for an empirical science; it lies in the purely logical interrelations of a theory and can carry in itself no predictive power or connection with the facts of experience. Nor should empirical statements, because they lack this certainty, be despised in comparison. Rather they can have their own kind of "certainty." The possibility that they may be proved false by later experience is not a disadvantage that they labor under, compared with the statements of mathematics, but rather the secret of their power. Only thus can they serve to distinguish one empirical state of affairs from another, and so assist us in understanding nature, and putting its processes to our use. Descartes, in common with other metaphysicians, had in mind the form which a completed science would assume; he gave a picture of what ideal knowledge would be, rather than of the actual methods of science, subject to the actual limitations of human knowledge.

[. . . I had long before noticed that, for the habits of ordinary life, it is sometimes necessary to adopt, as if above doubt, opinions which we discern to be highly uncertain, as has been already said; but as I then wanted to give my attention solely to the search after truth, I thought that a procedure exactly the opposite was called for, and that I ought to reject as absolutely false all opinions in regard to which I could suppose the least ground for doubt, in order to ascertain whether after that there remained anything in my belief that was wholly indubitable. Accordingly, seeing that our senses sometimes deceive us, I was willing to suppose that there existed nothing really such as they lead us to imagine; and because some men err in reasoning, and fall into paralogisms, even on the simplest matters of geometry, I, convinced that I was as open to error as any other, rejected as false all the reasonings that I had so far taken for demonstrations; and finally, when I considered that the very same thoughts which we have when awake may also come when we are asleep, while there is at that time not one of them true, I supposed that all the objects that had ever entered into my mind when awake, had in them no more truth than the illusions of my dreams. But immediately afterwards I observed that, whilst I thus wished to think that all was false, it was absolutely necessary that I, who thus thought, should be something; and as I observed that this truth, I think, therefore I am, was so certain and of such evidence, that no ground of doubt, however extravagant, could be alleged by the sceptics capable of shaking it, I concluded that I might, without scruple, accept it as the first principle of the philosophy of which I was in search.

In the next place, I attentively examined what I was and as I observed that I could suppose that I had no body, and that there was no world nor any place in which I might be; but that I could not therefore suppose that I was not; and that, on the contrary, from the very circumstance that I thought to doubt of the truth of other things, it most clearly and certainly followed that I was; while, on the other hand, if I had only ceased to think, although all the other objects which I had ever imagined had been in reality existent, I would have had no reason to believe that I existed; I thence concluded that I was a substance whose whole essence or nature consists only in thinking, and which, that it may exist, has need of no place, nor is dependent on any material thing; so that "I," that is to say, the mind by which I am what I am, is wholly distinct from the body, and is even more easily known than the latter, and is such, that although the latter were not, it would still continue to be all that it is.

After this I inquired in general into what is essential to the truth and certainty of a proposition; for since I had discovered one which I knew to be true, I thought that I must likewise be able to discover the ground of this certainty. And as I observed that in the words I think, therefore I am, there is nothing at all which gives me assurance of their truth beyond this, that I see very clearly that in order to think it is necessary to exist, I concluded that I might take, as a general rule, the principle, that all the things which we very clearly and distinctly conceive are true, only observing, however, that there is some difficulty in rightly determining the objects which we distinctly conceive.

In the next place, from reflecting on the circumstance that I doubted, and that consequently my being was not wholly perfect (for I clearly saw that it was a greater perfection to know than to doubt), I was led to inquire whence I had learned to think of something more perfect than myself; and I clearly recognised that I must hold this notion from some nature which in reality was more perfect. As for the thoughts of many other objects external to me, as of the sky, the earth, light, heat, and a thousand more, I was less at a loss to know whence these came; for since I remarked in them nothing which seemed to render them superior to myself, I could believe that, if these were true, they were dependencies on my own nature, in so far as it possessed a certain perfection, and, if they were false, that I held them from nothing, that is to say, that they were in me because of a certain imperfection of my nature. But this could not be the case with the idea of a nature more perfect than myself; for to receive it from nothing was a thing manifestly impossible; and, because it is not less repugnant that the more perfect should be an effect of, and dependent on, the less perfect, than that something should proceed from nothing, it was equally impossible that I could hold it from myself: accordingly, it only remained that it had been placed in me by a nature which was in reality more perfect than mine, and which even possessed within itself all the perfections of which I could form any idea; that is to say, in a single word, which was God. And to this I added that, since I knew some perfections which I did not possess, I was not the only being in existence (I will here, with your permission, freely use the terms of the Schools); but, on the contrary, that there was of necessity some other more perfect Being upon which I was dependent, and from whom I had received all that I possessed; for if I had existed alone, and independently of every other being, so as to have had from myself all the perfection, however little, which I actually possessed, I should have been able, for the same reason, to have had from myself the whole remainder of perfection, of the want of which I was conscious, and thus could of myself have become infinite, eternal, immutable, omniscient, all-powerful, and, in short, have possessed all the perfections which I could recognise in God. For in order to know the nature of God (following the arguments just mentioned), as far as my own nature permitted, I had only to consider in respect of all the properties of which I found in my mind some idea, whether their possession was a mark of perfection; and I was assured that no one which indicated any imperfection was in him, and that none of the rest was wanting. Thus I perceived that doubt, inconstancy, sadness, and such like, could not be found in God, since I myself would have been happy to be free from them. Besides, I had ideas of many sensible and corporeal things; for although I might suppose that I was dreaming, and that all which I saw or imagined was false, I could not, nevertheless, deny that the ideas were in reality in my thoughts. But, because I had already very clearly recognised in myself that the intelligent nature is distinct from the corporeal, and as I observed that all composition is an evidence of dependence, and that a state of dependence is manifestly a state of imperfection, I therefore determined that it could not be a perfection in God to be compounded of these two natures, and that consequently he was not so compounded; but that if there were any bodies in the world, or even any intelligences, or other natures that were not wholly perfect, their existence depended on his power in such a way that they could not subsist without him for a single moment.

I was disposed straightway to search for other truths; and when I had represented to myself the object of the geometers, which I conceived to be a continuous body, or a space indefinitely extended in length, breadth, and height or depth, divisible into various parts which admit of different figures and sizes, and of being moved or transposed in all manner of ways (for all this the geometers suppose to be in the object they consider), I went over some of their simplest demonstrations. And, in the first place, I observed, that the great certainty which by common consent is accorded to these demonstrations, is founded solely upon this, that they are clearly conceived in accordance with the rule I have already laid down. In the next place, I perceived that there was nothing at all in these demonstrations which could assure me of the existence of their object: thus, for example, supposing a triangle to be given, I distinctly perceived that its three angles were necessarily equal to two right angles, but I did not on that account perceive anything which could assure me that any triangle existed: while, on the contrary, recurring to the examination of the idea of a Perfect Being, I found that the existence of the Being was contained in the idea in the same way that the equality of its three angles to two right angles is contained in the idea of a triangle, or as in the idea of a sphere, the equidistance of all points on its surface from the centre, or even still more clearly; and that consequently it is at least as certain that God, who is this Perfect Being, is, or exists, as any demonstration of geometry can be.

.   .   .   .

Finally, if there be still persons who are not sufficiently persuaded of the existence of God and of the soul, by the reasons I have adduced, I very much wish that they should know that all the other propositions, of the truth of which they deem themselves perhaps more assured, as that we have a body, and that there exist stars and an earth, and such like, are less certain; for, although we have a moral assurance of these things, which is so strong that there is an appearance of extravagance in doubting their existence, yet at the same time no one, unless he takes leave of reason, can deny, when the question relates to a metaphysical certitude, that there is sufficient reason to exclude entire assurance, in the observation that when asleep we can in the same way imagine ourselves possessed of another body and that we see other stars and another earth, when there is nothing of the kind. For how do we know that the thoughts which occur in dreaming are false rather than those other which we experience when awake, since the former are often not less vivid and distinct than the latter? And though men of the highest genius study this question as long as they please, I do not believe that they will be able to give any reason which can be sufficient to remove this doubt, unless they presuppose the existence of God. For, in the first place, even the principle which I have already taken as a rule, viz., that all the things which we clearly and distinctly conceive are true, is certain only because God is or exists and because he is a Perfect Being, and because all that we possess is derived from him: whence it follows that our ideas or notions, which to the extent of their clearness and distinctness are real, and proceed from God, must to that extent be true. Accordingly, whereas we often enough have ideas or notions in which some falsity is contained, this can only be the case with such as are to some extent confused and obscure, and in this have some share of nullity, that is, exist in us thus confused because we are not wholly perfect. And it is evident that it is not less repugnant that falsity or imperfection, in so far as it is imperfection, should proceed from God, than that truth or perfection should proceed from nothing. But if we did not know that all which is in us of real and true proceeds from a Perfect and Infinite Being, however clear and distinct our ideas might be, we should have no ground on that account for the reassurance that they possessed the perfection of being true.

But after the knowledge of God and of the soul has made us certain of this rule, we can easily understand that the truth of the thoughts we have when awake, ought not in the slightest degree to be called in question on account of the imaginations of our dreams. For if it happened that an individual, even when asleep, had some very distinct idea, as, for example, if a geometer should discover some new demonstration, the circumstance of his being asleep would not militate against its truth; and as for the most ordinary error of our dreams, which consists in their representing to us various objects in the same way as our external senses, this is not significant as giving us an occasion to suspect the truth of the ideas of sense; for we are not infrequently deceived in the same manner when awake; as when persons who have jaundice see all objects yellow, or when the stars or bodies at a great distance appear to us much smaller than they are. For, in short, whether awake or asleep, we ought never to allow ourselves to be persuaded of the truth of anything unless on the evidence of our reason. And it must be noted that I say of our reason, and not of our imagination or of our senses: so, for example, although we very clearly see the sun, we ought not therefore to determine that it is only of the size which our sense of sight presents; and we may very distinctly imagine the head of a lion joined to the body of a goat, without being therefore driven to the conclusion that a chimaera exists; for it is not a dictate of reason that what we thus see or imagine is in reality existent; but it plainly tells us that all our ideas or notions must have some foundation in truth; for otherwise it could not be that God, who is wholly perfect and veracious, should have placed them in us. And because our arguments are never so clear or so complete during sleep as when we are awake, although sometimes the acts of our imagination are then as lively and distinct, if not more so, than in our waking moments, reason further dictates that, since all our thoughts cannot be true because of our partial imperfection, those possess-

ing truth must infallibly be found in the experience of our
waking moments rather than in that of our dreams.

.   .   .   .

. . . But as soon as I had acquired some general notions
in physics, and beginning to test them in various particular
difficulties, had observed how far they can carry us, and
how much they differ from the principles that have been
employed up to the present time, I believed that I could
not keep them concealed without offending gravely against
the law by which we are bound to promote, as far as in us
lies, the general good of mankind. For by them I perceived
it to be possible to arrive at knowledge highly useful in
life; and instead of the speculative philosophy usually
taught in the schools, to discover a practical philosophy,
by means of which, knowing the force and action of fire,
water, air, the stars, the heavens, and all the other bodies
that surround us, as distinctly as we know the various
crafts of our artisans, we might also apply them in the
same way to all the uses to which they are adapted, and
thus make ourselves the lords and possessors of nature. . . .]

THE PREVIOUS EXTRACT GAVE ONLY THE BARE BONES OF
Descartes's system; in the passages that follow, which are
taken from *Meditations on the First Philosophy, in which
the Existence of God and the Distinction between Mind
and Body are demonstrated* (1641), we can gain a greater
insight into some of its features. Here he gives at greater
length his views on the absolute distinction between mind
and body, the latter subject to mechanical causal laws, the
former free from them and existing independently. This
absolute distinction is of the first importance to Descartes's
purpose of showing that the doctrines of the Catholic faith
are reconcilable with progress and discovery in the physical
sciences; the doctrines of religion are concerned with the
soul, a substance quite separate from the processes of the
physical world. He elaborates, also, his proofs of the existence of God, and says more of the method of doubt—
a doubt which, it is worth noting, he considers as purely
philosophical: in the synopsis, referring to the proofs of
the external world which he offers in the sixth meditation,

he remarks that he does not deem them "of great utility in establishing what they prove, viz., that there is in reality a world, that men are possessed of bodies, and the like, the truth of which no-one of sound mind ever seriously doubted." His point in giving such proofs is to show that they are less clear and certain than the demonstrations of the existence of mind and of God.

About the method of doubt Descartes makes here two principal new points. In the first meditation, he faces the difficulty that he claims to have proved the existence of a Perfect Being who could not allow us to be deceived, and yet it is a fact that we can be and sometimes are deceived, and Descartes's method has been to work on the assumption that we are. But why should a God who could not allow us always to be deceived allow us to be deceived sometimes? Faced with the problem of justifying the continued use of a method, the conclusion of which is that the method itself is unnecessary and perhaps blasphemous, Descartes invokes the idea of a malignant demon who, for the purposes of the method, may be supposed to be doing his best to mislead men into falsehood. A more serious answer to the problem is found in the fourth meditation, where he argues that it is a wrong use of man's free will that leads him into error: that by arrogantly making up his mind to a judgment where there are insufficient reasons to support it, he brings falsehood upon himself. For error, as for moral wickedness, God is not responsible. By the first suggestion, the blame was on the devil; by this, it is on man. Only by setting ourselves to accept nothing but what is by the Cartesian criterion genuinely acceptable, will we avoid error. This connection of belief and will, and the notion of what one can *choose to believe,* is of particular importance in the views of Pascal, who argued (very differently from Descartes) that there could be no necessary and compulsive demonstration of the existence of God; for, if there was, failure to believe in him would be evidence merely of stupidity, a failure of the understanding, whereas to be an unbeliever must constitute a failure of the will, a moral and not merely an intellectual error.

In the third meditation Descartes adds importantly to

those things that I cannot doubt. The original demonstration of something indubitable was in terms of thinking: the proposition "I am doubting." Here Descartes shows that the same considerations apply to the "imagination"; if I have an idea (by which he seems to mean a mental image), then at least I am certain *that I have such an idea,* even if the thing of which it is an idea does not in fact exist. The same is true of hallucinations — even if what I seem to see is not there, at least something is indubitably true, viz., that I seem to see it. This notion, that whatever else may be uncertain, the facts of my own experience cannot be uncertain, has figured again and again in the history of philosophy, down to the present day.

Descartes makes several approaches in these passages to the problem of the nature and existence of material objects. He is careful to distinguish "the power of the imagination" from "the power of the intellect": that is, the ability to imagine what a thing looks like from the knowledge of what in fact it is, of its nature. Here again he employs the notion of "essence," both in connection with the faculty of imagination, which, unlike that of intellectual thought, he considers to be an inessential feature of the mind; and in connection with the nature of external bodies. In the second meditation he seeks to prove that the essence of a piece of wax, for instance, cannot lie in its sensible qualities; for its sensible qualities can all change, as when we melt it, without our denying that it is the same piece of wax. Here Descartes relies on the importance and recurrent connection of essence with *identity*—the essence of a body, what it really is, is that which persists through change. From the independence of the essence of the wax from its sensible qualities, Descartes argues that knowledge of the nature of things is gained only by the intellect and not by the senses; and here we have one of his fundamental reasons for supposing that science, as the investigation of essences, is something which ideally should be independent of observation.

For the *existence* of material objects Descartes comes back in the end to his former argument from the nature of God. Among "ideas" he distinguishes what he calls

innate, factitious, and adventitious ideas — that is, those
that are already in the mind, those that are constructed by
the mind, and those that seem to arise spontaneously in
the mind whether we want them to or not. In the occurrence of the last he finds a sufficient reason for our *believing* that there exist objects external to us. That this
belief is correct can be established only by considerations
of the unwillingness of a Perfect Being to deceive us. There
is no intrinsic necessity in the existence of material objects.

In the fourth meditation Descartes goes so far as to
invoke the belief in God as the only ultimate safeguard
against error even in the case of propositions that are
clearly and distinctly conceived to be true. While such
propositions are indeed self-evident, when properly viewed,
it is possible to lose confidence in them through a lack of
attention, a mass of conflicting evidence, and other such
contingent factors; and since we can perhaps never be certain that we are not in such circumstances, it is only the
belief in the undeceiving God that preserves one's balance.
Here piety seems to have got the better of consistency. For
it will be remembered that the existence of such a God was
itself only proved by reflection on "clear and distinct ideas";
and so at this point Descartes does seem to have fallen
into the vicious circle of which he has often been accused.

Despite all the criticisms that can be brought against
him, Descartes is one of the still living philosophers. His
was a truly philosophical enterprise: the attention he gave
to the fundamental problems of our thought and knowledge helped to bring about a revolution in ideas, and many
of his questions are still with us. He stands in a uniquely
important position, with one foot in the scholastic past
and one in the science of the future. The theory of knowledge, in its modern form, begins with him.

[*Synopsis of the Six Following Meditations*

In the First Meditation I put forward the grounds on
which we may doubt in general of all things, and especially
of material objects, so long, at least, as we have no other
foundations for the sciences than those we have had up to
now. Now, although the utility of a doubt so general may

not be apparent at first sight, it is nevertheless of the greatest utility, since it delivers us from all prejudice, and affords the easiest pathway by which the mind may detach itself from the senses; and, finally, it makes it impossible for us to doubt wherever we afterwards discover truth.

In the Second, the mind which, in exercise of the freedom peculiar to itself, supposes that no object exists, of the existence of which it has even the slightest doubt, finds that, meanwhile, it must itself exist. And this point is also of the highest moment, for the mind is thus enabled easily to distinguish what belongs to itself, that is, to the intellectual nature, from what belongs to the body. But since some, perhaps, will expect, at this state of our progress, a statement of the reasons which establish the doctrine of the immortality of the soul, I think it proper now to warn them that it was my aim to write nothing of which I could not give exact proof, and that I therefore felt myself obliged to adopt an order similar to that in use among the geometers, viz., to set down everything upon which the proposition in question depends, before coming to any conclusion respecting it. Now, the first and chief prerequisite for the knowledge of the immortality of the soul is our being able to form the clearest possible conception of the soul itself, and such as shall be absolutely distinct from all our notions of body; and this is what is done in the passage in question. There is required, besides this, the assurance that all things which we clearly and distinctly conceive are true, exactly as we conceive them: and this could not be established before the Fourth Meditation. Further, it is necessary, for the same purpose, that we possess a distinct conception of corporeal nature, which is given partly in the Second and partly in the Fifth and Sixth Meditations. And, finally, on these grounds, we must conclude that all those objects which are *clearly and distinctly conceived to be diverse substances,* as mind and body, are substances really reciprocally distinct; and this inference is made in the Sixth Meditation. The absolute distinction of mind and body is, besides, confirmed in the Second Meditation, by showing that we cannot conceive body unless as divisible; while, on the other hand, mind cannot be conceived unless as indivisible. For we are not able to conceive the half of a mind, as we can of any body, however small, so that the natures of these two substances are to be held, not only as diverse, but even in some measure as contraries. I have not, however, pursued this discussion further in the present treatise, both for the reason that these considerations are sufficient to show that the destruction of the mind does not follow from the corruption of the body, and thus to afford men the hope of a future life, and also because the premises from which one can infer the immortality of the soul involve an explanation of the whole of physics: in order to establish, in the first place, that generally all substances, that is, all things which can exist only in consequence of having been created by God, are in their own nature incorruptible, and can never cease to be, unless God himself, by refusing his concurrence to them, reduce them to nothing; and, in the second place that body, taken generally, is a substance, and therefore can never perish, but that the human body, in as far as it differs from other bodies, is constituted only by a certain configuration of members, and by other accidents of this sort, while the human mind is not made up of accidents, but is a pure substance. For although all the accidents of the mind be changed — although, for example, it think certain things, will others, and perceive others — the mind itself does not vary with these changes; while, on the contrary, the human body is no longer the same if a change take place in the form of any of its parts: from which it follows that the body may, indeed, without difficulty perish, but that the mind is in its own nature immortal.

In the Third Meditation, I have explained at sufficient length, as appears to me, my chief argument for the existence of God. But yet, since I wished there to avoid the use of comparisons taken from material objects, that I might withdraw, as far as possible, the minds of my readers from the senses, numerous obscurities perhaps remain, which will, I trust, be afterwards entirely removed in the replies to the objections: thus, among other things, it may be difficult to understand how the idea of a being absolutely perfect, which is found in our minds, possesses so much objective reality [i.e., participates by representation in so many degrees of being and perfection] that it must be held to arise from a cause absolutely perfect. This is illustrated in the replies by the comparison of a highly perfect machine, the idea of which exists in the mind of some workman; for as the objective [i.e., representative] perfection of this idea must have some cause, viz., either the science of the workman, or of some other person from whom he has received the idea, in the same way the idea of God, which is found in us, demands God himself for its cause.

In the Fourth, it is shown that all which we very clearly and distinctly conceive is true; and, at the same time, is explained wherein consists the nature of error; points that require to be known as well for confirming the preceding truths, as for the better understanding of those that are to follow. But, meanwhile, it must be observed that I do not at all there treat of Sin, that is, of error committed in the pursuit of good and evil, but of that sort alone which arises in the determination of the true and the false. Nor do I refer to matters of faith, or to the conduct of life, but only to what regards speculative truths, and such as are known by means of the natural light alone.

In the Fifth, besides the illustration of corporeal nature, taken generally, a new proof is given of the existence of God, not free, perhaps, any more than the former, from certain difficulties, but of these the solution will be found in the replies to the objections. I further show in what sense it is true that the certainty of geometrical demonstrations themselves is dependent on the knowledge of God.

Finally, in the Sixth, the working of the understanding is distinguished from that of the imagination; the marks of this distinction are described; the human mind is shown to be really distinct from the body, and, nevertheless, to be so closely conjoined therewith as together to form something like a unity. All the errors which arise from the senses are brought under review, while the means of avoiding them are pointed out; and, finally, all the grounds are adduced from which the existence of material objects may be inferred; not, however, because I thought them very useful in establishing what they prove, viz., that there is in reality a world, that men are possessed of bodies, and the like, the truth of which no one of sound mind ever seriously doubted; but because, from a close consideration of them, one realises that they are neither so strong nor clear as the reasonings which lead us to the knowledge of our mind and of God; so that the latter are, of all which come under human knowledge, the most certain and manifest—a conclusion which it was my single aim in these Meditations to establish; on this account I here omit mention of the various other questions which, in the course of the discussion, I also had occasion to consider.

. . . .

Meditation I. Of the Things of which we may Doubt

Let us suppose that we are asleep, and that all these particulars — namely the opening of the eyes, the motion of the head, the extending of the hands — are merely illusions; and even that we really possess neither a body nor hands such as we see. Nevertheless, it must be admitted at least that the objects which appear to us in sleep are, as it were, painted representations which could not have been formed unless in the likeness of realities; and, therefore, that those general objects, at all events — namely, eyes, a head, hands, and an entire body — are not simply imaginary, but really existent. For, in truth, painters themselves, even when they try to represent sirens and satyrs by forms the most fantastic and extraordinary, cannot bestow upon them forms and natures absolutely new, but can only make a certain mixture and composition of the limbs of different animals; or if they chance to imagine something so novel that nothing at all similar has ever been seen before, and such as is, therefore, purely fictitious and absolutely false, it is at least certain that the colours of which this is composed are real.

And on the same principle, although these general objects, viz., eyes, a head, hands and the like, be imaginary, we must nevertheless admit that there are at least some other objects still more simple and universal than these, of which are formed, just as of certain real colours, all those images of things, whether true and real or false and fantastic, that are found in our thought.

To this class of objects belong corporeal nature in general and its extension; the shape of extended things, their quantity or size and their number, as also the place in, and the time during which, they exist, and other things of the same sort. It will not, therefore, perhaps be an unsound conclusion from this that physics, astronomy, medicine and all the other sciences that have for their end the consideration of composite objects, are very much subject to doubt and uncertainty; but that arithmetic, geometry and the other sciences of the same class, which regard merely the simplest and most general objects, and scarcely inquire whether or not these exist in nature, contain something that is certain and indubitable: for whether I am awake or dreaming, it remains true that two and three make five, and that a square never has more than four sides; nor does it seem possible that truths so obvious could fall under a suspicion of falsity or uncertainty.

Nevertheless, the belief that there is a God who is all-powerful and who created me, such as I am, has for a long time been in my mind. How, then do I know that he has not arranged that there should be no earth, or sky or any extended things or shape or size or place, but that all the same I should have perceptions of all things and should think that they do not exist otherwise than as I perceive them? And further, as I sometimes think that others are in error in matters of which they believe themselves to possess a perfect knowledge, it is possible that God has decided that I should be deceived each time I add together two and three, or number the sides of a square, or form some judgment still more simple, if any more simple indeed can be imagined. But perhaps God is not willing that I should be thus deceived, for he is said to be supremely good. If, however, it were repugnant to the goodness of God to have created me subject to constant deception, it would seem likewise to be contrary to his goodness to allow me to be occasionally deceived; and yet it is clear that this is permitted. Some, indeed, might perhaps be found who would prefer to deny the existence of a being so powerful than to believe that everything else is uncertain. But let us not oppose their opinion for the moment, but suppose, as they would, that everything that has been said about God is a fiction: nevertheless, in whatever way they suppose that I reached the state in which I exist, whether by fate, or chance, or by an endless series of antecedents and consequents, or by any other means, it is clear (since to be deceived and to err is a kind of imperfection) that the less powerful the cause to which they assign my origin, the more probable it will be that I am imperfect enough to be deceived constantly. To these arguments I have assuredly nothing to reply, but am forced to declare that there is nothing at all that I formerly believed to be true which I could not now doubt, not in any light or unconsidered way, but from cogent and maturely considered reasons; so that henceforward I must stop and suspend judgment on these thoughts, and not assent to them any more readily than to those things that seem evidently false, if I am to discover anything fixed and certain in the sciences.

. . . .

I will suppose, then, not that God, who is sovereignly good and the fountain of truth, but that some malignant demon, who is at once exceedingly potent and deceitful, has employed all his artifice to deceive me; I will suppose that the sky, the air, the earth, colours, shapes, sounds, and all external things, are nothing better than illusion and deceit, by means of which this being has laid snares for my credulity; I will consider myself as without hands, eyes, flesh, blood, or any of the senses, and as falsely believing that I am possessed of these; I will continue resolutely fixed in this belief, and if indeed by this means it be not in my power to arrive at the knowledge of truth, I shall at least do what is in my power, viz. suspend my judgment and guard with settled purpose against giving my assent to what is false, and being imposed upon by this deceiver, whatever his power and artifice.

. . . .

Meditation II

. . . .

Let us consider the objects that are commonly thought to be the most distinctly known, the bodies we touch and see; I do not mean bodies in general, for these general notions are usually more confused, but some particular body. Take, for example, this piece of wax which has just been taken from the beehive; it has not yet lost the sweetness of the honey it contained; it still retains some of the odour of the flowers from which it was gathered; its colour, shape, size are apparent, it is hard, cold, easily handled; and when struck with the finger it produces a sound; everything that contributes to make a body as distinctly known as possible, is found in the one before us. But while I am speaking, let it be placed near the fire—what remains of the taste evaporates, the smell disappears, it loses its shape, its size increases, it becomes liquid, it grows hot, it can hardly be handled, and when struck emits no sound. Does the same wax still remain after this change? It must be admitted that it does remain: no one doubts it or judges otherwise. What, then, was it I knew with so much distinctness in the piece of wax? Certainly it can be nothing of all that I observed by means of the senses, since all of the things that fell under taste, smell, sight, touch and hearing are changed, and yet the same wax remains. It was perhaps what I now think, viz., that this was neither the sweetness of honey, the pleasant odour of flowers, the whiteness, the size nor the sound, but only a body that a little before appeared to me under these forms and which is now perceived under others. But what is it precisely that I imagine when I think of it in this way? Let us consider it carefully and, putting aside all that does not belong to the wax, see what remains. There certainly remains nothing except something extended, flexible and moveable. But what is meant by flexible and moveable? Is it that I imagine the piece of wax, being round, to be incapable of becoming square, or of passing from a square to a triangular shape? Assuredly this is not the case, because I conceive that it admits of an infinity of similar changes, but I am unable to compass this infinity by imagination; consequently this conception which I have of the wax is not the product of the faculty of imagination. But what now is this extension? Is it not also unknown? For it becomes greater when the wax is melting, greater when it has melted, and greater still when the heat goes on increasing; and I should not conceive, clearly and according to truth, the wax as it is if I did not suppose that it admitted even a wider variety of extension than I ever imagined. I must, therefore, admit that by imagination I cannot conceive what the piece of wax is, and that it is the mind alone that conceives it: I speak of one piece in particular; for, as to wax in general, this is still more evident. But what is the piece of wax that can be conceived only by the mind or understanding? It is certainly the same that I see, touch, imagine, and the same that I know from the beginning. But (and this it is of importance to notice) the perception of it is neither an act of sight, of touch, nor of imagination, and never was, though it might formerly seem so, but is simply an intuition of the mind, which may be imperfect and confused, as it formerly was, or very clear and distinct, as it is at present, according as the attention is more or less directed to the elements which it contains, and of which it is composed.

. . . .

But, finally, what shall I say of the mind itself, that is, of myself? for as yet I do not admit that I am anything but mind. What, then! I who seem to possess so distinct an apprehension of the piece of wax,—do I not know myself, both with greater truth and certitude, and also much more distinctly and clearly? For if I judge that the wax is or exists because I see it, it assuredly follows, much more evidently, that I myself am or exist, for the same reason; for it is possible that what I see may not in truth be wax, and that I do not even possess eyes with which to see anything; but it cannot be that when I see, or, which comes to the same thing, when I think I see, I myself who think am nothing. So likewise, if I judge that the wax exists because I touch it, it will still also follow that I am; and if I determine that my imagination, or any other cause, whatever it be, persuades me of the existence of the wax, I will still draw the same conclusion. And what I have remarked here about the piece of wax can be applied to all the other things that are external to me. And further, if the notion or knowledge of wax appeared to me more pre-

cise and distinct, after not only sight and touch, but many
other causes besides, with how much greater distinctness
must I now know myself, since all the reasons that contribute to the knowledge of the nature of wax, or of any
body whatever, manifest still better the nature of my mind?
And there are besides so many other things in the mind
itself that contribute to the illustration of its nature, that
those dependent on the body, to which I have here referred, scarcely merit to be taken into account.

But, in conclusion, I find I have, without noticing it,
returned to the point I intended; for, since it is now manifest to me that bodies themselves are not properly perceived by the senses nor by the faculty of imagination, but
by the intellect alone; and since we do not know them
because we see them, or because we touch them, but
solely because we conceive them in thought, I readily discover that there is nothing more easily or clearly apprehended than my own mind. . . .

Meditation III

I will now close my eyes, I will stop my ears, I will turn
away my senses, I will even efface from my consciousness
all the images of corporeal things; or at least, because this
can hardly be accomplished, I will consider them as empty
and false; and thus, holding converse only with myself,
and closely examining my inner self, I will try to obtain
by degrees a more intimate and familiar knowledge of
myself. I am a thinking (conscious) thing, that is, a being
who doubts, affirms, denies, knows little, and is ignorant
of much, who loves, hates, wills, refuses, who imagines
and perceives; for, as I remarked before, although the
things which I perceive or imagine are perhaps nothing
at all apart from me and in themselves, I am nevertheless
sure that those modes of consciousness which I call perceptions and imaginations, in as far only as they are modes
of consciousness, exist in me. And in the little I have said
I think I have summed up all that I really know, or at least
all that up to this time I have discovered that I know. Now,
I will consider more exactly whether I can still discover in
myself some further knowledge which I have not yet ob-

served. I am certain that I am a thinking thing; but do I not therefore likewise know what is required to render me certain of a truth? In this first knowledge, doubtless, there is nothing that gives me assurance of its truth except the clear and distinct perception of what I affirm, which would not indeed be sufficient to give me the assurance that what I say is true, if it could ever happen that anything I thus clearly and distinctly perceived should prove false; and accordingly it seems to me that I may now take as a general rule, that all that is very clearly and distinctly conceived is true.

. . . .

Of my thoughts some are, as it were, images of things and to these alone properly belongs the name idea; as when I have before my mind a man, a chimera, the sky, an angel, or even God. Others, again, have certain other forms; as when I will, fear, affirm, or deny, I always indeed conceive something as the object of my thought, but I also add something to the idea I have of two objects; and of this class of thoughts some are called volitions or affections, and other judgments.

Now, with respect to ideas, if these are considered only in themselves, and are not referred to any object beyond them, they cannot, properly speaking, be false; for whether I imagine a goat or a chimera, it is not less true that I imagine the one than the other. Nor need we fear that falsity may exist in the will or affections; for, although I may desire objects that are wrong, and even that never existed, it is still true that I desire them. There thus remain only judgments, in which I must take great care not to be deceived. But the chief error that arises in them consists in judging that the ideas that are in us are like, or conform to, the things that are external to us; for assuredly, if we but considered the ideas themselves as certain modes of our thought, without referring them to anything beyond, they would hardly afford any occasion of error.

But, among these ideas, some appear to me to be innate, others adventitious, and others to be made by myself (factitious); for, as I have the power of conceiving what is called a thing, or a truth, or a thought, it seems to me that I have this power from no other source than my own nature; but if I now hear a noise, if I see the sun, or if I feel heat, I have all along judged that these sensations proceeded from certain objects existing outside myself; and it appears to me that sirens, hippogryphs, and the like, are inventions of my own mind. But I may even perhaps come to believe that all my ideas are of the class that I call adventitious, or that they are all innate, or that they are all factitious, for I have not yet clearly discovered their true origin; and what I have here principally to do is to consider, with reference to those that appear to come from certain objects without me, what grounds there are for thinking that they are like these objects.

. . . .

Meditation IV

I have accustomed myself these past days to separating my mind from the senses, and I have accurately observed that there is exceedingly little that is known with certainty respecting corporeal objects,—that we know much more of the human mind, and still more of God himself. I am thus able now without difficulty to abstract my mind from the contemplation of sensible or imaginable objects, and apply it to those which, being free from all matter, are purely intelligible. And certainly the idea I have of the human mind in so far as it is a thinking thing, and not extended in length, breadth, and depth, and participating in none of the properties of body, is incomparably more distinct than the idea of any corporeal object; and when I consider that I doubt, in other words, that I am an incomplete and dependent being, the idea of a complete and independent being, that is to say of God, occurs to my mind with so much clearness and distinctness,—and from the fact alone that this idea is found in me, or that I who possess it exist, the conclusions that God exists, and that my own existence, each moment of its continuance, is absolutely dependent upon him, are so manifest,—as to lead me to believe it impossible that the human mind can know anything with more clearness and certitude. And now I seem to discover a path that will conduct us from the contemplation of the true God, in whom are contained all the treasures of science and wisdom, to the knowledge of the other things in the universe.

For, in the first place, I recognise that it is impossible for him ever to deceive me, for in all fraud and deceit there is a certain imperfection; and although it may seem that the ability to deceive is a mark of subtlety or power, yet the will to deceive provides unquestionable evidence of malice and weakness; and such, accordingly, cannot be found in God. In the next place, I experience in myself a certain faculty of judgment which I undoubtedly received from God, along with whatever else is mine; and since it is impossible that he should will to deceive me, it is likewise certain that he has not given me a faculty that will lead me into error, so long as I use it aright.

. . . .

Whence, then, spring my errors? They arise from this cause alone, that I do not restrain the will, which is of much wider range than the understanding, within the same limits, but extend it even to things I do not understand, and, as the will is of itself indifferent to them, it readily falls into error and sin by choosing the false instead of the true, and evil instead of good.

For example, when I lately considered whether anything really existed in the world, and found that because I considered this question, it very manifestly followed that I myself existed, I could not but judge that what I so clearly conceived was true, not that I was forced to this judgment by any external cause, but simply because great clearness of the understanding was succeeded by strong inclination in the will; and I believed this just as much the more freely as I was less indifferent with respect to it. But now I not only know that I exist, in so far as I am a thinking being, but there is likewise presented to my mind a certain idea of corporeal nature; hence I am in doubt as to whether the thinking nature which is in me, or rather that by which I am what I am, is different from that corporeal nature, or whether both are merely one and the same thing. Here I suppose that I am as yet ignorant of any reason that would determine me to adopt the one belief in preference to the other: whence it happens that it is a matter of perfect in-

difference to me which of the two suppositions I affirm or
deny, or whether I form any judgment at all in the matter.

This indifference, moreover, extends not only to things
of which the understanding has no knowledge at all, but
in general also to all those which it does not discover with
perfect clearness at the moment the will is deliberating upon
them; for, however probable the conjectures may be that
dispose me to form a judgment in a particular matter,
the simple knowledge that these are merely conjectures,
and not certain and indubitable reasons, makes it possible
for me to form one that is directly the opposite. Of this I
lately had abundant experience, when I laid aside as false
all that I had before held for true, on the single ground that
I could in some degree doubt of it. But if I abstain from
judging of a thing when I do not conceive it with sufficient
clearness and distinctness, it is plain that I act rightly, and
am not deceived; but if I resolve to deny or affirm, I then
do not make a right use of my free will; and if I affirm what
is false, it is evident that I am deceived: moreover, even if
I judge in accordance with the truth, I stumble upon it by
chance, and do not therefore escape the imputation of a
wrong use of my freedom; for it is a dictate of the natural
light, that the knowledge of the understanding ought always
to precede the determination of the will.

· · · · · · · · · · · · · ·

Meditation V

· · · · · · · · · · · · ·

Whatever proof or argument I use, it always returns
to this, that it is only the things I clearly and distinctly
conceive that have the power of completely persuading me.
And although, of the objects I conceive in this manner,
some, indeed, are obvious to every one, while others are
only discovered after close and careful investigation; nevertheless, after they are once discovered, the latter are not
esteemed less certain than the former. Thus, for example,
to take the case of the right-angled triangle, although it is
not so manifest at first that the square of the base is equal
to the squares of the other two sides, as that the base is
opposite to the greatest angle; nevertheless, after it is once
apprehended, we are as firmly persuaded of the truth of

the former as of the latter. And, with respect to God, if I were not preoccupied by prejudices, and my thoughts distracted by the continual presence of the images of sensible objects, I should know nothing sooner or more easily than the fact of his being. For is there any truth more clear than the existence of a Supreme Being, or of God, seeing it is to his essence alone that necessary and eternal existence pertains? And although the right conception of this truth has cost me much close thinking, nevertheless at present I feel not only as assured of it as of what I deem most certain, but I remark further that the certitude of all other truths is so absolutely dependent on it, that without this knowledge it is impossible ever to know anything perfectly.

Although I am of such a nature as to be unable, while I possess a very clear and distinct apprehension of a matter, to resist the conviction of its truth, yet because I am also of such a nature that I cannot keep my mind continually fixed on the same object, and as I frequently recollect having judged a thing to be true without recalling the reasons that made me so judge it, it may happen meanwhile that other reasons are presented to me which would readily cause me to change my opinion, if I did not know that God existed; and so I should possess no true and certain knowledge, but merely vague and vacillating opinions. Thus, for example, when I consider the nature of the triangle, it most clearly appears to me, who know little of the principles of geometry, that its three angles are equal to two right angles, and I find it impossible to believe otherwise, while I apply my mind to the proof; but as soon as I cease from attending to the process of proof, although I still remember that I had a clear comprehension of it, yet I may readily come to doubt of the truth demonstrated, if I do not know that there is a God: for I may persuade myself that I have been so constituted by nature as to be sometimes deceived, even in matters which I think I apprehend with the greatest evidence and certitude, especially when I recollect that I frequently considered many things to be true and certain which other reasons afterwards compelled me to reckon as wholly false.

But after I have discovered that God exists, since I at the same time observed that all things depend on him, and that he is no deceiver, and inferred from this that everything I clearly and distinctly perceive is of necessity true: although I no longer attend to the grounds of a judgment, no opposite reason can be alleged sufficient to lead me to doubt of its truth, provided only I remember that I once possessed a clear and distinct comprehension of it. My knowledge of it thus becomes true and certain. And this same knowledge extends similarly to whatever I remember to have formerly demonstrated, such as the truths of geometry and the like; for what can be alleged against them to lead me to doubt of them? Will it be that my nature is such that I may be frequently deceived? But I already know that I cannot be deceived in judgments of the grounds of which I possess a clear knowledge. Will it be that I formerly considered things to be true and certain which I afterwards discovered to be false? But I had no clear and distinct knowledge of any of those things, and, being as yet ignorant of the rule by which I am assured of the truth of a judgment, I was led to give my assent to them on grounds which I afterwards discovered were less strong than at the time I imagined them to be. What further objection, then, is there? Will it be said that perhaps I am asleep (an objection I lately myself raised), or that all the thoughts of which I am now conscious have no more truth than the reveries of my dreams? But although, in truth, I should be dreaming, the rule still holds that all which is clearly presented to my intellect is indisputably true.

And thus I very clearly see that the certitude and truth of all knowledge depends only on the knowledge of the true God, insomuch that, before I knew him, I could have no perfect knowledge of anything else. And now that I know him, I possess the means of acquiring a perfect knowledge about things, not only those that are in him, but also those connected with corporeal nature, in so far as it can serve as the subject of geometrical demonstrations, which do not concern themselves with the question whether it exists or not.

Meditation VI

There now only remains the inquiry as to whether material things exist. With regard to this question, I at least know with certainty that such things may exist, in as far as they constitute the subject of geometrical demonstrations, since, regarding them in this aspect, I can conceive them clearly and distinctly. For there can be no doubt that God possesses the power of producing all the objects I am able distinctly to conceive, and I never considered anything impossible to him, except when I found a contradiction in the attempt to conceive it aright. Further, the faculty of imagination which I possess, and of which I am conscious that I make use when I apply myself to the consideration of material things, is sufficient to persuade me of their existence: for, when I attentively consider what imagination is, I find that it is simply a certain application of the faculty of knowledge to a body which is immediately present to it, and which therefore exists.

And to render this quite clear, I remark in the first place, the difference there is between imagination and pure intellect. For example, when I imagine a triangle I not only conceive that it is a figure bounded by three lines, but at the same time also I look upon these three lines as present by the power and internal application of my mind, and this is what I call imagining. But if I want to think of a chiliogon, I indeed rightly conceive that it is a figure composed of a thousand sides, as easily as I conceive that a triangle is a figure composed of only three sides; but I cannot imagine the thousand sides of a chiliogon as I do the three sides of a triangle, nor, so to speak, view them as present with my mind's eyes. And although, in accordance with the habit I have of always imagining something when I think of corporeal things, it may happen that, in conceiving a chiliogon, I confusedly represent some figure to myself, yet it is quite evident that this is not a chiliogon, since it in no wise differs from that which I would represent to myself, if I were to think of a myriogon, or any other figure of many sides; nor would this reprensentation be of any use in discovering the properties that constitute the difference between a chili-

ogon and other polygons. But if it is a question of considering a pentagon, it is quite true that I can conceive its
figure, as well as that of a chiliogon, without the aid of imagination; but I can likewise imagine it by applying the
attention of my mind to its five sides, and at the same time
to the area which they contain. Thus I observe that a special
effort of mind is necessary to the act of imagination, which
is not required to conceiving or understanding; and this
special exertion of mind clearly shows the difference between imagination and pure intellect. I notice, besides,
that this power of imagination which I possess, in as far as
it differs from the power of conceiving, is in no way necessary to my nature or essence, that is, to the essence of my
mind; even if I did not possess it, I should still remain
the same that I now am, from which it seems we may conclude that it depends on something different from my mind.
And I easily conceive that, if some body exists, with which
my mind is so conjoined and united as to be able, as it
were, to consider it when it chooses, it may thus imagine
corporeal objects; so that this mode of thinking differs from
pure intellect only in this respect, that the mind in conceiving turns in some way upon itself, and considers some
one of the ideas it possesses within itself; but in imagining
it turns towards the body, and contemplates in it some
object that conforms to the idea which it either conceived
in itself or apprehended by the senses. I easily understand,
I say, that imagination may be thus formed, if it is true that
there are bodies; and because I find no other obvious mode
of explaining it, I thence, with probability, conjecture that
they exist, but only with probability; and although I carefully examine all things, nevertheless I do not find that,
from the distinct idea of corporeal nature I have in my
imagination, I can necessarily infer the existence of any
body.

. . . .

. . . I find in myself a certain passive faculty of perception, that is, of receiving and taking knowledge of the ideas
of sensible things; but this would be useless to me, if there
did not also exist in me, or in some other thing, another
active faculty capable of forming and producing those ideas.

But this active faculty cannot be in me in as far as I am but a thinking thing, seeing that it does not presuppose thought, and also that those ideas are frequently produced in my mind without my contributing to them in any way, and even frequently contrary to my will. This faculty must therefore exist in some substance different from me, in which all the objective reality of the ideas that are produced by this faculty is contained formally or eminently, as I before remarked: and this substance is either a body, that is to say, a corporeal nature in which is contained formally all that is objectively and by representation in those ideas; or it is God himself, or some other creature, of a rank superior to body, in which the same is contained eminently. But as God is no deceiver, it is manifest that he does not of himself and immediately communicate those ideas to me, nor even by the intervention of any creature in which their objective reality is not formally, but only eminently, contained. For as he has given me no faculty whereby I can discover this to be the case, but, on the contrary, a very strong inclination to believe that those ideas arise from corporeal objects, I do not see how he could be vindicated from the charge of deceit, if, in fact, they proceeded from some other source, or were produced by causes other than corporeal things: and accordingly it must be concluded that corporeal objects exist. Nevertheless they are not perhaps exactly such as we perceive by the senses, for their comprehension by the senses is, in many instances, very obscure and confused; but it is at least necessary to admit that everything I clearly and distinctly conceive as in them, that is, generally speaking, everything contained in the object of speculative geometry, really exists external to me.

. . . .

. . . And I ought to reject all the doubts of those bygone days as exaggerated and ridiculous, especially that general uncertainty respecting sleep, which I could not distinguish from the waking state: for I now find a very marked difference between the two states, in that our memory can never connect our dreams with each other and with the course of life, in the way it constantly does with events that occur when we are awake. And, in fact, if some one, when I was awake, appeared to me all of a sudden and suddenly disappeared, as do the images I see in sleep, so that I could not observe either where he came from or where he went, it would be quite reasonable for me to think it a spectre or phantom formed in my brain, rather than a real man. But when I perceive objects with regard to which I can distinctly determine both where they come from, and where they are, and the time at which they appear to me, and when, without interruption, I can connect the perception I have of them with the whole of the other parts of my life, I am perfectly sure that what I thus perceive occurs while I am awake and not during sleep. And I ought not in the least degree to doubt of the truth of those presentations, if, after having called together all my senses, my memory, and my understanding to examine them by any one of these faculties which is repugnant to that of any other: for since God is no deceiver, it necessarily follows that I am not herein deceived. But because the necessities of action frequently oblige us to come to a decision before we have had leisure for so careful an examination, it must be confessed that the life of man is liable to frequent error with respect to individual objects; and we must, in conclusion, acknowledge the weakness of our nature.]

CHAPTER V

Pascal

BLAISE PASCAL WAS BORN IN 1623 AND DIED IN 1662. HE was perhaps the most brilliant and profound Christian apologist that Europe has known since the Middle Ages. He was a great mathematician and a great thinker, but he was not an original philosopher, in the narrower sense of that word; for he was not primarily concerned to construct a systematic theory of knowledge or a rational scheme of reality. He wished only to show the inevitable weakness of human reason and the necessity of faith.

In the *Pensées* he describes, with unequaled force of language and psychological insight, the various phases of human despair, uncertainty and sense of unworthiness. But he asserts also the power and dignity of human thought, which at least makes men realize their own imperfection. This power to grasp his own imperfection is the greatness of man.

There is a peculiar vividness and tension in Pascal's writing; he himself had abandoned the study of mathematics for religious meditation, after showing great genius in his mathematical inventions. He invented a calculating machine and contributed to the theory of chance. No one was in a better position to understand the power of reason; in the two famous extracts from the *Pensées* printed below, he affirms the dignity of the human soul against the background of the new cosmology which was showing the immensities of the physical universe.

The original French is preserved, with a translation attached, because the words, as he wrote them, have their own force and place in history.

〖 CHAPTER XXIII. *Grandeur de l'Homme*

L'homme n'est qu'un roseau, le plus faible de la nature; mais c'est un roseau pensant. Il ne faut pas que l'univers entier s'arme pour l'écraser: une vapeur, une goutte d'eau, suffit pour le tuer. Mais, quand l'univers l'écraserait, l'homme serait encore plus noble que ce qui le tue, parce qu'il sait qu'il meurt, et l'avantage que l'univers a sur lui; l'univers n'en sait rien.

Toute notre dignité consiste donc en la pensée. C'est de là qu'il faut nous relever et non de l'espace et de la durée, que nous ne saurions remplir. Travaillons donc à bien penser: voilà le principe de la morale.

Man is only a reed, the weakest to be found in nature; but he is a thinking reed. It is not necessary for the whole of nature to take up arms to crush him: a puff of smoke, a drop of water, is enough to kill him. But, even if the universe should crush him, man would still be more noble than that which destroys him, because he knows that he dies and he realises the advantage which the universe possesses over him. The universe knows nothing of this.

All our dignity, then, consists in thought. It is upon this that we must depend, not on space and time, which we would not in any case be able to fill. Let us labour, then, to think well: this is the foundation of morality.

Appendix to Chapter XXIII

Roseau pensant.— Ce n'est point de l'espace que je dois chercher ma dignité, mais c'est du règlement de ma pensée. Je n'aurai pas d'avantage en possédant des terres: par l'espace, l'univers me comprend et m'engloutit comme un point; par la pensée, je le comprends.

Thinking reed.—It is not in space that I should look to find my dignity, but rather in the ordering of my thought. I would gain nothing further by owning territories: in point of space the universe embraces me and swallows me up like a mere point: in thought, I embrace the universe.〗

CHAPTER VI

Spinoza

BARUCH SPINOZA WAS BORN IN AMSTERDAM IN 1632 INTO a prosperous Jewish commercial family, which had come to Holland from Portugal in the sixteenth century. He was first educated at a Jewish school and spent his childhood and youth in the important Jewish community of Amsterdam. As a young man he came to know a circle of freethinkers interested in philosophy, who profoundly respected his gifts as a philosopher. His growing reputation as a freethinking philosopher led to his formal exclusion from the Jewish community in 1656. He was formally cursed and no Jew was to have any intercourse with him of any kind. For the remainder of his life he lived alone in various places in Holland, separated from the Jewish community; he was visited by, and corresponded with, a small circle of friends who knew of his philosophical work, most of which could not be published in his lifetime. He earned his living by grinding and polishing lenses. He corresponded with Oldenburg, Secretary of the Royal Society in London, and his work was known to Huygens, Boyle and other natural philosophers, and, although he lived in retirement from the world, his liberal attitude in politics became widely known. In 1665 he is believed to have intervened on the side of the de Witts by accepting a secret mission to the French. For reasons set out in his *Tractatus Theologico-Politicus,* he was an enemy of all persecuting churches, not excluding the Calvinists, who were active in Holland and who accepted the leadership of William of Orange. Like Hobbes, he wished to strengthen the secular power of the state against the warring, persecuting Christian churches; he demanded a purely secular

99

state, which would be indifferent in matters of religious
doctrine. He was the first great philosophical advocate of
toleration in the modern spirit. He refused an offer from
the Elector Palatine at Heidelberg to teach philosophy,
under conditions of complete freedom, at the University of Heidelberg; he explained that as a philosopher he
preferred to remain free of public commitments. He had
conversations with Leibniz, who visited him and subse-
quently denounced his dangerous errors. To know Spinoza
was in itself dangerous, so great was his reputation as an
implacable atheist and freethinker. He died of consump-
tion in 1677, having suffered from this disease for many
years.

The only work to be published under his own name in
his lifetime was the *Principles of Descartes's Philosophy,*
together with an appendix called *Metaphysical Thoughts.*
This is an exposition of Descartes's philosophy in geometrical order, and does not present his own thought. The
Theological-Political Treatise was published anonymously
in 1670 under a false imprint, and aroused scandal and
hostility because of its skepticism about religious doctrine.
That Spinoza was the author was generally known or inferred. Spinoza's masterpiece, the *Ethics,* plainly could
not be published in his lifetime. After his death his friends
produced his works in a single volume, which included
the *Ethics, On the Improvement of Understanding,
Treatise on Politics,* and his learned correspondence. The
Ethics was condemned as atheistical and morally subversive, and was largely neglected until towards the end of the
eighteenth century when Goethe, and later Shelley, Cole-
ridge and other romantic writers, aroused interest in Spinoza.

Throughout the nineteenth century Spinoza was admired, if not always understood, from many different points
of view: by some he was represented as a materialist and
rationalist critic of established morality, by others as a mystical pantheist. He was rightly seen as a precursor of the
Higher Criticism of the Bible, and as an advocate of liberalism and toleration. Some of the origins of his thought
have been found in earlier Jewish philosophy; on the other
hand some scholars have interpreted his philosophy as

solely a development of Descartes's. These interpretations are partial and incomplete. It is true that Spinoza was deeply influenced by the moral and intellectual traditions of the Jews, and it is true that his thought started from Descartes's conclusions and that he never abandoned Descartes's canons of clarity and deductive rigor. But, unlike Descartes, he was above all a moralist, who based his doctrine of the true salvation of man, and of the nature of society, on a metaphysical scheme which showed man's place in nature.

The following extracts do not include anything of the moral psychology, which is the subject of Parts III and IV of the *Ethics,* or of the picture of the free man, which is the subject of Part V. These extracts present only the main outlines of Spinoza's metaphysical system, which in the *Ethics* was set out in geometrical order, partly to achieve the greatest rigor and clarity that the subject admits, partly in order to achieve impersonality and detachment. In fact the argument does not, and indeed could not, follow a strictly deductive pattern, in which each step can be justified by reference to the previous proposition. Spinoza argues that there can be only a single substance, God or Nature, which necessarily exists and is the cause of itself; all other things or aspects of reality must be explained as attributes or modes of this single substance. There cannot be a Creator who is distinct from his creation; God or Nature must be eternally self-creating. Nor can there be any ultimate distinction between two substances, or quasi-substances, Mind and Matter (or Extension), as Descartes had supposed; thought and the system of things in space are only two aspects of the single reality, and are at every point inseparable. All particular things, including human things, must be thought of as having their determined place in the system of causes in Nature. As we advance in knowledge of the true order of causes in Nature, we realize that nothing in the world could possibly be other than it is. Spinoza was an uncompromising determinist, and he represented every human choice, attitude, or feeling as the necessary effect of causes in the infinite chain of causes. A man is no less a part of Nature than any other natural object, and his actions and reactions are to be studied and improved in a spirit of scientific detachment; most ordinary moral condemnation and exhortation is a mark of ignorance, and of not understanding the causes of human passions and actions. It was this determinism in the sphere of morality and human choice that seemed subversive to Spinoza's contemporaries, together with his identification of God with Nature.

Spinoza's argument in the *Ethics* turns on the notions of Cause and Substance and on the assumption that everything must have some rational explanation. In the order of explanation we must finally acknowledge something which is the cause of itself, the ultimate, terminating cause; but this substance can be nothing but God or Nature as a whole. In the development of this central notion there is much that is profoundly obscure, and one may read Spinoza's *Ethics* many times, as did his contemporaries, and still come back to some unsolved problems of interpretation. What is the relation of the two Infinite Attributes of Thought and Extension to each other? Why is God or Nature conceived by us under just these two Attributes? In what sense is everything in Nature to some degree animated? Is the existence and nature of the various finite modes, which are particular things, somehow deducible from the universal features of Nature, or is deduction confined to the eternal modes of Nature? What is the place allowed to experiment in natural knowledge? These are but a few of the many questions which a Spinozist must answer. But at least the outlines of this truly systematic philosophy are plain, and its vision of a complete knowledge of the necessary scheme of the natural order, infinite, eternal and self-creating, in which man can be free by understanding the true order of nature and so detaching himself from his transitory interests. Physics and medicine, including psychology, are the useful sciences, and all problems are soluble by the use of reason, which is the true happiness of man. In the *Tractatus Theologico-Politicus* he applied his metaphysical principles to the interpretation of religious belief and the problems of politics. He showed how the free man, who is a genuine philosopher, would behave as a citizen and in relation to the established church. And he advocated tolerance and liberalism as the necessary condition of any individual enlightenment.

Spinoza's main concern was with his moral philosophy; but he sought to demonstrate it as following directly from certain metaphysical views. It is with the latter that these extracts are concerned; they are drawn from Books I and II of the *Ethics*, which contain, in germ, the metaphysical view of the world from which Spinoza's doctrine of human bondage and of human freedom follow. These comments will mention only a few of his leading notions.

Spinoza's philosophy is in many ways the opposite of Leibniz's. Both are concerned with the notion of substance, but whereas Leibniz considers that there must be numberless substances, all different, Spinoza holds that there can be only one. Leibniz's God is the Creator of his substances; Spinoza's God is identical with the One Substance. Leibniz's God is a free agent who chooses between possibilities with a view to bringing about the best of all possible worlds; Spinoza denies that God can possess a Will, and considers the idea that all works for the best in human terms to be a vulgar superstition. Leibniz is not primarily concerned with the end of human action; he seeks to explain the nature of the universe, and merely finds free will of the traditional pattern which man enjoys. Spinoza allows no such freedom. His concern is with the struggle of the virtuous man to make himself free, by gaining an understanding of the nature and the origins of the passions from which he suffers. By arriving at knowledge of a higher order, a man can make himself free; for, as he gains knowledge, the passive ideas — the emotions — turn themselves into an active interest in eternal truths. All passionate interests in particular things are, for Spinoza, ultimately only a kind of misunderstanding: the failure to see the world as a whole and to grasp the essential connection of its internal necessities.

In Book I of the *Ethics* Spinoza sets up the structure of this world. He starts his definitions with the concept of something that is the cause of itself, with substance and with God. God is defined as a Being absolutely infinite, a substance of infinite attributes. Substance is defined as that the conception of which does not depend for its formation on anything else. This means that in replying to the question "What is it?", one does not need to mention any other being. Spinoza considers that the explanation of anything involves mentioning its cause, that which makes it what it is. Accordingly "the cause of itself" is defined as that whose essence involves existence. As the explanation of the existence of anything involves reference to its cause, the explanation of the existence of something which is cause of itself involves reference only to itself—i.e. its essence involves existence or, when one realizes what it is, one must realize that it exists.

These three concepts, God, Substance and Cause of Itself, are now shown to be identical. The substance and that which is cause of itself are seen to be identical in virtue of their definitions and of Axioms 1 to 4. If the explanation of substance does not involve reference to anything else, and the explanation of everything else does involve such a reference, except in the case of that which is cause of itself, evidently substance must be cause of itself. Substance is shown to be identical with God by means of Proposition 8 —"all substance is infinite, i.e., has infinite attributes" (Propositions 9 and 10, note), and Proposition 7, which asserts the identity of substance with that which is cause of itself and draws the conclusion that the substance necessarily exists. Hence substance is a necessary existent with infinite attributes, i.e., God. There can be only one such substance (Proposition 14). This follows in turn from Proposition 5, which shows that there cannot be two or more substances with the same attribute, together with the consideration that the ultimate explanation of everything, provided by the existence of God, rests on His attributes.

Spinoza distinguishes the attributes of God from the affections or modes of these attributes. God has, as we have seen, infinite attributes, and this includes the idea that He has an infinite number of attributes. But the human mind actually conceives God under only two attributes, Thought and Extension; that is, all our explanations of anything must come back to the single substance conceived either as a Thinking Thing or as an Extended Thing. Here Spinoza is in opposition to Descartes, who considered that there were two sorts of substance, thinking and extended substance. In Spinoza's system God comes to be *equated* with Nature, as the totality of things, each of which is to be understood as a modification of one of the two attributes of substance. God or Nature is eternal and self-creating.

Having given a priori proof of the existence of God, Spinoza gives also an a posteriori proof, which he considers independent. This proof has some similarities to Leibniz's argument in *The Ultimate Origin of Things,* from which an extract is given in Chapter VII. Here the argument is that any explanation of anything depends on stating its cause; so either there is an infinite regress of explanations, and therefore nothing is adequately explained at all, or there is a necessary Being, unless nothing exists at all. But evidently we exist, and some explanations are adequate, so there must be a necessary Being.

The core of this whole argument is that the universe, in order to be intelligible, must be conceived as a whole, and, as such, must be eternal, infinite, a single self-explaining system.

[Part I. *Concerning God: Definitions*

I. I understand that to be a Cause of Itself [*causa sui*] whose essence involves existence and whose nature cannot be conceived unless existing.

II. That thing is said to be Finite in Its Kind [*in suo genere finita*] which can be limited by another thing of the same kind. E.g., a body is said to be finite because we can conceive another larger than it. Thus a thought is limited by another thought. But a body cannot be limited by a thought, nor a thought by a body.

III. I understand Substance to be that which is in itself and is conceived through itself: I mean that, the conception of which does not depend on the conception of another thing from which it must be formed.

IV. An Attribute I understand to be that which the intellect perceives as constituting the essence of a substance.

V. By Mode I understand the Affections [*affectiones*] of a substance, or that which is in something else through which it may be conceived.

VI. God I understand to be a being absolutely infinite, that is, a substance consisting of infinite attributes, each of which expresses eternal and infinite essence.

Explanation. I say absolutely infinite, but not in its own kind. For, of whatever is infinite only in its own kind, we may deny an infinity of attributes, but to the essence of that which is absolutely infinite pertains everything that expresses essence and involves no denial.

VII. A thing is said to be Free which exists by the mere necessity of its own nature and is determined to act by itself alone. A thing is said to be Necessary, or rather Compelled, when it is determined to exist and to produce its effects by something else on a fixed and determined principle.

VIII. I understand Eternity to be existence itself, in so far as it is conceived to follow necessarily from the mere definition of an eternal thing.

Explanation. For such existence is conceived, like the essence of the thing, as an eternal truth; and therefore cannot be explained by duration or time, even if the duration is conceived as without beginning and end.

Axioms

I. All things, which are, are in themselves or in another thing.

II. That which cannot be conceived through another thing must be conceived through itself.

III. From a given determined cause an effect follows of necessity, and on the other hand, if no determined cause is granted, it is impossible that an effect should follow.

IV. The knowledge of effect depends on the knowledge of cause, and involves that knowledge.

V. Of two things that have nothing in common with each other, neither can be comprehended through the other.

VI. A true idea should agree with that of which it is the idea [*ideatum*].

VII. The essence of that which can be conceived as not existing does not involve existence.

Propositions

I. A substance is prior in its nature to its affections.

II. Two substances having different attributes have nothing in common with each other.

Proof. This is obvious from Def. 3. For each of them must be in itself and be conceived through itself; or, the conception of one of them does not involve the conception of the other.

III. Of two things having nothing in common with each other, one cannot be the cause of the other.

Proof. If they have nothing in common with each other, then (Ax. 5) they cannot be known through each other, and therefore (Ax. 4) one cannot be the cause of the other. Q.E.D.

IV. Two or more distinct things are distinguished one from the other by the difference of the attributes of the substance, or by the difference of their affections.

Proof. All things that are, are either in themselves or in other things (Ax. 1), that is (Defs. 3 and 5), outside the intellect, there is nothing save substances and their affections. Therefore there is nothing outside the intellect through which several things may be distinguished one from the other except substances, or, what is the same thing (Ax. 4), their attributes or affections. Q.E.D.

V. There cannot be in nature two or more substances having the same nature or attribute.

Proof. If several distinct substances were given, they would have to be distinguished one from another by the difference either of their attributes or of their affections. If they were to be distinguished just by the differences of their attributes, it would follow that there could not be granted two or more having the same attribute. Suppose, on the other hand, that they were to be distinguished by the difference of their affections; since a substance is prior in its nature to its affections, we may leave the affections outside, and consider the substance in itself, that is (Def. 3, Ax. 6), consider it truly; and then we could not conceive of it as distinct from another, that is (prev. Prop.) there could not be more than one substance possessing the same attributes. Q.E.D.

VI. One substance cannot be produced by another.

Proof. There cannot be in nature two substances with the same attribute (prev. Prop.), that is (Prop. 2), which have anything in common, and accordingly (Prop. 3) neither of them can be the cause of the other, or one cannot be produced by the other. Q.E.D.

Corollary. Hence it follows that a substance cannot be produced by anything else. For in the nature of things there is nothing save substances and their affections, as is obvious from Ax. 1 and Defs. 3 and 5; and substance cannot be produced by another substance (prev. Prop.). Therefore there is no way at all in which a substance could be produced by anything else. Q.E.D.

VII. Existence pertains to the nature of substance.

Proof. A substance cannot be produced by anything else (prev. Prop. Coroll.): it will therefore be its own cause, that is (Def. 1.), its essence necessarily involves existence, or existence pertains to its nature. Q.E.D.

VIII. All substance is necessarily infinite.

Proof. There can only be one substance that has any given attribute (Prop. 5) and it pertains to the nature of that substance that it should exist (Prop. 7). It must therefore exist either as finite or as infinite. But not as finite. For (Def. 2), it would then be limited by some other substance of the same nature, which would also necessarily have to exist (Prop. 7): and then two substances would be granted having the same attribute, which is absurd (Prop. 5). It exists, therefore, infinitely. Q.E.D.

Note 1. As to call anything finite is, really, in part, a denial, and to call it infinite is the absolute assertion of the existence of its nature, it follows therefore (from Prop. 7 alone) that all substance must be infinite.

Note 2. I do not doubt that to all those who are confused in their judgments about things, and are not accus-

tomed to know them by their first causes, it may be difficult to conceive the proof of the seventh Proposition; because, in fact, they do not distinguish between the modifications of substances and substances themselves, and do
not know how things are produced. The result is that
they ascribe to substances the origins that they see possessed
by things in nature. For those who do not know the real
causes of things confuse everything, and without the least
mental repugnance imagine trees speaking like men, and
that men can be conceived as made from stones as well
as from human seed, and imagine any form to be changed
into any other one likes. So also those who confuse divine
with human nature easily attribute human effects to God,
more especially while they do not know how effects are
produced in the mind. But if men would give heed to the
nature of substance they would not doubt at all the truth
of Prop. 7; rather everyone would consider it an axiom,
and it would take its place among common notions. For
by substance they would understand that which is in itself,
and is conceived through itself, or rather that the knowledge
of which does not depend on the knowledge of any other
thing; but by modification, that which is in something else,
and that the conception of which is formed from the conception of whatever it is in. Therefore we may have true
ideas of modifications which do not exist; since, although
they do not really exist outside the mind, yet their essence
is contained in something else in such a way that they may
be conceived through that thing. The truth of substances
does not exist outside the mind; they are conceived in themselves, because through themselves. If anyone should say,
then, that he has a clear and distinct, that is a true, idea
of substance, and should nevertheless doubt whether such
substance existed, he would indeed be like one who should
say that he has a true idea and yet should doubt whether it
were false (as will be manifest to anyone who pays a little
attention); or if anyone should say that substance was created, he would state at the same time that a false idea might
be made true; and it is difficult to conceive anything more
absurd than this. And therefore it must necessarily be acknowledged that the existence of substance, like its essence,

is an eternal truth. And hence we may conclude, in another manner, that there cannot be two substances of the same nature: which it is now perhaps worth while to show. But let me arrange this in its proper order. Therefore note (1) the true definition of each thing involves nothing, and expresses nothing, but the nature of the thing defined. From which it follows (2) that clearly no definition involves any certain number of individuals, nor expresses it, since the definition expresses nothing else than the nature of the thing defined. E.g., the definition of a triangle expresses nothing else than the simple nature of a triangle, but not a certain number of triangles. Let it be noted again, (3), that for each existing thing there is a cause by reason of which it exists. Note, moreover, that the cause by reason of which a thing exists should either be contained in the very nature and definition of the existing thing (simply because it pertains to its nature to exist), or should be given outside it. It follows from these positions that, if a certain number of individuals exist in nature, a cause must necessarily be given why those individuals, and not more or less, exist. E.g., if in nature twenty men were to exist (whom, for the sake of clarity, I will suppose to exist at the same time, and that none existed before them), it would not be enough, when giving a reason of why twenty men existed, to show the cause of human nature in general; it would first be necessary to show the cause why not more nor less than twenty existed: since (Note 3) a reason or cause should be given why each one existed. But this cause cannot be contained in human nature itself (Notes 2 and 3), since the true definition of man does not involve the number twenty. Hence (Note 4) the reason why these twenty men exist, and consequently why each one of them exists, must necessarily be given outside each one of them: and therefore we must conclude generally that whenever it is possible for several individuals of the same nature to exist, there must be an external cause for them in fact to exist. Since, as has been shown already in this Note, existence pertains to the nature of substance, its definition must of necessity involve existence, and therefore from its mere definition its existence can be concluded. But since in

Notes 2 and 3 we have shown that from its definition the existence of several substances cannot follow, it follows necessarily therefore that two or more substances cannot have the same nature; as was asserted.

IX. The more reality or being a thing has, the more attributes belong to it.

X. Each attribute of one substance must be conceived through itself.

Proof. An attribute is that which the intellect perceives of a substance as constituting its essence (Def. 4), therefore (Def. 3) it must be conceived through itself. Q.E.D.

Note. Hence it appears that even though two attributes are conceived as really distinct, that is, one is conceived without the aid of the other, we cannot thence conclude that they form two entities or two different substances. For it follows from the nature of a substance that each of its attributes can be conceived through itself: for all the attributes it ever had were always in it at the same time, nor could one of them be produced from another, but each of them expresses the reality or being of the substance. Therefore it is far from being absurd to attribute several attributes to one substance; since nothing is more clear than that each entity should be conceived under some attribute, and the more reality or being it has, the more attributes expressing necessity, or eternity and infinity, belong to it; and also nothing can be clearer than that an entity must be defined as absolutely infinite (as we defined it in Def. 6), which consists of infinite attributes, each of which expresses a certain eternal and infinite essence. But if anyone asks by what sign we shall be able to know the difference of substances, let him read the following Propositions, which will show that in the nature of things only one substance exists, and that it is absolutely infinite; therefore he will ask for that sign in vain.

XI. God, or a substance consisting of infinite attributes, each of which expresses eternal and infinite essence, necessarily exists.

Proof. If you deny it, conceive, if it be possible, that God does not exist. Then (Ax. 7) his essence does not involve existence. But this (Prop. 7) is absurd. Therefore God necessarily exists. Q.E.D.

Another Proof. A cause or reason ought to be assigned for each thing, why it exists or why it does not. E.g., if a triangle exists, there must be a reason or cause for its existence; but if it does not exist, there must be a reason or cause which prevents it from existing or which takes its existence from it. Now this reason or cause must be contained in the nature of the thing, or outside it. E.g., the reason why a square circle does not exist is shown by its nature, just because it involves a contradiction. On the other hand, the existence of substance follows from its nature alone, for that involves existence (*vide* Prop. 7). But the reason why a circle or triangle exists, or why it does not exist, does not follow from their nature, but from the order of universal corporeal nature; for it is from this that it must follow either that a triangle necessarily exists or that it is impossible that it can now exist. But this is in itself obvious. From which it follows that that must of necessity exist concerning which there is no reason or cause which could prevent its existence. If, thus, there is no reason or cause which could prevent the existence of God, or take his existence from him, it must certainly be concluded that he does exist of necessity. But if there is such a reason or cause, it must be either in the nature of God or outside it, that is, in another substance or another nature. For if the reasons lay in another substance of the same nature, the existence of God would be by this very fact admitted. But the substance of another nature has nothing in common with God (Prop. 2), and therefore can neither give him existence nor take it from him. And since the reason or cause which would take existence from God cannot be outside divine nature, i.e., the nature of God, it must of necessity lie, if indeed God does not exist, in his own nature, and this would involve a contradiction. But to assert this of a being absolutely infinite and perfect in all things is absurd: therefore neither within God nor without him is there any cause or reason that could take his existence from him, and consequently God must necessarily exist. Q.E.D.

Another Proof. Inability to exist is want of power, and, on the other hand, ability to exist is power (as is self-evident). And if that which now necessarily exists consists only of finite things, then finite things are more powerful than an absolutely infinite being; and this, as is self-evident, is absurd. Therefore, either nothing exists, or an absolutely infinite being necessarily exists. But we exist, either in ourselves or in something else that necessarily exists (*vide* Ax. 1 and Prop. 7). Therefore a being absolutely infinite, that is (Def. 6) God, necessarily exists. Q.E.D.

Note. In this last proof I wished to show the existence of God a posteriori, so that it might the more easily be understood, and not because the existence of God does not follow a priori from the same grounds. For since ability to exist is power, it follows that the more reality belongs to the nature of anything, the more power it will have to exist; and accordingly a being absolutely infinite, or God, has an absolutely infinite power of existence from itself, and on that account absolutely exists. Many, however, perhaps will not be able to see the force of this proof easily, because they are accustomed to consider those things which flow from external causes, and of these, those which are quickly made, that is, which exist easily, they see perish easily; and on the other hand, they judge those things to be harder to make, i.e., not existing so easily, to which they find more attributes belong. But, in truth, to deliver them from these prejudices, I need not show here in what manner or by what reason this statement "that which is quickly made perishes speedily" is true; or even, in considering the whole of nature, whether all things are equally difficult or not; but it suffices to note that I do not speak here of things which are made from external causes, but of substances alone which cannot be produced from any external cause. For those things which are made from external causes, whether they consist of many parts or few, whatever perfection or reality they have is only there by reason of their external cause; and therefore their existence arises merely from the perfection of some external cause and not from their own. On the other hand, whatever perfection a substance may have is due to no external cause: therefore its existence must follow from its nature alone, which is nothing else than its essence. Perfection, then, does not take existence from a thing, but, on the contrary, gives it existence; but imperfection, on the other hand, takes it away; and so we cannot be more certain of the existence of anything than of the existence of a being absolutely infinite or perfect, that is, God. Since his essence excludes all imperfection, and involves absolute perfection, by that very fact it removes all cause of doubt concerning his existence and makes it most certain; which will be manifest, I think, to such as pay a little attention.

XII. No attribute of a substance can be truly conceived, from which it would follow that substance can be divided into parts.

XIII. Substance absolutely infinite is indivisible.

XIV. Except God, no substance can be granted or conceived.

Corollary 1. Hence it distinctly follows that God is one and unique, that is (Def. 6), there is in nature only one substance, and that it is absolutely infinite, as we intimated in the *Note* of Prop. 10.

Corollary 2. It follows, in the second place, that extension and thought are either attributes of God or affections of attributes of God. . . .

XVII. God acts merely according to his own laws, and is compelled by no one.

Corollary 1. Hence it follows that there is no cause, either within God or outside of him, that can incite him to act, except the perfection of his own nature.

Corollary 2. Hence it follows that God alone is a free cause. For God alone exists from the mere necessity of his own nature. (Prop. 11 and Coroll. 1, Prop. 14), and by the mere necessity of his nature, he acts (prev. Prop.). And therefore (Def. 7) he is the only free cause. Q.E.D.

Note. Others think that God is a free cause because they think he can bring it to pass that those things which we say follow from his nature, that is, which are in his power, should not come about, or that they should not be produced by him. But this is the same as if they said that God can

bring it to pass that it should not follow from the nature
of a triangle that its three angles are equal to two right
angles, or that from a given cause no effect should follow,
which is absurd. Further on, without the aid of this proposition, I shall show that intellect and will do not apper-
tain to the nature of God. I am well aware that there are
many who say they can show that the greatest intellect
and free will belong to the nature of God: for they say
they know nothing more perfect to attribute to God than
that which amongst us is the greatest perfection. Further,
although they conceive God as possessing in fact the highest intellect, yet they do not believe that he can, in fact,
bring about the existence of anything which is in his intellect: for they think they would thus destroy the power
of God. They say that if he had created everything that
is in his intellect, he would then not be able to create anything more, which they think opposed to the omnipotence
of God; and accordingly they prefer to consider God as
indifferent to all things, and as creating nothing except
what he determines to create by a certain absolute will.
But I think I have sufficiently shown (*vide* Prop. 16) that
from God's supreme power or infinite nature, infinite things
in infinite modes, that is all things, have necessarily flowed,
or always follow by the same necessity; in the same manner
as from the nature of a triangle it always has followed, and
always will follow, that its three angles should be equal to
two right angles. Wherefore God's omnipotence was actual
from eternity, and will remain in the same state of actuality
through all eternity. And in this manner, in my opinion,
the perfection of God's omnipotence is asserted to be far
greater. On the other hand, the opponents of God seem
to deny (to speak freely) his omnipotence. For they are
obliged to confess that God's intellect perceives many
things that could be created which nevertheless he cannot
ever create. For, in other words, if he created all that his
intellect perceived, he would, according to them, exhaust
his omnipotence and render himself imperfect. As, therefore, they say that God is perfect, they are reduced to
state at the same time that he cannot complete all those
things to which his power extends; and anything more

absurd than this, or more opposed to the omnipotence of God, I cannot imagine could be conceived. Moreover (as I would like to say something concerning the intellect and will which we commonly attribute to God), if intellect and will pertain to the eternal essence of God, something far else must be understood by these two attributes than what is commonly understood by men. For the intellect and will that would constitute the essence of God must differ *toto coelo* from our will and intellect, nor can they agree in anything save name, any more than the dog, as a heavenly body, and the dog, as a barking animal, agree. This I shall show in the following manner. If intellect pertains to divine nature, it cannot, as with our intellect, be posterior (as many suppose) or even simultaneous in nature with the things conceived by the intellect, since (Coroll. 1, Prop. 16) God is prior in cause to all things; but on the other hand, truth and the formal essence of things is as it is, because it so exists objectively in God's intellect. Wherefore the intellect of God, as far as it can be conceived as forming his essence, is in truth the cause of things, both of their essence and their existence: which seems to have been noticed by those who have asserted that God's intellect, will, and power are one and the same thing. Now as God's intellect is the only cause of things, i.e., the cause both of their essence and of their existence, it must therefore necessarily differ from them in respect to its essence and in respect to its existence. For that which is caused differs from its cause precisely in that which it has from its cause. For example, a man is the cause of the existence but not the cause of the essence of another man (for the latter is an eternal truth) and so they can certainly agree in essence, but in existence they must differ, and on that account if the existence of one of them perish, that of the other does not consequently perish; but if the essence of one of them could be destroyed or be made false, the essence of the other must also be destroyed. On this account a thing that is the cause of the essence and existence of any effect must differ from that effect both in respect to its essence and in respect to its existence. Now the intellect of God is the cause of the essence and existence of our intellect: and therefore God's intellect, in so far as it can be conceived to form part of his essence, differs from our intellect both in respect to its essence and in respect to its existence, nor in any other thing save name can agree with it, which we wished to prove. And the argument concerning will would proceed in the same manner, as can easily be seen.

XVIII. God is the immanent and not the transient cause of all things.

XIX. God is eternal. That is, all his attributes are eternal.

XX. God's existence and his essence are one and the same thing.

Corollary 1. Hence it follows that the existence of God, like his essence, is an eternal truth. . . .

XXI. All things which follow from the absolute nature of any attribute of God must exist forever and infinitely, that is, as eternal and infinite.

XXII. Whatever follows from an attribute of God, in so far as it is modified by such a modification as exists of necessity and infinitely through the same attributes, must also exist of necessity and infinitely.

XXIII. Every mode which of necessity and infinitely exists must of necessity follow either from the absolute nature of some attribute of God, or from some attribute modified by a modification which exists of necessity and infinitely.

XXIV. The essence of things produced by God does not involve existence.

Corollary. Hence it follows that God is not only the cause that all things begin to exist, but also that they continue to exist, or (to use a scholastic term) God is the cause of the being [*causa essendi*] of things. For when we consider the essence of things, either existing or non-existing, we find it to involve neither existence nor duration; so their essence cannot be the cause either of their existence or their duration, but only God, to whose nature alone existence appertains (Coroll. 1, Prop. 14).

XXV. God is not only the effecting cause of the existence of things, but also of their essence.

Corollary. Particular things are nothing else than affec-

tions of attributes of God, or modes by which attributes
of God are expressed in a certain and determined manner.
The proof of this is clear from Prop. 15 and Def. 5.

XXVI. A thing which is determined necessarily by God,
and a thing which is not determined by God cannot determine of itself to do anything.

XXVII. A thing which is determined by God for the
performing of anything cannot render itself undetermined.

Proof. This is obvious from the third axiom.

XXVIII. Every individual thing, or any thing that is
finite and has a determined existence, cannot exist nor be
determined for action unless it is determined for action
and existence by another cause which is also finite and has
a determined existence; and again, this cause also cannot
exist nor be determined for action unless it be determined
for existence and action by another cause which also is finite
and has a determined existence: and so on to infinity. . . .

Note. As certain things must have been produced immediately by God, namely those things which necessarily
follow from his absolute nature; those primary products
being the mediating causes of other things, which nevertheless cannot exist nor be conceived without God, it follows that God is the proximate cause of those things immediately produced by him, absolutely, not, as some would
have it, in his kind. For the effects of God cannot exist
or be conceived without their cause (Prop. 15, and Coroll.,
Prop. 24). It follows, again, that God cannot be said in
truth to be the remote cause of individual things unless we
would thus distinguish these from the things which are
immediately produced by God, or rather which follow from
his absolute nature. For we understand by a remote cause
one which is in no wise connected with its effect. But all
things which are, are in God, and so depend on God that
without him they can neither exist nor be conceived.

XXIX. In nature there is nothing contingent but all
things are determined by the necessity of divine nature to
exist and act in a certain way.

Note. Before proceeding, I would wish to explain, or
rather to remind you, what we must understand by active
and passive nature [*natura naturans* and *natura naturata*],

for I think that from the past propositions it is agreed that by active nature we must understand that which is in itself and is conceived through itself, or such attributes of substance as express eternal and infinite essence, that is (Coroll. 1, Prop. 14, and Coroll. 2, Prop. 17), God, in so far as he is considered as a free cause. But by nature passive I understand all that follows from the necessity of the nature of God, or of any one of his attributes, that is, all the modes of the attributes of God, in so far as they are considered as things which are in God, and which cannot exist or be conceived without God.

XXX. Intellect, finite or infinite in actuality [*actus*], must comprehend the attributes of God and the affections of God and nothing else.

XXXI. The intellect in actuality, whether it be finite or infinite, together with will, desire, love, etc., must be referred not to active, but passive nature.

XXXII. Will can only be called a necessary cause, not a free one.

Corollary 1. Hence it follows that God does not act from freedom of will.

XXXIII. Things could not have been produced by God in any other manner or order than that in which they were produced.

Note 1. Although I have shown more clearly than the sun at noonday that there is absolutely nothing in things in virtue of which we can call them contingent, yet I would wish to explain here in a few words what is the signification of contingent; but first that of necessary and impossible. A thing is said to be necessary either by reason of its essence or its cause. For the existence of a thing necessarily follows either from its very essence or definition, or from a given effecting cause. A thing is said to be impossible for similar reasons: either because its essence or definition involves a contradiction, or because there is no external cause determined for the production of such a thing. But a thing cannot be called contingent save in respect to the imperfection of our knowledge. For when we are not aware that the essence of a thing involves a contradiction, or when we are quite certain that it does not involve a contradiction, and yet can affirm nothing with certainty concerning its existence, as the order of causes is hidden from us, such a thing can seem neither necessary or impossible to us: and therefore we call it either contingent or possible.

Note 2. It clearly follows from the preceding remarks that things were produced in consummate perfection by God, since they followed necessarily from an existing most perfect nature. Nor does this argue any imperfection in God, for his perfection has forced us to assert this. And from the contrary of this proposition it would have followed (as I have just shown) that God was not consummately perfect, inasmuch as if things were produced in any other way there must have been attributed to God a nature different to that which we are forced to attribute to him from the consideration of a perfect being. I make no doubt, however, that many will dismiss this opinion as absurd, nor will they agree to give up their minds to the contemplation of it and on no other account than that they are wont to ascribe to God a freedom far different to that which has been propounded by us (Def. 6). They attribute to him absolute will. Yet I make no doubt but that, if they would rightly consider the matter and follow our series of propositions, weighing well each of them, they would reject that freedom which they now attribute to God, not only as futile, but also clearly as an obstacle to knowledge. Nor is there any need for me here to repeat what was said in the note on Prop. 17. But for their benefit I shall show this much, that although it be conceded that will appertains to the essence of God, yet it nevertheless follows that things could not have been created in any other manner or order than that in which they were created; and this will be easy to show if first we consider the very thing which they themselves grant, namely, that it depends solely on the decree and will of God that each thing is what it is, for otherwise God would not be the cause of all things. They grant further that all the decrees of God have been appointed by him through and from all eternity: for otherwise it would argue mutability and imperfection in God. But as in eternity there are no such things as when, before, or after, it follows merely from the perfection of God that he never can or could decree anything else than what is decreed, that is, that God did not exist before his decrees, nor could exist without them. But they say that even if we suppose that God had made nature different or had decreed otherwise concerning nature and her order from all eternity, it would not thence follow that God was imperfect. Now if they say this, they must also admit that God can change his decrees. For had God decreed otherwise than he has concerning nature and her order, that is, had he willed and conceived anything else concerning nature, he would necessarily have had some other intellect and will than those which he now has. And if it is permitted to attribute to God another will and intellect than those which he now has, without any change in his essence or perfection, why should he not be able, even as it is, to change his decrees concerning things created, and yet remain perfect? For his intellect and will concerning things created and their order is the same in respect to his essence and perfection, however his intellect and will may be conceived. Furthermore, all the philosophers I have seen concede that there is no such thing as potential intellect in God, but only actual. But as they make no distinction between his intellect and will and his essence, being all agreed in this, it follows then that if God had another actual intellect and will, he must necessarily also have another essence; and thence, as I concluded in the beginning, that, were things produced in any other way than that in which they now exist, God's intellect and will, that is, as has been granted, his essence, also must have been other than they are, which is absurd.

Now since things could not have been produced in any other manner or order than that in which they were produced, and since this follows from the consummate perfection of God, there is no rational argument to persuade us to believe that God did not wish to create all the things which are in his intellect, in the same perfection as that in which his intellect conceived them. But they will say that in things there is no such thing as perfection or imperfection, but that which causes us to call a thing perfect or imperfect, good or bad, depends solely on the will of God; and so, if

God had willed it, he could have brought to pass that what
is now perfection might have been the greatest imperfection,
and vice versa. But what else is this than openly to assert
that God, who necessarily understands what he wishes,
could bring to pass by his own will that he should understand things in a manner different from that in which he understands them? This (as I have just shown) is the height of
absurdity. Wherefore I can turn their argument against
them in the following manner. All things depend on the
power of God. That things should be different from what
they are would involve a change in the will of God, and the
will of God cannot change (as we have most clearly shown
from the perfection of God): therefore things could not be
otherwise than as they are. I confess that the theory which
subjects all things to the will of an indifferent God, and
makes them dependent on his good will, is not so far from
the truth as that which states that God acts in all things
for the furthering of good. For these seem to place something beyond God which does not depend on God, and to
which God looks in his actions as to an example, or strives
after as an ultimate end. Now this is nothing else than subjecting God to fate, a greater absurdity than which it is
difficult to assert of God, whom we have shown to be the
first and only free cause of the essence of all things and
their existence. Wherefore let me not waste more time in
refuting such idle arguments.

XXXIV. The power of God is the same as his essence.

XXXV. Whatever we conceive to be in the power of
God necessarily exists.

XXXVI. Nothing exists from whose nature some effect
does not follow.

Appendix

In these propositions I have explained the nature and
properties of God: that he necessarily exists: that he is
one alone: that he exists and acts merely from the necessity of his nature: that he is the free cause of all things and
in what manner: that all things are in God, and so depend
upon him that without him they could neither exist nor be

conceived: and, finally, that all things were predetermined by God, not through his free or good will, but through his absolute nature or infinite power. I have endeavoured, moreover, whenever occasion prompted, to remove prejudices which might impede the good understanding of my propositions. Yet, as many prejudices still remain, which, to a very large extent, have prevented and do prevent men from embracing the concatenation of things in the manner in which I have explained it, I have thought it worth while to call these up for the scrutiny of reason. Now since the prejudices that I am here undertaking to point out depend upon this one point, that men commonly suppose that all natural things act like themselves with an end in view, and since they assert with assurance that God directs all things to a certain end (for they say that God made all things for man, and man that he might worship God), I shall therefore consider this one thing first, inquiring in the first place why so many fall into this error, and why all are by nature so prone to embrace it; then I shall show its falsity, and finally, how these prejudices have arisen concerning good and evil, virtue and sin, praise and blame, order and confusion, beauty and ugliness, and other things of this kind. But this is not the place to deduce these things from the nature of the human mind. It will suffice here for me to take as a basis of argument what must be admitted by all: that is, that all men are born ignorant of the causes of things, and that all have a desire of acquiring what is useful; that they are conscious, moreover, of this. From these premises it follows then, in the first place, that men think themselves free inasmuch as they are conscious of their volitions and desires, and as they are ignorant of the causes by which they are led to wish and desire, they do not even dream of the existence of these causes. It follows, in the second place, that men do all things with an end in view, that is, for that which is profitable, which they seek. Whence it comes to pass that they always seek out only the final causes of what has happened, and when they have divined these, they cease, for clearly then they have no cause of further doubt. If they are unable to learn these causes from someone, nothing remains for them but to turn to themselves and reflect what could in-

duce them personally to bring about such a thing, and thus
they necessarily estimate other natures by their own. Furthermore, as they find in themselves and outside themselves
many things which aid them not a little in their quest of
things useful to themselves, as, for example, eyes for seeing, teeth for mastication, vegetables and animals for food,
the sun for giving light, the sea for breeding fish, they consider all natural things alike to be made for their use; and
as they know that they found these things as they were, and
did not make them themselves, they have cause for believing that some one else prepared these things for their
use. Now having considered things as means, they cannot
believe them to be self-created; but they must conclude
from the means which they are wont to prepare for themselves, that there is some governor or governors of nature,
endowed with human freedom, who take care of all things
for them and make all things for their use. They must naturally form an estimate of the nature of these governors
from their own, for they have no information about it: and
hence they come to say that the Gods direct all things for
the use of men, that men may be bound down to them and
do them the highest honour. Whence it has come about that
each individual has devised a different manner in his own
mind for the worship of God, that God may love him above
the rest and direct the whole of nature for the gratification
of his blind cupidity and insatiable avarice. Thus this prejudice became a superstition, and fixed its roots deeply in
the mind, and this was the reason why all diligently tried
to understand and explain the final causes of all things.
But while they have sought to show that nature does nothing in vain (that is, nothing which is not of use to man),
they appear to have shown nothing else than that nature and the Gods are as mad as men. Behold now, I
pray you, what this thing has become. Among so many
conveniences of nature they were bound to find some incon-
veniences—storms, earthquakes, and diseases, etc.—and they
said these happened by reason of the anger of the Gods
aroused against men through some misdeed or some omis-
sion in worship; and although experience daily belied this,
and showed with infinite examples that conveniences and

their contraries happen promiscuously to the pious and impious, yet not even then did they turn from their inveterate prejudice. For it was easier for them to place this among other unknown things whose use they did not know, and thus retain their present and innate condition of ignorance, than to destroy the whole fabric of their philosophy and reconstruct it. So it came to pass that they stated with the greatest certainty that the judgments of God far surpassed human comprehension: and this by itself was enough to keep truth hidden from the human race through all eternity, had not mathematics, which deals not in the final causes, but in the essence and properties of forms, offered to men another standard of truth. And besides mathematics there are other causes (which need not be enumerated here) which enabled men to take notice of these general prejudices and to be led to the true knowledge of things.

Thus I have explained what I undertook in the first place. It is scarcely necessary that I should show that nature has no fixed aim in view, and that all final causes are merely fabrications of men. For I think this is sufficiently clear from the bases and causes from which I have traced the origin of this prejudice, from Prop. 16, and the corollaries of Prop. 32, and, above all, from all those propositions in which I have shown that all things are produced by a certain eternal necessity of nature and with the utmost perfection. Here, however, I shall pause to overthrow entirely that foolish doctrine of a final cause. For that which in truth is a cause it considers as an effect, and vice versa, and so it makes that which is first by nature to be last, and again, that which is highest and most perfect it renders imperfect. As these two questions are obvious, let us pass them over. It follows from Props. 21, 22 and 23 that the effect which is produced immediately from God is the most perfect, and that one is more imperfect according as it requires more intermediating causes. But if those things which are immediately produced by God are made by him for the attaining of some end, then it necessarily follows that the ultimate things for whose sake these first were made must transcend all others. Hence this doctrine destroys the perfection of God: for if God seeks an end, he necessarily de-

sires something which he lacks. And although theologians
and metaphysicians make a distinction between the end of
want and that of assimilation, they confess that God acts
on his own account, and not for the sake of creating things:
for before the creation they can assign nothing save God
on whose account God acted, and so necessarily they are
obliged to confess that God lacked and desired those things
for the attainment of which he wished to prepare means,
as is clear of itself. Nor must I omit at this point that
some of the adherents of this doctrine, who have wished to
show their ingenuity in assigning final causes to things,
have discovered a new manner of argument for the proving
of their doctrine, to wit, not a reduction to the impossible,
but a reduction to ignorance, which shows that they have
no other mode of arguing their doctrine. For example, if
a stone falls from a roof on the head of a passer-by and
kills him, they will show by their method of argument that
the stone was sent to fall and kill the man; for if it had not
fallen on him by God's will, how could so many circumstances (for often very many circumstances concur at the
same time) concur by chance? You will reply, perhaps:
"That the wind was blowing, and that the man had to pass
that way, and hence it happened." But they will retort:
"Why was the wind blowing at that time? and why was the
man going that way at that time?" If again you reply: "That
the wind had then arisen on account of the agitation of the
sea the day before, and the previous weather had been
calm, and that the man was going that way at the invitation of a friend," they will again retort, for there is no end
to their questioning: "Why was the sea agitated, and why
was the man invited at that time?" And thus they will pursue you from cause to cause until you are glad to take refuge
in the will of God, that is, the asylum of ignorance. Thus
again, when they see the human body they are amazed,
and as they do not know the cause of so much art, they conclude that it was made not by mechanical art, but divine
or supernatural art, and constructed in such a manner that
one part may not injure another. And hence it comes about
that those who wish to seek out the causes of miracles, and
who wish to understand the things of nature as learned men,

and not stare at them in amazement like fools, are soon deemed heretical and impious, and proclaimed such by those whom the mob adore as the interpreters of nature and the Gods. For these know that once ignorance is laid aside, that wonderment, on which alone they rely in argument and for the preservation of their authority, would be taken away from them. But I now leave this point and proceed to what I determined to discuss in the third place.

As soon as men had persuaded themselves that all things which were made, were made for their sakes, they were bound to consider as the best quality in everything that which was the most useful to them, and to esteem that above all things which brought them the most good. Hence they must have formed these notions by which they explain the things of nature, to wit, good, evil, order, confusion, hot, cold, beauty, and ugliness, etc.; and as they deemed themselves free agents, the notions of praise and blame, sin and merit, arose. The latter notions I will discuss when I deal with human nature later on, but the former I shall briefly explain here. They call all that which is conducive to health and the worship of God good, and all which is conducive to the contrary, evil. And forasmuch as those who do not understand the things of nature are certain of nothing concerning these things, but only imagine them and mistake their imagination for intellect, they firmly believe there is order in things, and are ignorant of them and their own nature. Now when things are so disposed that, when they are represented to us through our senses, we can easily imagine and consequently easily remember them, we call them well-ordered; and on the other hand, when we cannot do so, we call them ill-ordered or confused. Now forasmuch as those things, above all others, are pleasing to us which we can easily imagine, men accordingly prefer order to confusion, as if order were anything in nature save in respect to our imagination; and they say that God has created all things in order, and thus unwittingly they attribute imagination to God, unless indeed they mean that God, providing for human imagination, disposed all things in such a manner as would be most easy for our imagination; nor would they then find it perhaps a stumbling-block to their theory that infinite things are found which are far beyond the reach of our imagination, and many which confuse it through its weakness. But of this I have said enough. The other notions also are nothing other than modes of imagining in which the imagination is affected in diverse manners, and yet they are considered by the ignorant as the chief attributes of things: for, as we have said, they think all things were made for them, and call the nature of a thing good or bad, healthy, or rotten and corrupt, according as they are affected by it. For example, if motion, which the nerves receive by means of the eyes from the objects before us, is conducive to health, those objects by which it is caused are called beautiful; if it is not, then the objects are called ugly. Such things as affect the nerves by means of the nose are thus styled fragrant or evil-smelling; or when by means of the mouth, sweet or bitter, tasty or insipid; when by means of touch, hard or soft, rough or smooth, etc. And such things as affect the ear are called noises, and form discord or harmony, the last of which has delighted men to madness, so that they have believed that harmony delights God. Nor have there been wanting philosophers who assert that the movements of the heavenly spheres make up a harmony. All of which sufficiently shows that each man judges concerning things according to the disposition of his own mind, or rather takes for things what are really affections of his imagination. Wherefore it is not remarkable (as we may incidentally remark) that so many controversies as we find have arisen among men, and at last Scepticism. For although human bodies agree in many points, yet in many others they differ, and that which seems to one good may yet to another seem evil; to one order, yet to another confusion; to one pleasing, yet to another displeasing, and so on, for I need not treat further of these, as this is not the place to discuss them in detail, and indeed they must be sufficiently obvious to all. For it is in every one's mouth: "As many minds as men," "Each is wise in his own manner," "As tastes differ, so do minds"—all of which proverbs show clearly enough that men judge things according to the disposition of their minds, and had rather imagine things than understand them. For if they understood things, my argument would convince them at least, just as mathematics does, although they might not attract them.

We have thus seen that all the arguments by which the vulgar are wont to explain nature are nothing else than modes of imagination, and indicate the nature of nothing whatever, but only the constitution of the imagination; and although they have names as if they were entities existing outside the imagination, I call them entities, not of reality, but of the imagination; and so all arguments directed against us from such notions can easily be rebutted. For many are wont to argue thus: If all things have followed from the necessity of the most perfect nature of God, whence have so many imperfections in nature arisen? For example, the corruption of things till they stink, the ugliness of things which often nauseate, confusion, evil, sin, etc. But as I have just said, these are easily confuted. For the perfection of things is estimated solely from their nature and power; nor are things more or less perfect according as they delight or disgust human senses, or according as they are useful or useless to men. But to those who ask, "Why did not God create all men in such a manner that they might be governed by reason alone?" I make no answer but this: because material was not wanting to him for the creating of all things from the highest grade to the lowest; or speaking more accurately, because the laws of his nature were so comprehensive as to suffice for the creation of everything that infinite intellect can conceive, as I have shown in Prop. 16. These are the misunderstandings which I stopped here to point out. If any grains of them still remain, they can be easily dispersed by means of a little reflection.]

IN BOOK II OF THE *Ethics* SPINOZA CONSIDERS THE NATURE of the human mind. His argument hinges on his concept of "an idea," inherited from Descartes, but adapted. Already in Axiom 6 of Book I, he had stated that an idea is true in so far as it agrees with that of which it is the idea. Here (Definition 4) he defines "adequate idea" as that which has all the *intrinsic* marks of a true idea. Spinoza pictures the progress of the human mind to higher levels of knowledge as a substitution of adequate ideas for inadequate ones. This progress each man can begin for himself, but, being a finite mode, he can never complete it. The ideal of knowledge is knowledge of self-evidently true ideas which represent the relation between essences, and he holds that there is no real knowledge which does not show itself as indubitable and self-evident. Below this level there are two stages: reasoning, or inference, and, below that, mere common opinion about matters of fact and imagination. These three levels he illustrates with an example in Proposition 40, Note 2. In an earlier work, *The Treatise on the Correction of the Understanding,* in a passage which is given at the end of these extracts, he distinguishes four levels, dividing the lowest level into two. Spinoza's use of "idea" and "object of an idea" is peculiar to himself and is the kernel of his argument.

The human mind itself is an idea, and its object is the human body. Here it must be remembered that thought and extension are only attributes under which the one substance is conceived. Thus, the same event can, for Spinoza, be considered as something happening both in the sphere of thought, to a person's mind, and to his body. The thoughts are inseparable from happenings in the body. This is not, however Leibniz's "pre-established Harmony" of Soul and Body, where two sets of events are happily made coincident by God; for Spinoza, they are the same event looked at from different aspects. In sense perception and ordinary experience, the mind has only confused and inadequate ideas, reflecting what happens in the body. Such ideas do not bear the internal marks of adequacy (Proposition 29 and Corollary). Our knowledge of individual existents outside us is only obtained through affections of the body by external objects, and it is for this reason that sense perception can give us only confused and inadequate ideas. These last points are the parallel within the theory of knowledge of Spinoza's metaphysical doctrine that the chain of causes of particular things can never be brought to a conclusion, and that therefore they can never be directly deduced from the nature of God or reality as a whole. (See also the extract from the *Correction of the Understanding.*)

But we are not confined to such inadequate ideas, which

are the products of the "imagination." We all necessarily possess also some knowledge of the second and third order, some reason and intuition of self-evident truths. This is how we are able to distinguish the true from the false; for we each possess a model of the truth, since we each know some necessary truths about the Universe as a whole. These are the common notions—e.g., that everything has a cause—on which all our reasoning is founded. The path from bondage to freedom can be followed by each one of us if he sets himself to build up on the foundation of common notions a view of the Universe as a whole, including his own place in it. It is the purpose of the *Ethics* to point the way to this path.

Here, in accordance with the design of this book, the extracts from Spinoza must be concluded. But it must never be forgotten that Spinoza's metaphysics is designed as a background for his *Ethics*. He has explained how the mind, in so far as it remains at the ordinary level of empirical knowledge, is passive and affected mainly by things outside itself. In the third book he applies this distinction between pure thought, which is active, and perception and ordinary opinion, which are passive, to the life of feeling. He gives a theory of the emotions which represents them as passive ideas reflecting modifications of the body produced by external objects. At the highest level of knowledge, where the mind moves solely among eternal truths, applicable to the universe as a whole, we are free from the influence of particular things around us. Spinoza denies free will in the common sense. But the mind can set itself free, nevertheless, by its own efforts, and, in enjoyment of pure thought, become for a time occupied with eternal truths. From such understanding happiness and freedom will result; not in the sense of a stoical resignation to fate, but in the sense that the mind is free from particular interests, and the emotions which these engender, and is interested only in the unchanging features of the universe. This constitutes the love of God and of Nature.

Spinoza's whole manner of argument in the *Ethics* is open to the criticism which Hume and Kant were to bring later. He seeks to deduce from the nature of things what must be the highest type of life. Hume and Kant have shown that such a procedure cannot be defended in logic. Other critics have remarked that his arguments are less rigorous than they are made to appear; for the geometrical method does not in fact provide a series of strictly deductive proofs, and it could not be expected to do so. He is a philosopher whom people have tended generally either to revere or to revile, in both cases commonly without understanding his intentions. But he did not expect either his own works, or the manner of life he advocated, to be easy. As he says in the note to the last proposition of the last book *"omnia praeclara tam difficilia quam rara sunt"* ("All excellent things are as difficult as they are rare"). He is not a mystic, but a rationalist who makes greater claims for the powers of pure reason than any other great philosopher has ever made.

〔 Part II. *Concerning the Nature and Origin of the Mind. Preface.*

I now pass on to explain such things as must follow from the essence of God or of a being eternal and infinite: not all of them indeed (for they must follow in infinite number and infinite ways, as we have shown in Part I, Prop. 16), but only such as can lead us by the hand (so to speak) to the knowledge of the human mind and its consummate blessedness.

Definitions

I. By Body [*corpus*] I understand that mode which expresses in a certain determined manner the essence of God in so far as he is considered as an extended thing (*vide* Part I, Prop. 25, Coroll.).

II. I say that appertains to the essence of a thing which, when granted, necessarily involves the granting of the thing, and which, when removed, necessarily involves the removal of the thing; or that without which the thing can neither exist nor be conceived, and which, conversely, can neither exist nor be conceived without the thing.

III. By Idea I understand a conception of the mind which the mind forms by reason of its being a thinking thing.

Explanation. I say conception rather than perception, for the word perception seems to indicate that the mind is passive in relation to the object, while conception seems to express an action of the mind.

IV. By an Adequate Idea I understand an idea which in so far as it is considered with respect to the object, has all the properties or intrinsic marks of a true idea.

Explanation. I say intrinsic in order to exclude what is extrinsic, i.e., the agreement between the idea and its object. (See Book I, Ax. 6.)

V. Duration is indefinite continuation of existing.

Explanation. I say indefinite, because it can in no wise be determined by means of the nature itself of an existing thing nor by the efficient cause, which necessarily imposes existence on a thing but does not take it away.

VI. Reality and Perfection I understand to be one and the same thing.

VII. By Individual Things I understand things which are finite and have a determined existence; but if several of them so concur in one action that they all are at the same time the cause of one effect, I consider them all thus far as one individual thing.

Axioms

I. The essence of man does not involve necessary existence, that is, in the order of nature it can as well happen that this or that man exists as that he does not exist.

II. Man thinks.

III. The modes of thinking, such as love, desire, or any other name by which the affections of the mind are designated, do not exist unless there is an idea in the same individual of the thing loved, desired, etc. But the idea can exist although no other mode of thinking exists.

IV. We feel that a certain body is affected in many ways.

V. We neither feel nor perceive any individual things save bodies and modes of thinking.

Propositions

I. Thought is an attribute of God, or God is a thinking thing.

II. Extension is an attribute of God, or God is an extended thing.

VII. The order and connection of ideas is the same as the order and connection of things.

XI. The first thing that constitutes the actual being of the human mind is nothing else than the idea of an individual thing actually existing.

XII. Whatever happens in the object of the idea constituting the human mind must be perceived by the human mind; in other words the idea of that thing must necessarily be found in the human mind: that is, if the object of the idea constituting the human mind be a body, nothing can happen in that body which is not perceived by the mind.

XIII. The object of the idea constituting the human mind is a body, or a certain mode of extension actually existing and nothing else.

Note. Hence we understand not only that the human mind is united to the body, but also what must be understood by the union of the mind and body. But in truth no one will be able to understand this adequately or distinctly unless, at first, he is sufficiently acquainted with the nature of our body. For those things which we have so far propounded have been altogether general, and have not referred more to man than to the other individual things which are all, though in various grades, animate [*animata*]. For of all things there must necessarily be granted an idea in God, of which idea God is the cause, just as he is of the idea of the human body; and so whatever we say concerning the idea of the human body must necessarily be said concerning the idea of any other thing. Nevertheless we cannot deny that, like objects, ideas differ one from another, one transcending the others and having more reality, according as the object of one idea transcends the object of another or contains more reality than it. And so for the sake of determining in what the human mind differs from other things, and in what it excels other things, we must know the nature of its object, as we have said, that is, the human body. What this nature is, I am unable to explain here, but that is not necessary for what I am going to show. This, however, I will say in general, that according as one body is more adapted than others for doing and suffering many things at the same time, so is one mind more adapted than others for perceiving many things at the same time: and the more the actions of a body depend solely on itself, and the fewer other bodies concur with its action, so the mind is more apt for distinct understanding. And thus we may recognise how one mind is superior to all others, and likewise see the cause why we have only a very confused knowledge of our body, and many other things which I shall deduce from these.

XXVI. The human mind perceives no external body as actually existing save through ideas of affections of its body.

XXVII. The ideas of the affections of the human body, in so far as they are referred to the human mind alone, are not clear and distinct but confused.

XXIX. The idea of the idea of each affection of the human mind does not involve an adequate knowledge of the human mind.

Corollary. Hence it follows that the human mind, whenever it perceives a thing in the common order of nature, has no adequate knowledge of itself, nor of its body, nor of external bodies, but only a confused and mutilated knowledge thereof. For the mind does not know itself save in so far as it perceives ideas of affections of the body (Prop. 23, Part II). But it does not perceive its body save through the ideas of affections, through which also it only perceives external bodies (Props. 23 and 26, Part II). And therefore in so far as it has these ideas, it has no adequate knowledge of itself (Prop. 29, Part II), nor of its body (Prop. 27, Part II), nor of external bodies (Prop. 25, Part II), but only (Prop. 28 and Note, Part II) a confused and mutilated one. Q.E.D.

Note. I say expressly that the mind has no adequate but only confused knowledge of itself, of its body, and of external bodies, when it perceives a thing in the common order of nature, that is, whenever it is determined externally, that is, by fortuitous circumstances, to contemplate this or that, and not when it is determined internally, that is, by the fact that it regards many things at once, to understand their agreements, differences, and oppositions one to another. For whenever it is disposed in this or any other way from within, then it regards things clearly and distinctly, as I shall show further on.

XXXI. We can only have a very inadequate knowledge about the duration of individual things outside us.

XXXV. Falsity consists in privation of knowledge which is involved by inadequate or mutilated and confused ideas.

XXXVI. Inadequate and confused ideas follow from the same necessity as adequate or clear and distinct ideas.

XXXVII. Those things which are common to everything, and which are equally in a part and in the whole, can only be conceived as adequate.

XXXIX. That which is common to, and a property of, the human body and certain external bodies by which the human body is affected, and which is equally in the part and whole of these, has an adequate idea in the mind. . . .

Note 2. From all that has been said above it is now clearly apparent that we perceive many things and form universal notions, first, from individual things represented to our intellect in a mutilated, confused, and random manner (Coroll., Prop. 29, Part II), and therefore I am wont to call such perceptions knowledge from vague or casual experience [*cognitio ab experientia vaga*]; second, from signs, e.g., from the fact that we remember certain things through having read or heard certain words and form certain ideas of them similar to those through which we imagine things (Note, Prop. 18, Part II). Both of these ways of regarding things I shall call hereafter knowledge of the first kind, opinion [*opinio*], or imagination [*imaginatio*]. Third, from the fact that we have common notions and adequate ideas of the properties of things (Coroll., Prop. 38, Coroll. and Prop. 39, and Prop. 40, Part II). And I shall call this reason [*ratio*] and knowledge of the second kind. Besides these two kinds of knowledge there is a third, as I shall show in what follows, which we call intuition [*scientia intuitiva*], Now this kind of knowing proceeds from an adequate idea of the formal essence of certain attributes of God to the adequate knowledge of the essence of things. I shall illustrate these three by one example. Let three numbers be given to find the fourth, which is in the same proportion to the third as the second is to the first. Tradesmen without hesitation multiply the second by the third and divide the product by the first: either because they have not forgotten the rule which they received from the schoolmaster without any proof, or because they have often found it with very small numbers, or by conviction of the proof of Prop. 19, Book VII, of Euclid's elements, namely, the common property of proportionals. But with very small numbers there is no need of this, for when the numbers 1, 2, 3, are given, who is there who could not see that the fourth proportional is 6? And this is much clearer because we conclude the fourth number from the same ratio which intuitively we see the first bears to the second.

XLI. Knowledge of the first kind is the only cause of falsity; knowledge of the second and third kinds is necessarily true.

XLII. Knowledge of the second and third kinds, and not of the first kind, teaches us to distinguish the true from the false.

XLIII. He who has a true idea, knows at that same time that he has a true idea, nor can he doubt concerning the truth of the thing.

XLIV. It is not the nature of reason to regard things as contingent, but as necessary.

Corollary 1. Hence it follows that it depends solely on the imagination that we consider things, whether in respect to the past or future, as contingent.

Corollary 2. It is the nature of reason to perceive things under a certain form of eternity [*sub quadam aeternitatis specie*].

XLV. Every idea of every body or individual thing actually existing necessarily involves the eternal and infinite essence of God.

XLVI. The knowledge of the eternal and infinite essence of God which each idea involves is adequate and perfect.

XLVII. The human mind has an adequate knowledge of the eternal and infinite essence of God.

XLVIII. There is in no mind absolute or free will, but the mind is determined for willing this or that by a cause which is determined in its turn by another cause, and this one again by another, and so on to infinity.

On the Correction of the Understanding

I may now turn my attention to what is the most important subject of all, namely, to the correction of the understanding and to the means of making it able to understand things in such a way as is necessary to the attainment of our end. To bring this about, the natural order we observe demands that I should recapitulate all the modes of perception which I have used thus far for the indubitable affirmation or negation of anything, so that I may choose the best of all, and at the same time begin to know my powers and nature which I wish to perfect.

19. If I remember rightly, they can all be reduced to four headings, namely ——

I. Perception which we have *by hearsay* or from some sign, which may be called to suit any one's taste.

II. Perception which we have *from vague experience,* that is, from experience which is not determined by the intellect, but is only so called because it happened by chance and we have no experienced fact to oppose to it, and so it remains unchallenged in our minds.

III. Perception *wherein the essence of one thing is concluded from the essence of another,* but not adequately: this happens when we infer a cause from some effect, or when it is concluded from some general notion that it is accompanied always by some property.

IV. Finally, perception *wherein a thing is perceived through its essence alone* or through a knowledge of its proximate cause.

20. All these I shall illustrate by examples. *By hearsay*

alone I know my birthday, and that certain people were my parents, and the like: things of which I have never had any doubt. *By vague experience* I know that I shall die; and I assert that inasmuch as I have seen men like me undergo death, although they did not all live for the same space of time, nor died of the same illness. Again, *by vague experience* I know also that oil is good for feeding a flame, that water is good for extinguishing it. I know also that a dog is a barking animal, and man a rational animal: and in this way I know nearly all things that are useful in life. 21. We conclude one thing *from another* in the following manner: After we have clearly perceived that we feel a certain body and no other, we thence conclude clearly that a soul or mind is united to that body, and that the union is the cause of that feeling; but what is this feeling and union we cannot absolutely understand from that. Or after I know the nature of vision, and that it has such a property that we see a thing smaller when at a great distance than when we look at it close, I can conclude that the sun is larger than it appears, and other similar things.

22. Finally, a thing is said to be perceived *through its essence alone* when from the fact that I know something, I know what it is to know anything, or from the fact that I know the essence of the mind, I know it to be united to the body. By the same knowledge we know that two and three make five, and that if there are two lines parallel to the same line they are parallel to each other, etc. But the things which I have been able to know by this knowledge so far have been very few.

23. In order that all these things may be better understood I shall employ just one example, namely this: Three numbers are given to find the fourth, which is to the third as the second is to the first. Tradesmen will say at once that they know what is to be done to find the fourth number, inasmuch as they have not yet forgotten the operation, which they learned without proof from their teachers. Others again, from experimenting with small numbers where the fourth number is quite manifest, as with 2, 4, 3, and 6, where it is found that by multiplying the second by the third and dividing the answer by the first number, the

quotient is six, have made it an axiom, and when they find
this number which, without that working out, they knew
to be the proportional, they thence conclude that this
process is good invariably for finding the fourth proportional.

24. But mathematicians, by conviction of the proof of
Prop. 19, Bk. VII, *Elements* of Euclid, know what numbers
are proportionals from the nature and property of proportion, namely, that the first and fourth multiplied together
are equal to the product of the second and third. But they
do not see the adequate proportionality of the given numbers; if they do, it is not on the strength of that proposition, but intuitively without any process of working out.

XIV. *Of the Means by which Eternal Things are known*

. . . We can see that it is above all things necessary to us that we should deduce all our ideas from physical things or from real entities, proceeding, as far as
possible, according to the series of causes from one real
entity to another, and in such a manner that we never pass
over to generalities and abstractions, either in order to
conclude anything real from them or to deduce them from
anything real; for either of these interrupts the true progress of the intellect.

100. But it must be noted that I do not understand here
by that series of causes and real entities a series of individual mutable things, but only the series of fixed and
eternal things. For it would be impossible for human weakness to follow up the series of individual mutable things,
both on account of their number exceeding all count, and
on account of the many circumstances in one and the same
thing of which each one may be the cause that it exists
or does not. For indeed their existence has no connection
with their essence, or (as I have said) it is not an eternal
truth.

101. However, there is no need that we should understand this series, for the essences of individual mutable
things are not to be drawn from the series or order of
existence, which would afford us nothing save their ex-

trinsic denominations, relations, or at the most their circumstances, which are far removed from the inmost essence of things. But this is only to be sought from fixed and eternal things, and from the laws inscribed in those things as in their true codes, according to which all individual things are made and arranged: nay, these individual and mutable things depend so intimately and essentially (so to speak) on these fixed ones that without them they can neither exist nor be conceived. Whence these fixed and eternal things, although they are individual, yet on account of their presence everywhere and their widespread power, will be to us like generalities or kinds of definitions of individual mutable things, and the proximate causes of all things.

102. But although this be so, there seems to be no small difficulty to surmount in order that we may arrive at the knowledge of the individual things, for to conceive all things at once is a thing far beyond the power of human understanding. For one thing to be understood before another, however, the order, as we said, is not to be looked for from the series of existence, nor even from eternal things; for with these things all are simultaneous in nature. Whence other aids must necessarily be sought beside those which we employed to understand eternal things and their laws.}

CHAPTER VII

Leibniz

GOTTFRIED WILHELM VON LEIBNIZ WAS BORN AT LEIPZIG in 1646 and died in 1716. His father died when he was six, his mother when he was eighteen. He was a prodigy of learning and precocity as a young man, and described himself later as an "autodidact." He studied law, and at the age of twenty published an important treatise (*Ars Combinatoria*) which anticipated later discoveries in logic and mathematics and showed the foundations of his new philosophy. Germany at this time was still recovering from the horrors and divisions of the Thirty Years' War, still backward and chaotic, its intellectual life often centering round secret societies of alchemists and Rosicrucians and the remnants of Renaissance magic. Leibniz was then in contact with these secret societies, but soon found his way to the courts of Frankfurt and Mainz, where he codified laws and drafted schemes for the unification of the churches. He remained all his life a versatile courtier, civil servant and international lawyer, vastly prolific in learned and ingenious defenses of any case, religious or secular, which he was required to defend. At the same time he studied and assimilated the science, philosophy and mathematics of his time, particularly the work of Galileo, Descartes, Pascal, and Boyle. He entered into relations with the Royal Society in London and the Académie des Sciences in Paris; and he addressed works on physical theory to those societies. In 1672 he went first to Paris, on a diplomatic mission, and then to London, where he met Oldenburg, secretary of the Royal Society, the great chemist Boyle, and Christopher Wren. In 1676 he visited Spinoza at The Hague, and arrived at Hanover to take up his post as librarian to the Duke of Brunswick. He had already formulated the principle of the differential and integral calculus. The main outlines of his natural philosophy seem already to have been fixed in his mind. In addition to his work for the Dukes of Brunswick, he maintained a vast learned correspondence and elaborated, without publishing, his own mathematical and philosophical discoveries. In 1684 and 1685 the first of his essays on infinitesimals, and on knowledge and truth, appeared. After traveling through Vienna to Italy in the years 1687 to 1690, he returned to Hanover to find himself overwhelmed by the history of the House of Brunswick which he had undertaken to write, and by an astonishing variety of other projects, legal, scholarly, mathematical and philosophical. In 1700 he went to Berlin to found the Prussian Academy of the Sciences, and later he entered into relations with the Tsar with a view to founding an academy in Russia. In 1714 he fell ill in Vienna, and returned to Hanover to find that the Elector had left for London to become king of England. At this time began the celebrated controversy with the friends of Newton in England, who claimed that Leibniz had plagiarized the idea of the calculus, and that the credit for the discovery should go to Newton. In 1716, still with the great bulk of his mathematical and philosophical work unpublished, he died in Hanover. Only the *Theodicy,* subtitled "Essays on the Goodness of God, the Freedom of Man and the Origin of Evil," had been published, anonymously, in 1710.

Leibniz was perhaps the most universal genius of the modern world, comparable in insight with Newton, wider in range and lesser only in ultimate achievement. He rightly said of himself: "He who knows me only from published works, does not know me." He wrote many hundreds of treatises and fragments, touching on almost every branch of modern knowledge. Even now the whole of his work has not been published. He was the last man who could hope to master the whole range of modern knowledge, and to be an encyclopedia in himself. He was a visionary optimist, with an unlimited faith in reason and enlightenment, who prepared schemes for the reunion of the churches and for European peace, foresaw and designed in outline a new science of statistics, contributed to the theory of probability, was a founder of symbolic logic, projected a universal language, studied optics, conceived the idea of calculating machines, speculated on human history, organized scientific research, and foresaw a new age of invention in mechanics. His thought, and his vision of great academies of knowledge and enlightenment, was the foundation of eighteenth-century rationalism.

His philosophical system — and it is a tightly knit system — is scattered in different, and often occasional, works. The more complete statements are to be found in the *Discourse on Metaphysics,* in the *New Essays on the Understanding,* the *Monadology,* and in the *Letters* (to Samuel Clarke) *on Newton's Mathematical Principles of Philosophy.* The following extracts are taken also from some shorter essays and letters.

Leibniz distinguished two types of statements—those which state necessary truth, established as true by reference to the principle of non-contradiction alone, and contingent statements, which cannot be established to be true solely by reference to the principle of non-contradiction. This distinction is the center of Leibniz's philosophy. Necessary propositions define the limit of what is logically possible: but not everything which is logically possible is actual, and contingent propositions state which of the various possible arrangements of things is actually realized and exists. It is certain that a benevolent God exists, and since we know that he is benevolent and all-powerful, we know that he must have chosen the best of all the logically possible worlds. Therefore, in science, we must always, when we are concerned with the truth of contingent statements, prefer that hypothesis which shows the greatest possible number of effects as deducible from the smallest number of causes; that is, in judging of the truth of contingent statements, we must use the principle that God had a sufficient reason for creating things as he did. In this principle—which may be interpreted as the demand for simplicity in explanation—Leibniz thought that he had found a general method of discovery in science. He proposed a new and closer relationship between the different sciences, which he thought would everywhere illustrate a few simple and general principles of order. In the domain of necessary truths, Leibniz realized that there could be no essential distinction between logic and mathematics, and he looked forward to the possibility of a uniform and clear notation, in which any necessary truth could be established by mere calculation or the mechanical manipulation of symbols; to this end he proposed a universal logistic or calculus, anticipating, at least in outline, the work of Bertrand Russell and of symbolic logicians in this century. An extract is given below.

Closely following these doctrines of logic, Leibniz argued that the universe, created by the free and beneficent choice of God, must be conceived as consisting, in the last analysis, of ultimate substances, called Monads, each of which contains in itself all the attributes which can be truly predicated of it. Consequently there can be no interaction between these substances, and the monads must be, in Leibniz's phrase, "windowless." This theory of monads is the metaphysical counterpart of the logical doctrine that in any true judgment of the subject-predicate form, the predicate must be contained in the subject. All the attributes of a substance are necessarily connected, and, if our human minds were capable of carrying through an infinite analysis, we would be able to show that all true subject-predicate propositions are necessarily true. The only propositions which are not necessarily true in the last resort, even for God, are those which state that there exists a substance possessing such-and-such an attribute. But given that there exists a substance possessing a particular attribute, it is possible, in principle though not in practice, to deduce all the other attributes of the substance from the given one. From these principles it follows also that no two substances can have all their attributes in common—Leibniz's celebrated principle of the Identity of Indiscernibles; for a substance cannot be distinguished from the set of its properties.

Leibniz's system defines with unusual clarity the basic notions which must be related to each other in any systematic philosophy—Identity, Subject and Attribute, Necessity and Contingency, Existence, Truth and Knowledge. He adjusts his account of these organizing concepts in such a way as to allow a place for a benevolent God who has freely created a world which is entirely intelligible. The world which God has created must exhibit a few universal principles of order, which ought to guide us in framing hypotheses to explain phenomena; for we have in metaphysics an assurance that the actual world is the most rationally ordered of all possible worlds.

His arguments are of some complexity and are intended to fit tightly. Some, but not all, of the main difficulties of interpretation are mentioned below.

The first extract stands on its own, the formulation of the project which Leibniz conceived early in his life, and never carried out, although various scraps of work for it survive. The project of a "universal character," which would eliminate difficulties of ambiguity in one language, and of translation between several, by providing a general symbolism based on simple ideas, was widely discussed in the seventeenth and eighteenth centuries.

Leibniz's conception of such a language, to be modeled on the symbolism of arithmetic or geometry, has been noted as a forerunner of the systems of symbolic logic which, beginning with Boole and Schröder in the nineteenth century, were developed by Frege, Russell and Whitehead and others, and are widely employed and discussed today. Such systems have in fact proved of most value in the study of the logical foundation of mathematics itself; it is only in a few corners of the sciences that their application has been attempted.

Leibniz shows both far-sightedness and some caution in his formulation of the idea. The famous remark of *"calculemus* ("let us calculate") is a forerunner of that eighteenth-century optimism which hoped, in the phrase of Condorcet, to carry "les flambeaux de l'algèbre" into the darkest corners of human thought; yet his qualification "in so far as they are amenable to reasoning" leaves open the question of what subject matter we may be able to cast into the formalized language.

[*On Method.* Preface to the General Science (1677)

It is manifest that if we could find characters or signs appropriate to the expression of all our thoughts as definitely and as exactly as numbers are expressed by arithmetic or lines by geometrical analysis, we could in all subjects, in so far as they are amenable to reasoning, accomplish what is done in Arithmetic and Geometry.

All inquiries which depend on reasoning would be performed by the transposition of characters and by a kind of calculus which would directly assist the discovery of elegant results. We should not have to puzzle our heads as much as we have to-day, and yet we should be sure of accomplishing everything the given facts allowed.

Moreover, we should be able to convince the world of what we had discovered or inferred, since it would be easy to verify the calculation either by doing it again or by trying tests similar to that of casting out nines in arithmetic. And if someone doubted my results, I should say to him "Let us calculate, Sir," and so by taking pen and ink we should soon settle the question.]

THE PHILOSOPHY OF LEIBNIZ, TO A GREATER EXTENT THAN any other, can be seen as following from a few simple axioms; and Leibniz himself did not fail to single these out, emphasize them, name them, and often incorporate them in some telling phrase. Another great merit of his system is that his metaphysics is connected integrally and naturally with his logic; his view of the world as consisting of "windowless monads," and his theory of free will, are both based firmly on his logical doctrines about predication, and necessity and contingency, and on the law of sufficient reason. These basic logical notions are what will principally concern us in the first set of extracts.

1. *Subject, Predicate and Substance.* We may start with the law of non-contradiction; this is merely the requirement that a proposition and its opposite cannot both be true—and that any proposition which implies a contradiction, or contains elements that implicitly deny each other, is false, and, indeed, absurd. Leibniz is able, using this principle, to

distinguish what he calls "truths of reason" and "truths of fact" and, correspondingly, the concepts of necessity and contingency. A truth of reason is a proposition which is "true in virtue of the law of non-contradiction alone"; that is, its *denial* implies a contradiction. Such propositions are necessarily true. Truths of fact, on the other hand, are propositions which are indeed true, but not *necessarily* so, in the strong sense of "logical necessity"; their denial does not imply a contradiction, and so is possible and conceivable. Truths of fact are only *contingently* true. Kant (himself in his earlier years a Leibnizian) gave the terms "analytic" and "synthetic" respectively to these two types of proposition; and under these terms the distinction remains of great importance in philosophy today.

The terms "analytic" and "synthetic," which were not employed by Leibniz himself, do in fact imply his own way of presenting the distinctions: even though radically different types of proposition were attached to either side of the division by Leibniz and by Kant. The point of formulating the distinction in this way is seen if one considers any proposition as being of the form of a subject with a predicate attached to it. A proposition will then be analytic if the predicate is logically *contained* in the subject—as for instance "all bachelors are male," where the subject "bachelors" already contains in its meaning the predicate concept "male"; in the case of synthetic propositions this is not so, and the predicate is externally attached to the subject. It is at this point that we find the greatest difference between Leibniz and the philosophers who have used this distinction after him. Leibniz held that *all* predicates, except that of "existence," were contained in their subjects: he held that predication simply consisted of stating the properties which inhere in a substance. This might seem to destroy the distinction between analytic and synthetic propositions, because if all predicates are contained in their subjects, then all propositions will be analytic. But it is the exception, the predicate of "existence," that allows a place for synthetic propositions. On Leibniz's view, while it is a matter of necessity that a certain substance should possess a certain property, it is not a matter of necessity, and it is contingent, that that substance should exist rather than some other. His doctrine, therefore, is that it is impossible that a certain substance which has a certain property should not have had that property–in that case it would have been a different substance–but it is possible that some other substance might have been created in place of this one, which indeed had the other properties of this, but lacked the one in question.

This exception for existence is not an arbitrary postulate of Leibniz's. So different in fact are ascriptions of existence from ascriptions of properties that philosophers after Kant have said that existence is not a property at all. Leibniz does not himself take this view, and does consider existence as a property; but he could have put his theory of predication even more clearly and forcefully if he had anticipated Kant. This would, however, have been inconsistent with his view that there is *one* existential proposition which is not, like all the others, contingent, viz., the proposition asserting the existence of God: For Leibniz *does* want to keep an argument (shown in the extract from *The Ultimate Origin of Things*) to prove that there must be one substance whose essence includes existence, i.e., the existence of which is a necessary truth.

The question now arises, how can the properties of a substance change? For if the properties are necessarily connected with the substance, and it could not fail to have the properties it has, and still be the same substance, how do we account for the evident fact that things change, losing some properties and gaining others? Leibniz's answer to this is that the properties of a substance are, in a sense, eternal: that is, it is always true of it that it should have, at various times, the properties it does have at those times. This conclusion is in fact merely the consequence of a strict application of Leibniz's doctrine about predicates. In such a proposition as "Caesar is going to cross the Rubicon," " . . . is going to cross the Rubicon" is as much a predicate of Caesar as ". . . is crossing the Rubicon" is in "Caesar is crossing the Rubicon"; and so the same principle holds, that predicates referring to the future (and similarly those referring to the past) inhere in the subject, and are part of its nature. Each substance, according to Leibniz, is marked with its past and is "big with its future." The process in which one state of a substance follows on another Leibniz calls the "activity" of the substance (cf. *Monadology, 22*).

The action of an individual substance, which has been introduced in this way, is central to Leibniz's philosophy. A substance is something the name of which can *only* be a subject in a proposition, and cannot be predicated of anything: the word "I" refers to such a substance. This substance is also that which persists through any change; it is the same "I" who now does one thing and now another; and therefore it cannot be the things I do, or the things that happen to me, or the thoughts I have, that make up the real "I": all these things are predicated of the "I," which must be something behind all these. This Leibniz explains in the third extract, from *Identity in Individuals and in Propositions*. . . . Hence we have the doctrine that substances are timeless or eternal; this is closely integrated with the doctrine of predication just mentioned.

It follows from these considerations that no substance can affect any other; for if all the properties of a substance are eternally inherent in it, clearly nothing outside it can bring about a change in them. But if this is so, how do we explain the causal relations which we observe between one thing and another? Leibniz answers this by postulating a *pre-established harmony* between substances, such that the changes that spontaneously occur in each of them are correlated with every other. These correlations can be detected and formulated in scientific laws; these laws will be contingent in Leibniz's system, that is, it makes sense to suppose that the correlation might have worked out differently. The doctrine of the pre-established harmony perhaps sounds gratuitous; but it both follows from the system and contains an important insight. Leibniz has seen some distinctions that were put very differently by Hume: that to speak of a causal connection as a kind of influence of one thing over another is to adopt a kind of imaginative picture; all that is in fact given in experience as the basis of causal connection is observed uniformities between events. But

Leibniz's doctrine is in one way more fruitful than Hume's, for Hume was concerned only with causal laws, but Leibniz is concerned with *functional* laws — laws, that is, that state not what causes what, but what precise mathematical relation relates variations in one thing with variations in another; and functions play a much larger part in physics than causes do. So we find Leibniz in a passage from the *Discourse on Metaphysics* explaining what he means in terms of finding an equation for the line drawn through any arbitrarily selected set of points.

2. *The Principle of Sufficient Reason.* In this last example, Leibniz has given something that characteristically illuminates his thought. It can be proved that a function can be found to fit any line drawn through any set of points: but the function will be of greater or less complexity, depending on how regular the arrangement of the points is. Leibniz has a principle which governs the nature of the functions and of the laws which fit what actually happens: one will always find in explaining the world in this way a combination of the *greatest simplicity with the greatest diversity*. This is is one formulation of the *Principle of Sufficient Reason*. The principle of non-contradiction constitutes a general test for truths of reason, the principle of sufficient reason constitutes a general test for truths of fact. It is established in Leibniz's system that whether a particular substance exists, having certain properties, is a matter of contingent fact; it is not self-contradictory to suppose that different ones might have existed instead. It has also been shown that, since it is a contingent fact that certain substances exist with certain properties, the laws which state a correlation between the properties of different substances must be contingent truths. We now want to know why just *these* substances exist, and just *these* laws are true: it is this question that the principle of sufficient reason is designed to answer. It states that, for every contingent truth, a reason or cause can be given, why it should be so; there is an overruling principle in accordance with which all things come about, viz., the requirements of "good order, and perfection." God had an infinity of worlds to choose from in creating. He must have chosen,

on Leibniz's view, that which is the most perfect, and that which has the greatest diversity of contents arranged in the most economical manner. This principle has for Leibniz a moral significance, which will be considered later; but he employs it widely as a logical or methodological postulate, and it seems to express the requirement that a scientific hypothesis or explanation should combine so far as possible simplicity with breadth and fruitfulness of explanation. A particular application of the principle is to be found in Leibniz's principle of continuity—that "Nature never makes leaps."

Is the principle of sufficient reason itself necessary or contingent? It might seem that, at least in the form in which it can be used to explain what actually and contingently happens, it must be contingent; for if it were necessary, then it would be a matter of necessity that certain contingent laws of nature should hold; and then it would seem that the laws of nature would have to be both necessary and contingent, which is absurd. Again, God has a free choice of what world to create; and for this to be so (as will be seen later) the principle on which He chooses must be contingent. Nevertheless the question is not as simple as this; for there is at least one form of the principle which is necessary, viz., that which states that there must be *some* reason for everything. About this it can be said (as Bertrand Russell has said in his admirable book on Leibniz) that there are two forms of the principle: the general, which just postulates *some* reason, applies to possible worlds and is necessary, and the particular, which postulates a certain kind of reason (the requirement of order, perfection, and good), applies to the actual world, and is contingent.

But it is not clear that this solution is correct. In the essay on *The Ultimate Nature of Things* Leibniz argues from the contingent nature of things in the world to the existence of a necessary being. Without God, he argues, nothing could be explained at all; all explanations would be left hanging in the air, incomplete, if there were no necessary being who was the reason for them all. He further states that it must be possible in principle to argue downwards from the nature of God to what must be the case in the world; ultimately one gets to particulars, which, because they each have an infinite number of properties, must be incomprehensible except to an infinite mind. This last consideration certainly leaves contingency in the knowledge of particulars, at least so far as finite minds are concerned; but above that level it may be that Leibniz had some idea that contingencies could be seen as necessities if —what he considered in fact impossible—we succeeded in deducing the whole system of natural laws from the perfection of God.

3. *The Identity of Indiscernibles*. By the principle of sufficient reason in its particular application, God has arranged for the greatest possible diversity in the world; and from this it follows that no two substances can have all their properties in common. If two substances were to have all their properties in common, i.e., were indiscernible, they would be identical, i.e., not two substances at all, but one. This principle is known as that of the *Identity of Indiscernibles*.

Again, it is not entirely clear whether Leibniz regarded this principle as contingent or necessary. In general he seems to have thought it contingent; logically, it could be otherwise, but actually it would not be, because God would not so choose. Yet there are some grounds for thinking it to be necessary. First, in his remarks on Newton's *Principles* he refers to the idea of two indiscernible universes as an *impossible* fiction; and impossibility in Leibniz generally means metaphysical or logical impossibility. Second, he supports the principle by a different appeal to the principle of Sufficient Reason—that God could have had no reason for choosing between two indiscernible substances in choosing what to create. But God chooses between what is possible, not what is actual; the actual is what he has in fact chosen. So this argument must mean that there could not be two *possible* indiscernibles, and not just that there could not be two actual ones. But from this it follows that two indiscernibles are not even possible, and hence, by all Leibniz's doctrines about necessity, that the Indentity of Indiscernibles is a necessary truth.

However this may be, there is one clear and important

feature of the doctrine that must be noted: the differences in place and time are not included in the differences required to make two substances discernible. It may be easily agreed that there cannot be two things in the same place at the same time; but Leibniz's requirement is more stringent—that even at different places, or at different times, there cannot be two things which are exactly alike. Leibniz believed this because of his doctrines of time and space; he held, against Newton, that these were relative, and were themselves only to be explained in terms of the relations between particulars, which accordingly had to be distinguished without reference to space and time.

[*Logic and the Foundations of the Sciences. The Principle of Sufficient Reason.*

There are two basic principles of all reasonings, the principle of contradiction . . . and the principle that a reason must be given, i.e., that every true proposition which is not known to be so per se, has an a priori proof, or that for every truth a reason can be given, or, in the common phrase, that nothing happens without a cause. Arithmetic and Geometry do not need the latter principle, but Physics and Mechanics do, and Archimedes employed it. . . .

I use two principles in demonstration, one, that whatever implies a contradiction is false, the other that a reason can be given for every truth that is not immediate or a statement of an identity, that is, that the concept of the predicate is always explicitly or implicitly contained in the concept of its subject, and that this holds good no less in extrinsic than in intrinsic denominations, no less in contingent than in necessary truths. . . .

As there is an infinity of possible worlds, there is also an infinity of laws, some of which are proper to one, and others to another, and each possible individual of any world contains in its own notion the laws of its world. . . .

I think you will concede that not everything that is possible exists. . . . But when this is admitted, it follows that it is not from absolute necessity, but from some other reason (such as good order, perfection) that some possibles obtain existence rather than others.

Identity in Individuals and true Propositions (1686)

Let a certain straight line A B C represent a certain time, and let a certain individual, say myself, endure or exist during this period. Then let us consider the me that exists during the time A B and the me that exists during the time B C. Since we suppose that it is the same individual substance that persists in me during the time A B while I am in Paris and the time B C while I am in Germany, there must be some reason for our truly saying that I persist, or that it is the same I who was in Paris and is now in Germany; if there were no reason, then it would be correct to say it was not I but another person. Certainly I am convinced a posteriori of this identity, from introspection, but there must also be some a priori reason. The only reason that can be found is the fact that the attributes of the preceding time and state and the attributes of the succeeding time and state are all predicates of the same subject [*insunt eodem subjecto*]. Now, what is it to say that the predicate is in the subject, if not that the concept of the predicate is in some manner involved in the concept of the subject? Since from the moment that I began to exist it could be truly said of me that this or that would happen to me, we must allow that the predicates in question are principles involved in the subject or in the complete concept of me, which constitutes what is called the ego and is the basis of the interconnection of all my different states. These have been known to God from all eternity. . . . When I say that the individual concept of Adam entails all that will ever happen to him, I mean no more than what philosophers understand when they say of a true proposition that the predicate is contained in the subject. . . .

I consider a true proposition as such that every predicate, necessary or contingent, past, present or future, is contained in the concept of the subject. . . . This is a very important proposition which ought to be well established, for it follows from it that every soul is as a world apart, independent of everything else except God; that the soul is not only immortal and impenetrable, but retains in its substance traces of everything that happens to it. This proposition also determines the nature of the relations and communication between substances and, in particular, the union of the soul and body. The latter is not explained by the ordinary hypothesis that one physically influences the other; rather each present state of a subject occurs in it spontaneously, and is nothing but a consequence of its preceding state. Nor does the hypothesis of occasional causes explain, as Descartes and his followers imagine . . . My hypothesis of concomitant harmony seems to me to show how it happens. That is to say, every substance expresses the whole sequence of the universe in accordance with its own view-point or relationship to the rest, so that all are in perfect correspondence with one another.

On Newton's Mathematical Principles of Philosophy

5. These great principles of a sufficient reason and of the identity of indiscernibles change the state of metaphysics. That science becomes real and demonstrative by means of these principles; before it generally consisted of empty words.

6. To suppose two things indiscernible, is to suppose the same thing under two names. Therefore to suppose that the universe could have had another position of time and place than it actually had, and yet that all the parts of the universe should have had the same relation among themselves as that which they actually have, such a supposition, I say, is an impossible fiction.

. . . .

There are necessities that ought to be admitted. For we must distinguish between an absolute and an hypothetical necessity, and also between a necessity that is so because the opposite implies a contradiction (which is called logical, metaphysical or mathematical necessity), and a necessity that is moral, whereby a wise being chooses the best, and every mind follows the strongest inclination.

5. Hypothetical necessity is that which the supposition or hypothesis of God's foresight and preordination imposes on future contingents. This must be admitted, unless we

deny, as the Socinians do, God's foreknowledge of future
contingents and his providence which regulates and governs
every particular thing.

6. But neither the foreknowledge nor the preordination
derogate from liberty. For God being moved by his supreme
reason to choose, among many series of possible things or
worlds, the one in which free creatures should make such
or such resolutions (though not without his concourse),
has thereby rendered every event certain and determined
once for all; but he has not derogated thereby from the
liberty of those creatures: that simple decree or choice
did not change, but only actualised, their free natures,
which he saw in his ideas.

7. Neither does moral necessity derogate from liberty.
For when a wise being, and especially God, who has supreme wisdom, chooses what is best, he is not on that account less free: on the contrary, not to be hindered from
acting in the best manner on that account is the most perfect liberty. And when anyone else chooses according to
the most apparent and the most strongly inclining good, he
imitates therein the liberty of a truly wise being as far as
he is able. Without this, the choice would be a blind chance.

8. But the good, either true or apparent, that is to say
the motive, inclines without necessitating; that is, without
imposing an absolute necessity. For when God (for instance) chooses the best, what he does not choose, although less perfect, is nevertheless possible. If what he
chose were absolutely necessary, any alternative to it would
be impossible: which is against the hypothesis. God chooses
among possibles, that is among many ways of which none
implies a contradiction.

9. To say, on the other hand, that God can only choose
what is best; and to infer from this that what he does not
choose is impossible; this, I say, is a confusion of terms;
it is mixing up power and will, metaphysical necessity and
moral necessity, essences and existences. For what is necessary is so by its essence, as the opposite implies a contradiction; but a contingent thing that exists owes its existence to the principle of what is best, which is a sufficient
reason for the existence of things. Therefore I say that

motives incline without necessitating; and that in contingent things there is a certainty and infallibility, but not an absolute necessity.

10. This moral necessity is a good thing, consistent with the divine perfection, and with the great principle or ground of existence, which is the need of a sufficient reason: whereas absolute and metaphysical necessity depends upon the other great principle of our reasoning, viz., that of essences, that is the principle of identity or contradiction: for when something is absolutely necessary, it is the only possible way, and its contrary implies a contradiction.

89. The harmony, or correspondence, between the soul and the body, is not a perpetual miracle; but the effect or consequence of an original miracle which was worked at the creation of things; as all natural things are. Certainly it is a perpetual wonder, as many natural things are.

90. The phrase pre-established harmony is a term of art, I confess; but it is not a phrase without content, since it is explained very intelligibly.

91. The nature of every simple substance, soul, or true monad, is such that each subsequent state is a consequence of the preceding one; in this lies the cause of the harmony. For God needs only to make a simple substance once to be from the beginning a representation of the universe, according to its point of view; it follows from this alone that it will be so perpetually, and that all simple substances will always have a harmony among themselves, because they always represent the same universe.

92. The soul, on my view, does not disturb the laws of the body, nor the body those of the soul; the soul and body only agree together; the one acting freely, according to the rules of final causes, and the other acting mechanically, according to the rules of efficient causes. But this does not derogate from the liberty of our souls; for every agent that acts according to final causes is free, though it happens to agree with an agent acting only by efficient causes without knowledge, or mechanically; because God, foreseeing what the free cause would do, from the beginning regulated the machine in such manner that it could not fail to agree with that free cause.

Reflections on Knowledge, Truth and Ideas

We insist here on a distinction between nominal definitions, which contain only characters by which we can distinguish one thing from another, and real definitions, from which the possibility of things can be demonstrated. So we may refute the view of Hobbes, who held that all truths are arbitrary because they depend on nominal definitions: for he did not recognise that the reality of a definition is not a matter of our choice, and that we cannot consistently connect together any concepts we like. Finally, all this makes clear the distinction between true and false ideas. An idea is true if what it represents is possible; false if the representation contains a contradiction. The possibility of a thing, however, is known either a priori or a posteriori. It is known a priori, when we analyse the idea into its elements (that is, into other ideas whose possibility is already known) and establish that it contains nothing incompatible. For example, this is the case when we see the way in which an object is produced, whence causal definitions are of such paramount significance. On the other hand, we recognise the a posteriori possibility of a thing when its actual existence is known to us through experience. For anything that exists or has existed must certainly be possible. Wherever we have adequate knowledge we have at the same time an a priori knowledge of the possibility; that is, if we have completed the analysis and no contradiction has appeared, the possibility of the idea is demonstrated. Whether human knowledge will ever attain to a perfect analysis of ideas, and so to the first possibility and to unanalysable concepts —in other words whether it will be able to reduce all thoughts to the absolute attributes of God himself, to first causes and the final reason of things—that is a question which I do not want to discuss or to decide just now. Usually we are content to ascertain the reality of certain concepts by experience, in order then to combine them synthetically according to the model of nature.

On the Ultimate Origin of Things

In addition to the world, or aggregate of finite things, we find a certain unity which is dominant, not just like the soul in me, or rather the Ego itself in my body, but in a much higher sense. For the unity dominating the universe not only rules the world, but creates and fashions it, is superior to the world and is, so to speak, extramundane, and is thus the ultimate reason of things. For neither in any particular thing nor in the whole aggregate and series can be found the sufficient reason of existence. Suppose a book on the elements of geometry to have been eternal and that one copy had been successfully made from another; it is evident that, although we might account for the present book by the book which was its model, we could never, by assuming any number of books whatever, reach a perfect reason for them; for we might always wonder why there should have been such books from all time; that is, why there should be books at all and why they are so written.

What is true of books is also true of the different states of the world; for although there are certain laws of change, a succeeding state is in a certain way only a copy of the preceding, and to whatever earlier state you may go back, you will never find in them a complete reason why there should be any world at all, and why this world rather than some other. Even if you imagine the world eternal, you are still supposing nothing but a succession of states; and as you find in none of them a sufficient reason for them, and as no number of them, however great, helps you in giving a reason for them, it is evident that the reason must be sought elsewhere. For in eternal things, even where there is no cause, there must be a reason which, in permanent things, is necessity itself or essence, but in the series of changing things, if it were supposed that they succeed each other eternally, this reason would be, as will soon be seen, the prevailing of inclinations, where the reasons do not necessitate (by an absolute or metaphysical necessity, the opposite of which would imply a contradiction), but incline. From which it follows that even by supposing the world to be eternal, an ultimate extramundane reason of things, or God, cannot be escaped.

The reasons which explain the world, therefore, lie in something extramundane, different from the chain of states, or theories of things, the aggregate of which constitutes the world. We must therefore pass from physical or hypothetical necessity, which determines the later states of the world by the earlier, to something which is of absolute or metaphysical necessity, for which itself no reason can be given. For the present world is necessary, physically or hypothetically, but not absolutely or metaphysically. That is, once it is determined that the world is to be such as it is, it follows that things must happen in it just as they do. But as the ultimate origin must be in something which is metaphysically necessary, and as the reason of the existing must lie in the existing, there must exist some one being metaphysically necessary, that is, whose essence involves existence; and so there must exist something which differs from the plurality of beings that is the world, which, as we have recognised and shown, is not metaphysically necessary.

But in order to explain a little more clearly how, from truths that are eternal, essential or metaphysical, there arise truths that are temporary, contingent or physical, we ought first to recognise that from the very fact that something exists rather than nothing, there is in possible things, that is, in the very possibility or essence itself, a certain need of existence, or, so to speak, a claim to existence; in a word that essence tends of itself towards existence. From this it follows that all possible things, expressing essence or possible reality, tend by equal right towards existence, in proportion to their quantity of essence or reality, or in proportion to the degree of perfection they contain; for perfection is nothing else than quantity of essence.

From this it is most evident that out of infinite combinations of possibles and possible series, that one actually exists by which the most essence or possibility is brought into existence. Indeed there is always in things a principle of determination which turns on consideration of maximum and minimum, such that the maximum effect is obtained with the minimum, so to speak, expenditure. And the time, place, or, in a word, the receptivity or capacity of the world may here be considered as the expenditure, or the ground upon which a building can be most easily erected, whereas the varieties of forms correspond to the commodiousness of the building and the number and elegance of its rooms.

It is rather like those games where all the spaces on the board have to be filled according to certain rules and where, unless some skill is employed, you will be in the end shut out of some unfavourable spaces and will be forced to leave many more places empty than you either needed or wished. But there is a certain formula for filling most easily the most space. Just as, therefore, if we have to construct a triangle, and there is no further determining reason, it will be an equilateral one; and if we have to go from one point to another, without any further determination as to the way, we shall choose the easiest and shortest path; so, once it is granted that being is better than not being, that is, that there is a reason why something rather than nothing should be, or that we must pass from the possible to the actual, it follows that, even if nothing further is determined, the quantity of existence must be as great as possible, with regard to the capacity of time and place (or to the possible order of existence), much as tiles are fitted together in a given area in such a way that it shall contain the greatest number of them possible.

From this it is now wonderfully clear how in the very origin of things a kind of divine mathematics or metaphysical mechanics was employed, and how the greatest quantity of existence comes to be determined. It is thus that of all angles the determinate angle in geometry is the right angle, and that liquids placed in heterogeneous media take the form that has the most capacity, the spherical; but the best example is that in ordinary mechanics itself: when several heavy bodies act against each other, the resultant motion constitutes, on the whole, the greatest descent. For just as all possibles tend by equal right to existence in proportion to their reality, so all weights tend to descend by an equal right in proportion to their gravity; and as here a motion is produced which involves the greatest possible descent of heavy bodies, so there a world is produced in which the greatest number of possibles comes into existence.

Thus we now have physical necessity based on metaphysical necessity; for although the world is not metaphysically necessary, in the sense that its contrary implies a contradiction or a logical absurdity; it is nevertheless physically necessary, or determined in such a way that its contrary implies imperfection or moral absurdity, and as possibility is the principle of essence, so perfection or degree of essence (through which the greatest number of things is compossible) is the principle of existence. From this it is at the same time evident how the author of the world can be free, although he makes all things determinately; for he acts according to a principle of wisdom or perfection. Indifference arises from ignorance, and the wiser one is, the more determined one is to the action which is most perfect.

But, you will say, this comparison of a certain metaphysical determining mechanism to the physical mechanism of heavy bodies, however elegant it appears, nevertheless fails in this; that there really exist heavy bodies, whereas possibilities and essences prior to existence, or outside of it, are only fancies or fictions, in which accordingly the reason of existence cannot be sought. I answer that neither these essences nor the truths about them which are called eternal, are fictions, but that they exist in a certain region of ideas, if I may so put it, that is in God himself, the source of all essences and of the existence of everything else. The existence of the actual series of things shows of itself that this is not just a gratuitous assertion. For since the reason for the series is not found in itself, as we have shown above, but must be sought in metaphysical necessities or eternal truths; and since what exists can only come from something that exists, as we have remarked above; therefore eternal truths must have their existence in a subject which is absolutely and metaphysically necessary, that is, in God, through whom those things which otherwise would be imaginary are (to use a barbarous but significant expression) realised.

Indeed, we discover that everything takes place in the world according to the laws of eternal truths, not only geometrical but also metaphysical; that is, not only according to material necessities but also according to formal necessities. This is true not only generally, with regard to the reason (which we have just explained) why the world exists rather than not, and exists thus rather than otherwise (a reason which can only be found in the tendency of the possible to existence); but if we come down to detail we see the metaphysical laws of cause, of power, of activity, holding good in admirable manner in all nature, and prevailing even over the purely geometrical laws of matter, as I found in accounting for the laws of motion; a thing which struck me with such astonishment that, as I have explained at great length elsewhere, I was forced to abandon the law of the geometrical composition of forces, which I had defended in my youth when I was more of a materialist.]

LEIBNIZ'S DOCTRINES RECEIVE THEIR FULL EXPRESSION IN the form, not merely of logical doctrines about predication, but also of a metaphysical system; the metaphysical system provides an imaginative picture of the structure of the universe from which certain conclusions are drawn about God's relation to man and human freedom. The extracts that follow show Leibniz's scheme of reality.

1. *Monads*. The logical doctrine of ultimate subjects provide a picture of the universe as consisting of numberless substances called *monads*. These must be (a) completely independent of each other—they "have no windows by which anything could go out or come in"; (b) they must be indestructible by natural processes, and could not come into existence except by an act of God's creation, and they have no parts; (c) they are unchanging, in the sense that their "activity" is the product entirely of their inner nature, which contains in germ all that will happen to them; (d) they are all different. Furthermore they form a system; not, in such a way, that they can affect one another, but they have been so arranged by God that the spontaneous activity of each in fact mirrors the whole of the universe, more or less clearly or confusedly, from its particular point of view.

The monads, Leibniz says, are the "real atoms of nature": but they are unlike the physical atoms of the scientist, and have no extension of any kind. Their inner activity Leibniz calls "perception," in virtue of its feature of mirroring the universe (i.e., the activity of other monads); the tendency within the monad to change these perceptions he calls "appetition." Everything consists of such monads; and so Leibniz has given us a picture of the universe as consisting entirely of substances whose essence is, in some sense, to have perceptions. But this does not make each monad a *soul,* or every part of the universe animate; for Leibniz insists against Descartes that there can be perceptions of which one is not conscious; this conclusion he reaches partly by his Law of Continuity, partly by the a priori consideration that the activity of the monad must be unceasing, as there is nothing to start it off again if it stopped. Only those monads with memory and the power of reflective thinking are properly to be called "souls" *(Monadology,* 19). In an early writing Leibniz had remarked that body was "momentary mind, i.e., mind without memory."

The connection between soul and body is a connection between monads: and therefore is not a *connection* at all, but a case of the pre-established harmony. Leibniz was very proud of this doctrine, which he opposed to the Cartesian theory of two interacting substances. It certainly contains some valuable insights: Leibniz was aware, for instance, that no amount of scientific investigation of the brain could lead to the locating of perception or of thought itself: (cf. the image of the mill, *Monadology,* 17). Leibniz's conclusions, are par excellence metaphysical, that is, they assert that any adequate knowledge of reality must assume a certain form, which can be determined in advance. He uses what would seem to many modern philosophers quite different *kinds* of argument to make the same point; for instance, as has been seen, the doctrine of the continuous activity of the monad is ultimately deduced from a logical doctrine about the function of predicates, but is reinforced by arguments from experience. By pure thought we can anticipate the structure of science; and then we may look in actual science for confirmation of this metaphysical insight.

2. *Theory of Knowledge and the External World.* In his *New Essays,* Leibniz criticizes the views of Locke, whose *Essay concerning Human Understanding* (1690) had created a great impression. The extract from the *New Essays* which is given below is concerned principally with the question of "innate ideas," concepts, that is, not given in expe-

rience; Locke had denied that there could be such concepts. Leibniz insists that there are; and his method of argument here shows his great philosophical subtlety. Locke had treated the question in such a way as to suggest that the existence or non-existence of innate ideas was an empirical matter, to be settled by introspection and research. Leibniz seems to realize that it is not an empirical but a logical issue; the question is—can all our concepts be satisfactorily reduced to, or analyzed into, concepts which are given in experience? But he adds the consideration that if it were an empirical issue, it would be undecidable, since one could not tell by introspection whether a concept had been given in experience or not. And this by itself shows that it cannot be an empirical issue.

Leibniz's objections to Locke go deeper than this; because of his theory of the activity of the monad, the whole distinction between what is given in experience and what is "innate" seems ultimately to collapse; in a sense, all the perceptions of a monad are innate, for all proceed spontaneously from its inner nature. Leibniz is here faced with a difficulty about the existence of the external world: if he starts from the Cartesian position of the existence of his own thoughts, it is unclear how he can proceed outside himself to establish the independent existence of numberless other substances; for, on his own thesis, these can never have any effect on him. To this question Leibniz gives no ultimately satisfactory answer. His answer is, so far as it goes, convincing: the coherence of observed phenomena, he suggests, constitutes an external world; that phenomena should hang together in the way they do is enough for us to say that there is a world outside. But this does not answer the question of how one establishes the existence of other substances beyond the phenomena which appear to oneself. Here Leibniz has failed to give an epistemological answer (an answer to the question "how do we know what exists?") which measures up to his metaphysical answer (an answer to the question "what exists?"). This missing answer, Kant, who was deeply influenced by Leibniz, tried to supply.

3. *Necessity and Human Freedom.* Leibniz had said that

everything which happens to a man is contained from the beginning in his essence; and therefore he was urgently faced with the problem of free will. If God had created a certain substance, say Caesar, who must by his nature act in a certain way, e.g., cross the Rubicon, how can it be that Caesar had a free choice when standing at the Rubicon? For, being Caesar, he could not have acted otherwise. Leibniz's answer to this problem is in terms of his distinction between the different senses of "necessary." One sense of "necessity" is that of logical or metaphysical necessity, necessity expressed in a truth of reason; the other is that of physical or hypothetical necessity, necessity expressed in a truth of fact. The opposite of a metaphysical necessity is logically impossible; the opposite of a hypothetical necessity is possible, but will not actually happen. The necessity by which a man acts as he does is of the second kind, for it merely follows from the principle of sufficient reason; it is a contingent matter that this substance, Caesar, who will act in this way, should have been created rather than some other substance. Therefore it is not (logically) impossible that Caesar should act otherwise than he does: although it is already fixed in his nature which way he will choose, he still chooses between alternatives, either of which is possible. Thus human freedom is preserved.

Leibniz, who is not free from self-congratulation, was evidently pleased by this solution; but it is hardly satisfactory. For the sense of "possibility" in which it is possible for a man to act otherwise than as he does, is merely that in which it *makes sense* to suppose that he does act otherwise, that this does not contain a contradiction; it is still an actual impossibility for him to do so. But if a man is gagged and bound, for instance, and is in this way prevented from stopping his house from being robbed, it still *makes sense* to suppose that he could have prevented the burglary: that he cannot in this case is just an actual impossibility. Yet no one would suppose that such a man was *free* to prevent the burglary. We need for freedom *more* than the mere logical possibility of the alternatives, which is all that Leibniz gives us. Yet Leibniz's treatment is not so easily dismissed: he is surely right, for instance, in argu-

ing that a man is still free in doing something which flows
from his character—that is, that the mere fact that one
could have predicted that a man would choose in a certain
way, because he was that sort of man, does not show that
he was not free in so choosing. This is a tangled and still
unsolved problem; Leibniz's doctrine is of value in drawing distinctions within it, even if he has perhaps not drawn
all that are needed, or drawn the main one in the right place.

4. *The Best of All Possible Worlds*. Leibniz's optimism,
his doctrine that God has chosen the best of all possible
worlds, became notorious. His views were violently attacked
by Voltaire, who in *Candide* represents the Leibnizian philosopher Panglosse complacently justifying God's choices
in the face of ghastly and meaningless disasters. Such criticism, though directed against a wilful parody of Leibniz,
has a point: for Leibniz's system, like all great metaphysical
constructions, embodies together with its arguments a particular view of the world, with moral implications, which
may be found either sympathetic or repugnant.

The comments on Leibniz given here have illustrated
only a few of Leibniz's doctrines and have discussed only
a few of the criticisms that may be made of them. It is a
tribute to his genius that proper criticism of him would
involve extensive discussion of all the leading issues of
philosophy. On all of them he held views still important
and fruitful, formulated in a system of such elegance, ingenuity and profundity that he stands as the model of one
type of systematic metaphysician and remains one of the
most suggestive philosophers of all time.

〔 *Discourse on Metaphysics* (1685)

VI. God's actions or acts of will are commonly divided
into ordinary and extraordinary. But it is well to consider
that God does nothing out of order. Thus what passes for
extraordinary is so only with regard to a particular order
established among created things; as regards the universal order, everything conforms to it. This is so true that
not only does nothing happen in the world which is absolutely irregular, but one cannot even imagine such a thing.

Let us suppose, for example, that someone jots down a number of points upon a sheet of paper at random, as do those who practice the ridiculous art of Geomancy; now I say that it is possible to find a geometrical line the concept of which will be constant and uniform, that is, in accordance with a certain formula, and at the same time such that it will pass through all these points, and in the same order as the hand jotted them down; also, if a continuous line is drawn which is now straight, now circular and now of any other description, it is possible to find a notion, a formula, or an equation, common to all the points on this line in virtue of which the changes must occur. There is no face, for instance, the outline of which does not form part of a geometric line and which cannot be traced completely by a certain movement according to rule. But when the formula is very complex, what conforms to it passes for irregular. Thus we may say that, in whatever manner God created the world, it would always have been regular and in a certain general order. God, however, has chosen the most perfect, that is to say, the one which is at the same time the simplest in hypothesis and the richest in phenomena, as might be the case with a geometric line, the construction of which was easy, but whose properties and effects were very remarkable and extensive. . . .

IX. There follow from this [the inclusion of predicates in their subject] several notable paradoxes; among others that it is not true that two substances may be exactly alike and differ only numerically [*solo numero*], and that what St. Thomas says on this point about angels and intelligences (*quod ibi omne individuum sit species infima*) is true of all substances, provided that one takes the specific difference, as Geometers take it in the case of figures; again that a substance can begin only through creation and perish only through annihilation; that a substance cannot be divided into two, nor one be made of two, and so the number of substances neither increases nor diminishes through natural means, although they are frequently transformed. Furthermore every substance is like a whole world, and like a mirror of God or of the universe, which they portray, each one in its own fashion; much as the same city is variously represented according to the various viewpoints from which it is regarded. Thus the universe is in some sort multiplied as many times as there are substances, and the glory of God in the same way is multiplied by as many wholly different representations of his work. It can even be said that every substance bears in some sort the character of God's infinite wisdom and omnipotence and imitates him as much as it can; for it expresses, even though confusedly, all that happens in the universe, past, present and future, and thus has some resemblance to an infinite perception or power of knowing. And since all other substances express this substance in turn, and accommodate themselves to it, we can say that it extends its power over all the others in imitation of the omnipotence of the creator.

XIII. . . . We have said that the concept of an individual substance includes once for all everything which can ever happen to it, and that in considering the concept one will be able to see everything that can be truly predicated of the individual, just as we can see in the nature of a circle all the properties that can be derived from it. But it seems that in this way the difference between contingent and necessary truths will be destroyed, that there will be no place for human liberty, and that an absolute fatality will rule over all our actions as well as over all the other events of the world. To this I reply that a distinction must be made between what is certain and what is necessary. Everyone grants that future contingencies are assured, since God foresees them; but, for all that, we do not say that they are necessary. But (it will be said) if a conclusion can be deduced infallibly from a definition or concept, it is necessary; and since we maintain that everything which is to happen to anyone is already virtually included in his nature or concept, as all the properties are contained in the definition of a circle, therefore the difficulty still remains. To meet this objection satisfactorily, I say that connection or sequence is of two kinds: the one absolutely necessary, whose contrary implies contradiction, and this has its place among the eternal verities, like the truths of geometry; the other is necessary only *ex hypothesi,* and so to speak by accident, and in itself is contingent, since the contrary does not imply a contradiction. This latter sequence is not founded just upon pure ideas and the understanding of God, but upon his free decrees and upon the processes of the universe. Let us take an example. Since Julius Caesar will become perpetual Dictator and master of the Republic, and will overthrow the liberty of Rome, this action is contained in his concept, for we have supposed that it is the nature of such a perfect concept of a subject to involve everything, in order that the predicate may be included in the subject, *ut possit inesse subjecto*. We may say that it is not in virtue of this concept or idea that he must perform this action, since it pertains to him only because God knows everything. But it will be insisted in reply that his nature or form corresponds to this concept, and since God has imposed upon him this personality, he is compelled henceforth to satisfy it. I could reply with the similar case of future contingencies, which as yet have no reality save in the understanding and will of God, and which, since God has given them in advance this form, must correspond to it. But I prefer to meet a difficulty rather than to excuse it by instancing other difficulties, and what I am about to say will serve to illuminate the one as well as the other. It is here then that one must apply the distinction between kinds of connection, and I say that what happens in conformity to these decrees is assured, but that it is not necessary; and if anyone did the contrary, he would do nothing impossible in itself, although it is impossible, *ex hypothesi,* that this should happen. For if anyone were capable of carrying out the complete demonstration to prove this connection of the subject, Caesar, and the predicate, his successful enterprise, he would in fact show that the future dictatorship of Caesar had its ground in his concept or nature, so that one would see there a reason why he resolved to cross the Rubicon rather than to stop, and why he gained rather than lost the day at Pharsala, and that it was reasonable, and consequently assured, that this would occur; but one would not prove that it was necessary in itself, nor that the contrary implied a contradiction. In much the same way it is reasonable and assured that God will always do what is best, although that which is less perfect does not imply a contradiction. For it would be found that this demonstration of this predicate of Caesar was not as absolute as those of numbers or geometry, but that this predicate supposes the sequence of things that God has freely chosen and which is grounded in the first free decree of God, which was to do always that which is the most perfect; also in the decree that God made following the first one, regarding human nature, which is that men should always do, although freely, that which appears to be the best. Every truth that is founded upon this kind of decree is contingent, although certain, for the decrees of God do not change the possibilities of things and, as I have already said, although God assuredly chooses the best, this does not prevent what is less perfect from being possible in itself. It will never happen, but it is not its impossibility but its imperfection which causes him to reject it. Now, nothing is necessary the opposite of which is possible. One will be in a position, then, to meet these kinds of difficulties, however great they may appear (and in fact they have not been less vexing to all other thinkers who have ever treated this matter), provided that he considers well that all contingent propositions have reasons for being thus rather than otherwise, or (what is the same thing), that they have proofs a priori of their truth, which make them certain, and show that the connection of the subject and predicate in these propositions has its basis in the nature of one and of the other; but that they do not have demonstrations of necessity, since their reasons are founded only on the principle of contingency, or of the existence of things, that is to say, upon that which is, or appears to be, the best among several equally possible things. Necessary truths, on the other hand, are founded upon the principle of contradiction, and upon the possibility or impossibility of the essences themselves, without regard in this to the free will of God or of creatures.

New Essays on the Human Understanding

. . . The question at issue is whether the soul in itself is entirely empty, like the tablet upon which nothing has yet been written [*tabula rasa*], as is the view of Aristotle and the author of the *Essay* [Locke], and whether all that is traced on it comes solely from the senses and from experience; or whether the soul contains originally the principles of various notions and doctrines which external objects merely awaken from time to time, as I believe, with Plato and even with the Schoolmen, and with all those who take in this sense the passage of St. Paul (Romans, 2:15) where he remarks that the law of God is written in the heart. . . . From this there arises another question, whether all truths depend on experience, that is to say, on induction and examples, or whether there are some that have some other basis. For if some events can be foreseen before any trial has been made of them, it is clear that we must here contribute something of our own. The senses, although necessary for all our actual knowledge, are not sufficient to give us the whole of it, since the senses never give anything except examples, that is to say, particular or individual truths. All examples which confirm a general truth, however numerous they may be, are not enough to establish the universal necessity of this same truth; for it does not follow that what has happened will happen again in the same way.

. . . It would seem that necessary truths, such as are found in pure mathematics, and especially in arithmetic and in geometry, must have principles the proof of which does not depend on examples, nor, consequently, on the testimony of the senses, although without the senses it would never have occurred to us to think of them. This ought to be well recognised; Euclid has so well understood it that he often demonstrates by reason what is obvious enough through experience and by sensible images. Logic also, together with metaphysics and ethics, one of which forms natural theology and the other natural jurisprudence, are full of such truths; and consequently their proof can only come from internal principles, which are called innate. It is true that we must not imagine that these eternal laws of the reason can be read in the soul as in an open book, as the edict of the praetor can be read in his *album* without difficulty or research; but it is enough that they can be discovered in us by dint of attention, for which opportunities are given by the senses. The success of experiments serves also as confirmation of the reason, very much as proofs serve in arithmetic for better avoiding error of reckoning when the reasoning is long. . . .

It seems that our able author claims that there is nothing potential in us and nothing even of which we are not at any time actually conscious; but he cannot mean this strictly, or his opinion would be too paradoxical; for acquired habits and the contents of our memory are not always consciously perceived and do not even always come to our aid at need, although we often easily bring them back to mind on some slight occasion which makes us remember them, just as we need only the beginning of a song to remember the song. Also he modifies his assertion in other places by saying that there is nothing in us of which we have not been at least formerly conscious. But besides the fact that no one can be sure by reason alone how far our past apperceptions, which we may have forgotten, may have gone, especially in view of the Platonic doctrine of reminiscence, which, mythical as it is, is not, in part at least, incompatible with bare reason; in addition to this, I say, why is it necessary that everything should be acquired by us through the perceptions of external things, and that nothing can be unearthed in ourselves? Is our soul, then, such a blank that, besides the images borrowed from without, it is nothing? . . . there are a thousand indications that lead us to think that there are at every moment numberless perceptions in us, but without apperception and without reflection; that is to say, changes in the soul itself of which we are not conscious, because the impressions are either too slight and too numerous, or too even, so that they have nothing sufficient to distinguish them one from the other; but, joined to others, they do not fail to produce their effect and to make themselves felt at least confusedly in the mass. . . .

In a word, insensible perceptions are of as great use in psychology as insensible corpuscles are in physics, and it is as unreasonable to reject the one as the other under the pretext that they are beyond the reach of our senses. Nothing takes place all at once, and it is one of my great maxims, and one of the best confirmed, that nature never makes leaps: this is what I called the Law of Continuity, when I spoke of it in the first *Nouvelles de la République des Lettres;* and the use of this law is very considerable in physics. It teaches that the small always passes into the great, and vice versa, through the intermediate magnitudes, in degree as in quantity; and that a motion never comes about immediately from rest, nor is reduced to it except through a smaller motion, just as one never completes running any line or length before having completed a shorter line; although hitherto those who have exhibited the laws of motion have not observed this law, believing that a body could receive in an instant a motion contrary to the one immediately preceding. All this leads us to conclude rightly that noticeable perceptions also come by degrees from those that are too minute to be noticed. To think otherwise is to have little comprehension of the enormous subtlety of things, which always and everywhere include an actual infinity.

I have also noticed that, in virtue of insensible variations, two individual things cannot be perfectly alike, and that they must always differ by more than a mere numerical difference. This destroys the concept of the blank tablets of the soul, a soul without thought, a substance without action, a void in space, atoms and even particles not actually divided in matter, absolute rest, complete uniformity in one part of time, of space, or of matter, perfect globes of the second element, original, perfect cubes, and a thousand other fictions of the philosophers, which arise from their incomplete notions and are not admitted by the nature of things, and which our ignorance, and the little attention we give to the insensible, let pass. These cannot be tolerated, unless they are limited to abstractions of the mind — the mind insisting that it does not deny the things which it considers irrelevant to any particular enquiry, but merely sets them on one side. . . .

1. (Intuitive.) Primitive truths, which are known by intuition, are, like the derivative, of two kinds. They are either truths of reason or truths of fact. Truths of reason are necessary and those of fact are contingent. Primitive truths of reason are those which I call by the general name of

identical, because it seems that they do nothing but repeat the same thing without giving us any information. They are affirmative or negative. . . .

Primitive truths of fact, on the other hand, are the immediate internal experiences of an immediateness of feeling. Here it is that the first truth of the Cartesians, or of St. Augustine, *I think therefore I am,* that is, *I am a thing that thinks,* holds good. It should be recognised, however, that just as the identicals can be either general or particular, and that the one class is as clear as the other (since it is just as clear to say that A is A, as to say that a thing is what it is) so it is also with the first truths of fact. For not only is it clear to me immediately that I think; but it is just as clear to me that I have different thoughts; that sometimes I think of A, and that sometimes I think of B, etc. Thus the Cartesian principle is sound, but it is not the only one of its kind. You see by this that all primitive truths, of reason or of fact, have this in common, that they cannot be proved by anything more certain.

I believe that the proper criterion concerning the objects of the senses is the connection of phenomena, that is, the connection of what happens at different places and times, and in the experience of different men, who are themselves, each to the others, very important phenomena on this score. And the connection of phenomena, which validates truths of fact concerning sensible things outside us, is verified by means of truths of reason; as the phenomena of optics are explained by geometry. However, it must be confessed that none of this certainty is of the highest degree, as you have well recognised. For it is not a metaphysical impossibility that there should be a dream as continuous and lasting as the life of man; but it is a thing as contrary to reason as the idea that the plot of a book should be formed haphazard by throwing the type together at random. Beyond that, it is true that, so long as the phenomena are connected, it does not matter whether they are called dreams or not, since experience shows that we are mistaken in the measures we take concerning phenomena, when they are understood according to the truths of reason.

The *Monadology* (1714)

1. The *monad,* of which we shall here speak, is nothing but a simple substance which enters into compounds; simple, that is to say, without parts.

2. And there must be simple substances, since there are compounds; for the compound is only a collection, or aggregate of simple substances.

3. Now where there are no parts, neither extension, nor figures, nor divisibility, is possible. These monads are the real atoms of nature and, in a word, the elements of things.

4. No dissolution of them is to be feared, and there is no conceivable way in which a simple substance can be destroyed by natural means.

5. For the same reason there is no conceivable way in which a simple substance can come about by natural means, since it cannot be formed by composition.

6. Thus it may be said that a monad can only begin or end all at once, that is to say it can only begin by creation and end by annihilation; whereas that which is compound begins or ends by parts.

7. Further, there is no way of explaining how a monad can be altered or internally changed by any other created thing; for nothing can be transposed within it, nor can any internal movement be conceived in it which could be directed, increased or diminished within it, as is possible with compounds, where there is change among the parts. The monads have no windows through which anything could come in or go out. Accidents cannot detach themselves from substances, or go about outside of them, as the "sensible species" of the Schoolmen used to do. Thus neither substance nor accident can come into a monad from outside.

8. Nevertheless the monads must have some qualities, or they would not even be entities. And if simple substances did not differ at all in their qualities, there would be no way of perceiving any change in things; for that which is in the compound can only come from the simple ingredients, and

the monads, if they had no qualities, would be indistinguishable from one another, seeing they do not differ in quantity. Consequently, space being a plenum, each part of it would always receive, in any motion, only the equivalent of what it had had before, and one state of things would be indistinguishable from another.

9. Indeed, each monad must be different from every other. For there are never in nature two beings which are exactly alike and in which it is not possible to find an internal difference, or at least one founded upon an intrinsic quality.

10. I take it also for granted that every created being, and consequently the created monad, is subject to change, and further that this change is continuous in each.

11. It follows from what has just been said that the natural changes of the monads come from an internal principle, since an external cause could not influence their inner being.

12. But, besides the principle of change, there must be a particular series of changes which constitutes, so to speak, the specifications and variety of the simple substances.

13. This series must involve a multiplicity in the unit, or in that which is simple. For since every natural change takes place by degrees, something changes and something remains; and, consequently, there must be in the simple substance a plurality of affections and of relations, although it has no parts.

14. The passing state, which involves and represents multiplicity in the unit, or in the simple substance, is nothing but what is called *perception,* which must be distinguished from apperception or consciousness, as will appear in what follows. Here the Cartesian view especially fails, since it considers as non-existent the perceptions of which we are not conscious. It is this also which made Cartesians believe that only spirits are monads, and that there are no souls of brutes or of other entelechies. They, with most people, have failed to distinguish between a prolonged state of unconsciousness and death strictly speaking, and have therefore agreed with the old scholastic prejudice of

entirely separate souls, and have even confirmed ill-balanced minds in the belief that souls are mortal.

15. The activity of the internal principle which causes the change or passage from one perception to another, may be called *appetition;* it is true that desire cannot always completely attain to the whole perception at which it aims, but it always attains something of it and reaches new perceptions.

16. We experience in ourselves a multiplicity in a simple substance, when we find that the least thought of which we are conscious involves a variety in the object. Thus all who admit that the soul is a simple substance ought to admit this multiplicity in the monad.

17. It must be confessed, moreover, that perception, and that which depends on it, are inexplicable by mechanical causes, that is, by figures and motions. And supposing that there were a machine so constructed as to think, feel and have perception, we could conceive it as enlarged and yet preserving the same proportions, so that we might enter it like a mill. If this were so, we should, when we looked around inside, find only pieces pushing one against another, but never anything by which to explain a perception. This must be sought for, therefore, in the simple substance and not in a compound or a machine. Furthermore, nothing but this (namely perceptions and their changes) can be found in the simple substance. It is also in this alone that all the internal activities of simple substances can consist.

18. The name of *entelechies* might be given to all simple substances or created monads, for they have within themselves a certain perfection; they have a certain self-sufficiency which makes them the sources of their internal activities, and, so to speak, incorporeal automata.

19. If we choose to give the name *soul* to everything that has perceptions and desires in the general sense which I have just explained, all simple substances or created monads may be called souls; but as feeling is something more than a simple perception, I think it right that the general name of monads or entelechies should suffice for those

simple substances which have only perception, and that those substances only should be called souls whose perception is more distinct and is accompanied by memory.

20. We experience in ourselves a state in which we remember nothing and have no distinguishable perception, as when we fall into a swoon, or when we are overcome by a profound and dreamless sleep. In this state the soul does not differ sensibly from a simple monad; but as this state is not continuous and the soul comes out of it, the soul is something more than a mere monad.

21. And it does not at all follow that in such a state the simple substance is without any perception. That is indeed impossible, for the reasons already given; for it cannot perish, and it cannot continue to exist without some affection, and this affection is nothing else than its perception. But when there are a great number of minute perceptions, in which nothing is distinct, we are stunned; as when we turn round continuously in the same way several times in succession, from which there arises a dizziness that may make us swoon, and which prevents us from distinguishing anything. And death may produce for a time this condition in animals.

22. And as every present state of a simple substance is naturally the consequence of its preceding state, so its present is big with its future;

23. And as on being awakened from a stupor, we are aware of our perceptions, we must have had them immediately before, although we were unconscious of them; for one perception can come in a natural way only from another perception, as a motion can come in a natural way only from a motion.

29. The knowledge of necessary and eternal truths is what distinguishes us from mere animals, and furnishes us with reason and the sciences, raising us to a knowledge of ourselves and of God. This is what we call the rational soul or spirit in us.

30. It is also by the knowledge of necessary truths, and by their abstractions, that we rise to acts of reflection, which makes us think of what is called "I," and to observe

that this or that is within us; and it is thus that, in thinking of ourselves, we think of being, of substance, simple or compound, of the immaterial and of God himself, conceiving that what is limited in us is in him without limits. And these acts of reflection provide the principal objects of our reasonings.

38. The final reason of things must be found in a necessary substance, in which the variety of particular changes exists only eminently, as in their source; and that is what we call God.

39. As this substance is a sufficient reason of all this variety, which also is linked together throughout, there is but one God and this God is sufficient.

40. We may also conclude that this supreme substance, which is unique, universal and necessary, having nothing outside itself which is independent of it, and being a pure consequence of possible being, must be incapable of limitations and must contain as much reality as is possible.

46. But we must not imagine, as some do, that the eternal truths, being dependent upon God, are arbitrary and depend upon his will, as Descartes seems to have held. This is true only of contingent truths, the principle of which is fitness, or the choice of the best, whereas necessary truths depend solely on his understanding and are its internal object.

53. Now, as there is an infinity of possible universes in the ideas of God, and as only one of them can exist, there must be a sufficient reason for the choice of God, which determines him to select one rather than another.

54. And this reason can be found only in the fitness, or in the degrees of perfection that these worlds contain, each possible world having a right to claim existence in proportion to the measure of perfection which it possesses.

60. Besides, we can see, in what I have just said, the a priori reasons why things could not be otherwise than they are. For God, in regulating the whole, has had regard to each part, and particularly to each monad, whose nature being to represent, nothing can limit it to representing only a part of things; although it is true that this representation

is but confused, as regards the detail of the whole universe, and can be distinct only in the case of a small part of things, namely, those that are nearest or greatest in relation to each of the monads; otherwise each monad would be a divinity. It is not as regards the object, but only as regards the modification of their knowledge of the object, that monads are limited. They all confusedly strive after the infinite, the whole; but they are limited and differentiated by the degrees of their distinct perceptions.]

Recommended Further Reading

BACON

The Philosophical Works of Francis Bacon, edited by J. M. Robertson. London: George Routledge & Sons Ltd., 1905.

Works, edited by James Spedding, R. L. Ellis and D. D. Heath. London: 1857-74 (14 v.).

Selected Writings of Francis Bacon, edited by Hugh G. Dick. New York: Random House, 1955. (Modern Library.)

GALILEO

Dialogues Concerning the Two New Sciences, translated by Henry Crew and Alfonso de Salvio. New York: The Dover Publishing Company, 1952.

Dialogue on the Great World Systems, edited by Giorgio de Santillana. Chicago: University of Chicago Press, 1953.

HOBBES

Leviathan, edited by A. R. Waller. New York: The Macmillan Company, 1904.

Leviathan, New York: E. P. Dutton & Co., Inc., 1950. (Everyman's Library.)

Selections, edited by F. J. E. Woodbridge. New York: Charles Scribner's Sons, 1930.

De Cive; or The Citizen, edited by Sterling P. Lamprecht. New York: Appleton-Century-Crofts, 1949.

DESCARTES

The Philosophical Works of Descartes, translated by Elizabeth S. Haldane and G. R. T. Ross. Cambridge: The University Press, 1931-34 (2 v.). The most useful English edition.

A Discourse on Method and Selected Writings, translated by John Veitch. London and Toronto: J. M. Dent & Sons Ltd. New York: E. P. Dutton & Co., Inc., 1951. (Everyman's Library).

Selections, edited by Ralph M. Eaton. New York: Charles Scribner's Sons, 1927.

PASCAL

Pensées, translated by W. F. Trotter. New York: E. P. Dutton & Co., Inc., 1954. (Everyman's Library.)

Pensées and The Provincial Letters, translated by W. F. Trotter and Thomas McCrie. New York: Random House, 1941. (Modern Library.)

SPINOZA

The Chief Works of Benedict de Spinoza, translated from the Latin by R. H. M. Elwes. New York: The Dover Publishing Company, 1952.

Ethics, and On the Improvement of the Understanding, translated from the Latin by William H. White, edited by James Gutmann. New York: Hafner Publishing Company, 1949.

The Correspondence of Spinoza, translated and edited by A. Wolf. London: George Allen & Unwin Ltd. New York: The Dial Press, 1928. The best edition of the letters.

The Philosophy of Spinoza, edited by Joseph Ratner, translated by R. H. M. Elwes. New York: The Tudor Publishing Company, 1926.

Selections, edited by John D. Wild. New York: Charles Scribner's Sons, 1930.

Principles of Descartes Philosophy, translated by Halbert Hains Britan. LaSalle, Illinois: Open Court Publishing Company. (Religion of Science Library, No. 59.)

LEIBNIZ

The Monadology and Other Philosophical Writings, translated by Robert Latta. London: Oxford University Press, 1925. Includes *New Essays* and *On the Ultimate Origin of Things.*

Selections, edited by Philip Wiener. New York: Charles Scribner's Sons, 1951.

New Essays Concerning Human Understanding, translated by A. G. Langley. LaSalle, Illinois: Open Court Publishing Company, 1949.

Discourse on Metaphysics, Correspondence with Arnauld, and Monadology, translated by G. R. Montgomery. LaSalle, Illinois: Open Court Publishing Company.

Philosophical Writings, selected and translated by Mary Morris. New York: E. P. Dutton & Co., Inc., 1934. (Everyman's Library.)

The Leibniz-Clarke Correspondence with Extracts from Newton's Principia Mathematica, edited by H. G. Alexander. Manchester: The University Press, 1956. (Philosophical Classics).

Index of Names

THE
MENTOR PHILOSOPHERS

☆

A DISTINGUISHED SERIES of six volumes presenting, in historical order, the basic writings of the outstanding philosophers of the Western world — from the Middle Ages to the present time. Each volume is self-contained and presents a single phase of the great development. Each is edited by a noted scholar who contributes an introduction and interpretive commentary explaining in what way the significant thought of each period has influenced the development of Western philosophy.

"A very important and interesting series."
—*Gilbert Highet*

"Mentor Books is to be congratulated."
—*New York Times*

"The New American Library, publishers of Mentor Books, has done the academic world and general reading public a service."
—*The Classical Bulletin*

"This is a gallant affirmation of a belief that Americans can not only read, but think. Thank you!"
—*St. Louis Post Dispatch*

*The Nature of Man,
of Being, of God*

THE AGE OF BELIEF
The Medieval Philosophers

BY ANNE FREMANTLE

HERE, IN one volume, is the wisdom of the most spiritually harmonious age that Western man has known. In this age of belief, the period from the fifth to the fifteenth centuries, when religion and social institutions were closely related, philosophers discussed the nature of God, of Being, and of Man, with an intensity not known before or since.

In this remarkable book, Anne Fremantle, religious scholar and author, presents selections from the basic writings of such dominant philosophers of the medieval period as St. Augustine, St. Thomas Aquinas, Boethius, Erigena, Anselm, Abelard, Bonaventura, and Averroës, with an interpretation of their work woven throughout the texts. (#MT126—75¢)

> **"Highly commendable . . . provides an excellent beginning volume."**
> —*The Classical Bulletin.*

ANNE FREMANTLE, an associate editor of Commonweal, *an editor of the Catholic Book Club, an associate professor at Fordham University, an editor-on-loan to the United Nations during the General Assembly, is also the author of numerous books, reviews and articles. Mrs. Fremantle also edited The Papal Encyclicals in Their Historical Context (Mentor #MT256—75¢) and A Treasury of Early Christianity (Mentor #MT285).*

Uncharted Paths

THE AGE OF ADVENTURE

The Renaissance Philosophers

By Giorgio de Santillana

THE RENAISSANCE was a time when men turned from abstractions, from thoughts of other-worldly perfection, to explore new seas, new continents, new notions, new images of man. They studied the giants of the past in the belief that they had already discovered man's true nature and then brought forth such bold creations —in art, psychology, politics and manners—as were never known in the ancient world.

Giorgio de Santillana presents in this volume the basic writings of the great innovators of the Renaissance—Da Vinci, More, Machiavelli, Michelangelo, Erasmus, Copernicus, Montaigne, Kepler, Galileo, and Giordano Bruno—and contributes an introduction and connecting commentary which illustrates the love of life that characterized this age of adventure.

(#MT184—75¢)

"The most exciting and varied in the series."
—New York Times

GIORGIO de SANTILLANA was born in Rome in 1902. He studied and worked in Rome and Paris until 1935, when he came to the United States. Mr. de Santillana has taught at Harvard and is currently Professor of the History and Philosophy of Science at M.I.T. He edited Galileo's Dialogue on the Great World Systems *and is the author of* The Crime of Galileo. *Mr. de Santillana is the general editor of the new series, tentatively called The Mentor history of Scientific Thought and author of the first volume,* The Origins of Scientific Thought (#MQ336)

The Emergence of Science

THE AGE OF ENLIGHTENMENT

The 18th Century Philosophers

By Sir Isaiah Berlin

THE PHILOSOPHY of the 18th century begins with a systematic effort to apply to the study of man those methods which Newton had so triumphantly applied to nature. The editor of this volume, Sir Isaiah Berlin, traces the development of the influence of scientific thought through the writings of the great philosophers and popularizers whose work remains the foundation of liberal humanism and rationalism in the West.

Sir Isaiah's selections, and his penetrating introduction and interpretive commentary, shed light upon the philosophy of Locke, Berkeley, Voltaire, Hume, Reid, Condillac, and their German critics.

(#MT172—75¢)

"(Sir Isaiah) has one of the liveliest and most stimulating minds among contemporary philosophers."

—N. Y. Herald Tribune

SIR ISAIAH BERLIN is a Fellow of All Souls College, Oxford, and a University Lecturer in Philosophy. Born in 1909, he is a graduate of Corpus Christi College, Oxford, where he took First Class Honors in Philosophy and Ancient History, Politics and Economics. He has been a visiting lecturer at Harvard University and Bryn Mawr College, has written widely on philosophical, historical and political topics, and is also author of The Hedgehog and the Fox *(Mentor #MD198—50¢)*

A New View

THE AGE OF IDEOLOGY

The 19th Century Philosophers

BY HENRY D. AIKEN

ONE GREAT new development of philosophy in the 19th century was the attempt to construct consistent attitudes toward the human situation. In this time of great religious, political and economic change, philosophy became a technique for adjustment to a changing environment. An effort was made to synthesize the traditions of the 17th and 18th centuries. Idealism and romanticism, empiricism and positivism, the philosophy of history and existentialism were developed.

The major thought of the period is elucidated here through Henry D. Aiken's commentary and his selections from the great thinkers of the age—Kant, Fichte, Hegel, Schopenhauer, Comte, Mill, Spencer, Marx, Mach, Nietzsche and Kierkegaard. (#MT185—75¢)

> **"Mr. Aiken's writing is original and stimulating, perhaps the most distinct intellectual contribution made in the series."**
> **—*New York Times***

HENRY D. AIKEN, now professor of philosophy at Harvard, was born in Portland, Oregon, in 1912. He studied at Reed College, Stanford, and later received his Ph.D. from Harvard. Mr. Aiken has been on the teaching staffs of Columbia University and the University of Washington. His writings on ethics and aesthetics have appeared in many philosophy journals. He has edited two volumes of Hume and is completing a work on ethics.

THE AGE OF ANALYSIS

20th Century Philosophers

By Morton White

This volume emphasizes those ideas of the philosophers of the 20th century which are most important to philosophy and least familiar to the general reader—ideas in the field of logic, and of philosophical and linguistic analysis. Yet the better-known studies of time and instinct, existentialism, phenomenology, and organism are also represented.

Philosophy in the 20th century is by no means remote from the concerns of the ordinary man and the problems of culture. In his introduction and commentary, Morton White illustrates this, and illuminates the background of the selections themselves. The 20th century philosophers included are: Peirce, Whitehead, James, Dewey, Bertrand Russell, Wittgenstein, Croce, Bergson, Sartre and Santayana. (#MT353—75¢)

> "No other book remotely rivals this as the best available introduction to 20th century philosophy."
>
> —*N. Y. Herald Tribune*

MORTON WHITE, Professor of Philosophy at Harvard University, has taught at Columbia University and at the University of Pennsylvania. He has also held a Guggenheim Fellowship and was visiting professor at Tokyo University. The author of numerous articles and reviews, he has written three books, The Origin of Dewey's Instrumentalism, Social Thought in America, *and* Toward Reunion in Philosophy.